THE CIVILIZATION OF THE AMERICAN INDIAN SERIES

The Kalispel Indians

The Kalispel Indians

BY

John Fahey

UNIVERSITY OF OKLAHOMA PRESS: NORMAN AND LONDON

BY JOHN FAHEY

Inland Empire: D. C. Corbin and Spokane (Seattle, 1965)
Ballyhoo Bonanza: Charles Sweeny and the Idaho Mines (Seattle, 1971)
The Flathead Indians (Norman, 1974)
Days of the Hercules (Moscow, Idaho, 1978)
The Inland Empire, 1879–1929 (Seattle, 1986)
The Kalispel Indians (Norman, 1986)

Library of Congress Cataloging-in-Publication Data

Fahey, John.
   The Kalispel Indians.

   Bibliography: p.
   Includes index.
   1. Kalispel Indians—History.   2. Indians of North
America—Washington (State)—History.   I. Title.
E99.K17F34   1986   979.6'00497   86-40073
ISBN 0-8061-2000-2 (alk. paper)

Contents

Illustrations

Preface

THE Kalispels are one of the neglected tribes of the inland northwest, although they live in the names of towns, rivers, lakes, mountains, and streets with variations in spelling. As this book shows, however, the Kalispels are very much in business on a remnant of their ancient homeland tucked in the northeastern corner of Washington state.

Throughout their relations with white men, Kalispels have been confused with Pend Oreilles. Many accounts call them Lower Pend Oreilles because they live downriver from Upper Pend Oreilles. And because the United States never assigned an agent to the Kalispels, the record of government administration is scattered through the files of several agencies, mainly the Coeur d'Alene, Colville, Flathead, and Spokane.

Part of the historical confusion about the Kalispels, as about other northwest tribes, arises from the government's arbitrary designation of tribes for the purpose of making agreements with them. But, in fact, Indians of the interior northwest comprised relatively fluid societies. Kalispels intermarried with Spokanes, Pend Oreilles, and Flatheads frequently and with others infrequently. An Indian marrying into another tribe never wholly lost childhood identity. A Spokane might marry a Kalispel, for example, and live with the Kalispels the rest of his life, functioning as a member of Kalispel society, but forever be a Spokane to the Kalispels. Today only one group, Victor's band, is known as Kalispels, but its members are related to a half dozen other tribes: Coeur d'Alenes, Spokanes, Flatheads, Chewelahs, Pend Oreilles, Colvilles, and so on.

In standard anthropological classifications of Indians, Kalispels are regarded as Pend Oreilles on the basis of language, and are often identified as Lower Pend Oreilles. But that is not the way the Kalispels see themselves, or is it the way other tribes see the Kalispels. In the Indian view, the Kalispels are a distinct people with their own territory, their own culture, and their own chiefs. The Kalispels have a different name for Pend Oreilles, *slketekumschi.*

If one matches the tribes with geography, the separations among them seem clearer. In such a matching, the Kalispels show their separate identity. The United States negotiated with the Kalispels as a tribe separate from others, asking them to give up land regarded as distinctly theirs.

For these reasons, and because modern Kalispels are emphatic in asserting their singularity, I regard them as separate, not as a branch of the Pend Oreilles. In environmental studies of the Pend Oreille River Valley preliminary to construction of a paper mill, archaeologists find that people have been cooking roots there for four thousand years. The Calispell Valley Archaeological Project, over the period of roughly one year, excavated and analyzed a 100-acre site, finding the remnants of root ovens, some tools, and a limited number of points and flakes. To me, their findings suggest that Kalispels may have lived in their valley longer than anyone previously suspected.

The Kalispel story is one of struggle—struggle for identity, for recognition, and for justice. As this is written, the Kalispels continue their quest for justice, to establish their rights and to regain a portion of their homeland. This book originated with the tribe's need for a documented account of its history, initiated by the tribal counsel, Robert D. Dellwo. As we reconstructed the story, we concluded that using it only as an appendage to lawsuits and applications would deny the Kalispels the wider audience their history deserves.

The Kalispels are actors in "the fundamental drama of Indian law [which] continues to be whether Indian tribes will vanish by assimilation into American society or remain legally and culturally apart," to quote Eric R. Biggs in the *Washington Law Review* (54:633, 1979). "Tribal ability to make reservations economically viable will play a major role in this drama." The Kalispels are working hard to make themselves economically self-sufficient, as you will see.

One barrier to a definitive Kalispel history is the lack of general archaeological research in their territory. Another is the sparse anthropological data available. This book, of necessity, relies on the field work of Allan H. Smith who supplied most of the anthropological interpretation for the Kalispels' case before the Indian Claims Commission.

My search for Kalispel history received a welcome boost from the attorneys who prepared the Kalispels' claim case and other suits; their files contain hundreds of letters, reports, excerpts from books, and other material pertaining to the Kalispels from public and private archives. The Kalispel files of the Wilkinson and Dellwo law firms hold much of the record of the tribe since passage of the Indian Reorganization Act. Citations from these sources in the notes show how much I depended on them.

I was gratified to have the invaluable counsel of Kalispels, attorneys, and Indian bureau personnel who took part in some of the events recorded here. And I appreciate the patience of Alice Ignace O'Connor, Frank Nick, and Francis Cullooyah who searched for identities of persons in faded snapshots. Even so, some of those pictured have been forgotten. The map is by David Anderson, Eastern Washington University cartographic laboratory.

To write a book, I rely foremost on the encouragement and understanding of my wife, Peggy. She also leafed through agency reports in the National Archives to find mentions of the Kalispels.

I thank these and the other contributors to this book.

JOHN FAHEY

Spokane, Washington

The Kalispel Indians

CHAPTER 1

White Man's Religion; White Man's Vengeance

Jesuits who settled a Catholic mission among the Flathead Indians on the Bitterroot River in September 1841 sent messengers to tell other tribes they had come at last to the Pacific Northwest. One of the tribes to receive the news was the Kalispel —nomadic hunters, diggers, and fishers, noted for their sturgeon-nosed canoes, who clustered in the secluded valley of the Pend Oreille River. To the Kalispels, neither white men nor the Christian religion were novel, and they were as eager as other tribes of the northwest interior for the ministry of priests who possessed, to the Indian mind, strong spiritual powers. The Congregationalists Elkanah Walker and Cushing Eells had visited the Kalispels on the Pend Oreille River several times, and earlier in 1841 Father Modeste Demers, passing through Kalispel territory on his way from Quebec to Vancouver with Father Francis N. Blanchet, had baptised some Kalispels. [1]

Demers, who converted Angus McDonald, the Hudson's Bay trader at Colville to the Catholic faith, told the Kalispels to stay away from Protestant missionaries. A few Kalispels rode up to the Bitterroot to inspect the priests at St. Mary's, the Flathead mission set on a grassy river plain with a log cross marking it, rude cottonwood huts, a log chapel, and a palisade of upright timbers for protection against marauding Blackfeet—whom the Jesuits in-

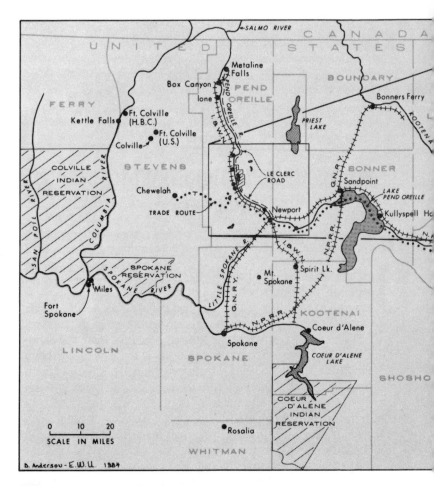

This map compresses Kalispel history, showing not only the vanished east-west trade route, Kullyspell House, abandoned posts and missions, and railroads with their names when built, but also modern towns and present county and reservation boundaries. Drawn by David Anderson, Eastern Washington University.

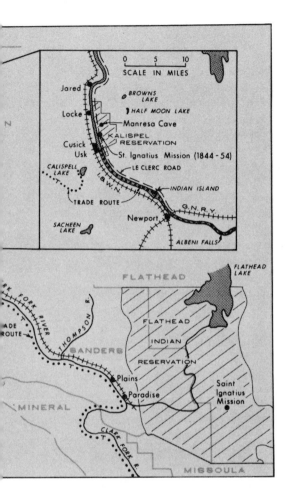

tended to pacify eventually. Some Kalispels had children baptized there.[2]

The Coeur d'Alene tribe, the Kalispels' neighbors on the southeast, sent a delegation to implore the priests to settle among them, too. In answer, the leader of the missionary band, a stocky Belgian, Father Peter John De Smet, went to talk with the Coeur d'Alene chiefs, leaving two other priests, Nicholas Point and Gregory Mengarini, and three lay brothers, to build the huts and stockade and teach the Indians.[3]

De Smet's impetuous departure for Coeur d'Alene country was typical of him; he would range far—down the Columbia to concoct a broad mission enterprise with the vicar general at Vancouver, Blanchet—among the interior tribes of the northwest; and across North America and Europe raising money and recruiting priests for the Rocky Mountain missions. He would name mountains, lakes, or streams for generous donors and then write to tell them that their names had been memorialized.

In the fall of 1841 De Smet dashed for the Hudson's Bay Company post at Fort Colville to buy mission supplies, taking a circuitous route to visit Indians. On the Clark Fork River near modern Paradise, Montana, he encountered two Kalispel camps that he thought had come out to meet him; on the eastern shore of Pend Oreille lake, he found three Kalispel families; and as he moved down the Pend Oreille River, he met increasing clusters of Kalispels all the way to the tribe's main camp on a flatland by a wide place in the river that De Smet called a bay. Thereafter he named these people the Kalispel of the Bay to distinguish them from Kalispels on the lakes and from Pend Oreilles with whom many whites, including De Smet, often confused Kalispels.[4]

After briefly instructing the Kalispels, De Smet found them disposed and baptized 160. (Here a distinction needs to be made: Catholic priests, by the term "disposed," meant readiness to accept the Catholic faith, while Methodist and Presbyterian ministers, working among other tribes, declined to baptize Indians not fully instructed in the tenets of their sects.) De Smet regarded the Kalispels as truthful, generous, and docile. Like the novelists who wrote romantic yarns of "noble savages," he tended, in fact, to endow Indians with sterling virtues learned from nature. De Smet would never abandon his first favorable impressions of Indian peoples. Although he did not learn their language and spent no more than six years among them, De Smet attracted the lasting esteem and trust of a generation of interior Indians, and returned their affection. Shortly after placing a mission among the Blackfeet in 1846, he would be called to St. Louis to be treasurer of the Jesuits' Missouri Province, fund-raiser and promoter of missions, but he would not lose his concern for "his" Indians. By his efforts, the Indians' trust in him, and his recruitment of priests—he made 36 trips across the Atlantic—this hard-working, visionary Jesuit, as much as any one man, changed the Indian way of life. De Smet and other missionaries, foreseeing the effects of America's westward thrust, aimed to turn Indians into pious farmers living in stable communities for religious ministry.

A year after starting St. Mary's among the Flatheads, De Smet sent Point to open a mission among the Coeur d'Alenes and, as the small party of Jesuit missionaries at St. Mary's received new men, he directed a Dutch priest, Adrian Hoecken, with Brother John B. McGean, to found a mission among the Kalispels.[5]

Hoecken had been working among the Coeur d'Alenes; he had visited the Kalispels several times and baptized some. In the fall of 1844, he arranged to meet Father Peter DeVos at the Kalispels' main camp on the Pend Oreille to see the lay of the land (DeVos was the superior while De Smet was absent, recruiting in Europe). Then in November, Hoecken and De Smet himself went to the Kalispels, who greeted them joyfully with musketry and trumpets. With winter coming on, they quickly chose a flat by the river near Albeni Falls for a mission—too hastily—the river overflowed the spot every spring. Kalispel men cut fir trees for a frame and women brought bark and mats to cover it, completing a chapel in two days. They called it St. Michael's. With priests among them, the Kalispels celebrated Christmas with discharges of guns, a mass, and baptisms. In howling snowstorms, the river icy and the sky windswept gray, De Smet, Hoecken, and McGean huddled for the winter in a hut made of fir posts covered with bark and mats. De Smet, on a clearing day in February, left to visit the Flathead.[6]

Hoecken found the Kalispels, as he later confided to a visiting

army surgeon, "poor, miserable, half-starved . . . with an insuffi-
ciency of food and nearly naked, living upon fish, camas, and other
roots and, at the last extremity, upon the pine-tree moss . . . in
utter misery and want—*in want of everything.*" But they listened
eagerly to this bald, angular, soft-hearted Dutchman with the stern
face. From their earlier instruction by priests and Catholic trappers, many Kalispels recited Christian prayers as augurs for success in the hunt and warfare. And their trades for guns, steel
knives, woolens, metal canisters, and similar items, suggested that
like his goods, the white man's religion must be superior. Having
embraced the Catholic faith, many were fervent, although they
tended to interpret Christian teaching in naturalistic ways. Eells
had found the Kalispels praying morning and evening—to the sun.[7]

The Kalispels' taciturn chief, Standing Grizzly, whom Hoecken
christened Loyola, renounced buffalo hunting because the hunt
would take him away from the mission for months or even years.
Each evening the chief gathered headmen to hear the lessons
Hoecken had taught him during the day through an interpreter. A
wise, forceful man, Standing Grizzly was respected by his people
and their neighbors; he was often elected chief for a buffalo hunt
by intertribal parties. Loyola, following the custom among many
tribes, shared large game killed in winter with the entire camp.
Famed as a hunter, now he cast aside his hunting prestige, knowing
that a few warriors and hunters ridiculed his conversion, declaring
to Hoecken, "The rascals may kill me, but as long as I am breath-
ing, they must go straight." And under this compelling chief, the
Kalispels embraced Catholicism.[8]

After Easter, De Smet returned to choose a better mission site,
"a vast and beautiful prairie . . . surrounded by cedar and pine"
near a cave he named New Manresa and used for a chapel. In the
next few years, the lay brother and Kalispel men, with an occasional hired artisan, built a church of dressed logs, a priest's house,
stable, barn, shops, and a small grist mill; they erected log shanties for Kalispels who lived near the mission, named St. Ignatius.
With seeds from the Hudson's Bay Company they planted a 160-
acre mission farm with plots for any Indians who agreed to try
cultivating the soil. In July, De Smet came again bringing eleven
horses laden with plows, axes, spades, scythes, carpenter's tools,
and other equipment for a permanent settlement and farm.[9]

A hillside cave on Kalispel ground so enchanted Father De Smet that he named it New Manresa and used it as a chapel. Now an historic site, the cave looks across LeClerc road and the Pend Oreille River toward Cusick.

But the ground was poor. The river flooded the fields in 1845 and again the next year. Kalispels complained that tilling this earth was useless. A few inches below the topsoil lay barren bluish clay and ashes from a volcanic eruption. (Some Indians still recalled the night of fiery skies and falling cinders; they had supposed that the sun had burned, and when it rose in the morning, celebrated its return with dancing and feasting.) Their crops of potatoes and wheat shrunken and thin, the Kalispels were obliged to continue hunting, fishing, and digging to sustain life, activities that took them away from the mission for weeks at a time.[10]

Doubtless some Kalispels felt shamed by their failure at farming; others blamed the missionary for demanding the impossible. Leaving the mission to hunt and fish loosened their close ties to the priest and allowed them to escape the eye of Loyola. Some of the particularly adventurous young men welcomed their time away;

they revelled in the chase, gambling, and stealing horses and women. Others gravely continued morning and evening prayers. The Kalispels had been of several minds before the missionaries came, torn by loyalties to relatives in other tribes and by the buffalo hunt. One segment preferred canoes, fishing, hunting small game, and the comparative security of their rivers and lakes; another looked forward to furious buffalo chases on the prairies, convivial companions, the danger of Blackfeet encounters, and the rivalry of horsemen. Tales of debauchery drifted back from the buffalo hunts to appal the priests at St. Mary's and St. Ignatius.[11]

Catholic teaching widened the rifts within the tribe. Most Kalispels accepted the Christian faith; others could not put aside shamans, talismans, and fetishes, fearing retribution from the spirits that guided them; and still others cared little for any supernatural notions, concerning themselves with gaining prestige in hunting and fighting. One Kalispel who had had the priest baptize his children explained that he could not become a Christian himself because he had two wives. The priests insisted on one spouse, but they compromised by recognizing Indian-custom marriage and divorce. Surely the Kalispels were confused by talking about religion with mountain men or visiting their Presbyterian friends, the Spokanes. Some of the Kalispels visited Eells and Walker at their mission in June and again in September 1845 to talk.[12]

Conflicts rent the tribe again when the Jesuit superior, DeVos, visiting poor St. Ignatius, asked Loyola if he would move to ground more suited to farming with another tribe. The chief discussed this proposal overnight with his people, finding them divided on it, too, and the next day spoke for them, declaring, "God gave us this land. Let us keep it!" But forceful chief Loyola died April 6, 1846, succeeded by his gentler son, Victor, whom the priests thought irresolute as a willow in the wind. He was a brave hunter, chosen chief by election, and sat sadly before his lodge as warriors in their finest costumes marched up, discharged their muskets, and one by one shook hands and pledged fealty to him. Victor could not bring himself to whip an Indian malefactor, a chief's usual punishment, without begging the miscreant's permission. Said a priest, Loyola's death was "the beginning of the end" of the mission among the Kalispels.[13]

Perhaps the Kalispel disaffection was a part of the malaise creeping across the interior, a swing of the pendulum away from the Indians' first enthusiasm for Christian teaching, resistance to changing old ways, and foreboding at the swelling trains of immigrants moving into the Oregon country. Doubtless the Kalispel—and the Indian—alienation was compounded of all of these. Cushing Eells and his wife, Myra, missionaries since 1837 to the Spokanes, disheartened now by flagging interest in their message, reluctantly prepared to leave. At St. Mary's, the Jesuits saw the Indians edging away from the mission. A harsh winter in 1846–47 depleted the game in Kalispel territory; the hunters killed so thoroughly that they nearly exterminated the animals, leaving too few to breed. They prayed—but the game did not come back. As missionaries soon discovered, Indians expected instant answers to prayer, as they had from their talismans and guardian spirits. Immigrant trains had doubled the white population of the Oregon country in 1845 and more came; an 1848 train brought smallpox carriers, infecting interior Indians. [14]

Although the Kalispels lived well north of immigrant pathways, the rippling disruption of Indian life lapped against them. In November 1847 Cayuse Indians murdered Marcus and Narcissa Whitman, missionaries near Walla Walla, spreading unfounded tales that whites had retaliated by killing 60 Indians on the Columbia River. Such news raised fear in Indian camps. Probably some mounted Kalispels, accompanying Flathead and Nez Perce trading parties, had seen for themselves the ranks of worn settlers trudging inexorably into the Bitterroot and Walla Walla valleys. A second severe winter, 1848–49, pushed the Jesuit missions of the interior northwest near collapse from lack of supplies and Indian discontent. Funding for the missions dried up, due to revolution in Paris. Jesuits even considered prospecting in California's gold fields to pay their bills. After a Blackfeet raiding party thoroughly frightened the fortified community of St. Mary's, the Jesuit superior in 1850 ordered the mission closed, mourning that it now served "nothing but a handful of undisciplined and corrupted youth which cares nothing about priests and religion." Its priests scattered. Joseph Joset spent the winter with Hoecken among the Kalispels and there learned that St. Ignatius, too, was tottering. [15]

Joset, now the superior, went on to Colville. Letters followed him, asserting that the Kalispels "clamored" to move to a place where they could live. In 1853 he received four such letters, one quoting Victor as saying, "The superior does not love us, since he wants us to die here of starvation." Thereupon Joset authorized Father Joseph Menetrey and Brother McGean to seek a new location and, with the assent of the Pend Oreilles, they chose a site south of Flathead Lake, a traditional trading and gaming place regarded as common ground. A brother built five river barges and several dozen wooden boxes and the Pend Oreilles came with a hundred horses to help the Kalispels move. In September 1854 the train moved out from the riverbay mission. At that final moment, the Kalispels changed their minds; they decided to stay in their homeland. Joset snapped, "We are not children. Go on!" Then Victor stepped out with the caravan and most of the tribe followed him to the new St. Ignatius in Montana. Two or three families stayed behind. Hoecken had sold the mission cattle for $2,000, money "to put the new place on a good footing."[16]

During the ten years that a mission existed among the Kalispels, United States Indian policy changed, as it would many times. Management of Indians shifted in 1849 from the War to the Interior department and, although the army continued to represent Indian policy in the northwest, the separation of Washington from Oregon territory in 1853 passed Indian control to civilians. The army had tried to protect natives within an unofficial interior "Indian territory" by discouraging white settlement north of the Snake River and punishing traders who sold whiskey to Indians. But alcohol was not the only threat. Smallpox, like wildfire sweeping Indian bands north of the Columbia, devastated interior tribes. This time, the Kalispels escaped because the Jesuits had vaccinated them with pus from the infected. Perhaps earlier Kalispels had not been so fortunate: the Kalispels say that a band near Calispell Lake was wiped out long ago, and at an old winter camp near Indian Creek, they know a place called "many human bones," where Indians died so fast the living could not bury them all. Now in the 1850s, Indians fled the pestilence, spreading it, again leaving their dead unburied. Coyotes tore at the corpses and the pox soon decimated the coyotes.[17]

A conviction took root in the national capital, meanwhile, that the policy of Indian removal was not working. The Commissioner of Indian Affairs, George W. Manypenny, advocated instead that Indians be placed on permanent reserves. Thus when the 35-year-old Isaac Ingalls Stevens, who had resigned his commission as a major of engineers, set out to cross the northern United States to Washington as the territory's first governor and Indian superintendent, he was committed by federal fiat to persuade the Indians to cede their aboriginal lands in return for reservations. Stevens was simultaneously scouting a route for a northern transcontinental railroad which, if built, would penetrate the buffalo country, breach tribal domains, and increase white immigration. On his journey west, Stevens met in council with Indian chiefs; he arrived at Olympia, the territorial capital, convinced that most tribes would go peacefully onto reservations.

Stevens did not meet the Kalispels but he heard about them, largely from Dr. George Suckley, army physician in the governor's party, who had visited St. Ignatius in November 1853 before the mission moved from the Pend Oreille. The "Kalispelms proper, Pend Oreilles," as Stevens called them in his report of explorations, numbered about 450. When he learned that they had moved to Montana, Stevens assumed that the Kalispels could be combined with the Pend Oreilles and Flatheads on a future reservation. Washington territory at this time extended into Montana. Of this region, Stevens wrote the commissioner, "There is much valuable land and an inexhaustible supply of timber east of the Cascades. I consider its speedy settlement so desirable that all impediments should be removed," and to his territorial legislature, Stevens recommended passage of a law to extinguish Indian claims to land east of the Cascades so that settlers could secure valid homestead titles. During 1854 the governor and Indian superintendent treated with Indians west of the Cascades, intending in 1855 to meet those east of the mountains.[18]

In the meantime, the Kalispels were drifting back, family by family, from the new St. Ignatius to their old home on the Pend Oreille River. Within a year, Victor and most of the Kalispels had returned. They had found the new St. Ignatius a crossroads for Indian hunting and trading parties; it attracted a good many white

Pagh-Pagh. sem-i-am -   1 3 0, 305
"The woman of good sense
(Kalispel)

Private Gustavus Sohon, a barometric observer with Isaac Stevens' exploring expedition, also sketched Indians. Sohon drew this portrait of a Kalispel woman in the spring of 1854. (Smithsonian Institution, National Anthropological Archives, No. 32876–G)

men; Indians of several tribes settled near it, and as the mission thrived, the Kalispels felt themselves being fused into a conglomerate camp where they could retain neither their identity nor their tribal autonomy. They went home to find their tribesmen who had stayed on the river miserable, drunk, gambling—all of the vices the missionaries had tried to stamp out. Joset was furious with Victor, who, he snapped, "instead of standing for order, is following downstream and there is no one to keep order." When the Kalispels wailed that they had been abandoned by the Jesuits, Joset retorted that they would have a priest if they settled where they could farm. But his words reached "deaf ears."[19]

By going home, the Kalispels put themselves in danger of being pushed aside, for Stevens' purpose was to open eastern Washington to settlers and commerce, including the army's Indian zone north of the Snake. The governor proposed to group the Indians on two reservations between the Cascades and the Rocky Mountains, one for tribes consolidated with the Flatheads and the other for combined tribes near Spokane Plains, although his intent was not yet conveyed to the chiefs. His secretary, James Doty, and a pioneer Puget Sound physician who had enlisted in Stevens' Indian service, Richard H. Lansdale, scheduled councils with tribes east of the Cascades. On May 29, 1855, Stevens convened his first council in eastern Washington at Walla Walla with the Nez Perces, Umatillas, Cayuses, Walla Wallas, and Yakimas. Slight, short, peremptory in manner, Stevens held the center of attention wherever he went, listening impatiently to the long speeches of chiefs. From his first meeting he went to the Bitterroot valley to meet the Flatheads, Pend Oreilles, and Kutenais, and after that, to the confluence of the Judith and Missouri rivers to treat with the Blackfeet tribes. The Kalispels sent no observers to these parleys. To each council, Stevens came with a document already drafted; he was willing to make minor changes but his program, calling for Indians to cede their land and move to reservations, did not allow the chiefs much room for negotiation.

Because they spoke through interpreters, neither the governor nor the Indians understood one another well. The Indians left the Walla Walla and Bitterroot councils confused and dissatisfied. Indeed, a conspiracy for war buzzed through the Walla Walla council even while it was in session. On the other hand, the Blackfeet conclave produced an artificial peace that lasted for months on the buffalo prairies. [20]

Stevens at first expected to invite the Kalispels to his council with the Spokanes, Okanogans, Coeur d'Alenes, and Colvilles near Antoine Plante's ferry on the Spokane River. After St. Ignatius moved, however, he concluded instead to meet the Kalispels and Coeur d'Alenes "at their respective missions." He wrote the priests asking their help to assemble the tribes, and assigned to Colonel H. R. Crosbie the task of preparing the Kalispel and Coeur d'Alene councils, intending to hold them on his way back to Olympia from the Missouri. Father Menetrey warned Stevens that the Kalispel mission could offer little in the way of sustenance: "Our crop was very poor, we have little to spare." [21]

When Governor Stevens heard that Kalispels were straying back
to the Pend Oreille he offered Crosbie the alternative of bringing
them, instead, to the Spokane council "as originally intended." To
Special Agent A. J. Bolin, who was to arrange the Spokane meeting, he wrote that "great caution" must be used in dealing with the
Indians. "The general object of treaties, . . . cession of their lands
and placing them on reservations should distinctly be made known.
But as to the particular reservation, whilst every effort should be
taken to ascertain the views of the Indians," the agent should not
promise the Indians a specific location. "I am unwilling to establish
a third reservation between the Cascades and the Bitterroot,"
he warned Bolin, "especially in view of the gold excitement now
breaking out."[22]

The gold excitement had nearly dispersed Stevens' escort before he reached Walla Walla. He had trouble keeping his men from
bolting to the Colville valley where gold had been washed in 1854,
although the news did not spread until a year later. As Stevens
crossed Washington territory eastward, prospectors, packers, and
traders scurried northward. "A gold fever has broken out . . . and
adventurers and miners are resorting thither in thousands," he advised the Commissioner of Indian Affairs. Then gold was discovered near the mouth of the Pend Oreille and, with business slow on
the Coast, thousands more rushed inland. Wagons to the Colville
valley wore tracks that three years later the army followed to open
a post near Colville. And from the first discovery, prospectors
fanned along the streams, looking for other strikes. Gold seekers
spilled into Kalispel country.[23]

But Stevens did not come to talk with the Kalispels. Instead, he
chafed at Fort Benton, held there by delay of his goods for the
Blackfeet council, while the Indian participants scattered to hunt
buffalo. Finally, realizing that he could not hope to reach the Kalispels on schedule, he dispatched Lansdale to St. Ignatius to "call
together into council the Lower Pend Oreilles [Kalispels] . . . and
lay before them the wish of the government to treat with them for
the sale of their lands . . . and to place them on the Flathead reservation." If the Kalispels agreed, Lansdale was to bring a delegation
to meet Stevens at Hell Gate (near Missoula) "invested with full
powers from the Tribe to make the treaty."[24]

Lansdale, of course, discovered that the Kalispels were not at St. Ignatius; he was told they were on their way "but, being poor in horses, and having frail bark canoes only, and compelled to hunt and fish for subsistence, they have been unable to reach the Mission . . . and cannot be brought into council . . . this fall," he wrote Stevens. Between the lines, Lansdale summed up the tragic dilemma of the Kalispels: Unwilling to settle near the mission but reluctant to give up their priests, some toiled back and forth between St. Ignatius and their Pend Oreille River home, living off the country as they went, a people torn by indecision.[25]

Not only was a Kalispel council out of the question but Stevens' Walla Walla negotiations also aborted, for a messenger intercepted his returning caravan to report Indians at war on both sides of the Cascades, settlers and miners murdered, and a large hostile force waiting near Walla Walla to kill the governor. With his guide and one man, Stevens skirted the Indians and reached Olympia. He immediately closed the interior to settlers, traders, and missionaries, directing whites already in the area to deal with Indians only under military supervision.

The Kalispels stayed out of this war but they could not escape its currents; their relatives to the south were fighting and white men, often unable to tell one Indian from another, turned suspicious and belligerent. The Hudson's Bay Company curtailed its sales of guns and ammunition to Indians. Tied by war and territorial affairs to Olympia, Stevens again instructed Lansdale, agent to the Flatheads, to treat with the Kalispels. Before Christmas 1855 Lansdale talked at his agency with Victor and several principal Kalispel men, met them again on December 27, and in the spring of 1856, on March 24, convened a treaty council at St. Ignatius. Here, with the blind Flathead Michel Revais as interpreter, the agent conveyed the terms of Stevens' draft treaty.

The terms were standard stuff. In return for ceding their lands, not specified, the government promised the Kalispels $40,000 to be paid in increments over 20 years, a grist mill, a sawmill, a hospital and physician, an agricultural-industrial school with teachers, and various shops with men to work in them and teach Indians to be carpenters, blacksmiths, or gun, wagon, or plow makers, "by means of which they would be elevated and incited to acquire additional knowledge of farming and trades, and the white man's way of living." The Kalispels were to be united with the Flathead nation on the Flatheads' Montana reservation.[26]

Over the months they had waited for treaty-making, the Kalispels had weighed their situation. Now Victor, small and diffident, stepped forward with their counterproposal, a generous one from the tribe's viewpoint: The Kalispels would cede half their land, that south and west of the Pend Oreille River, and keep the land north and east. "We spoke together about it, and concluded to give what I said. . . . I would be glad if the big father [the President] would give his red children a small piece of land in their own country," he concluded.

Lansdale: "I have not the power to change it [the treaty draft]."

Simon, Victor's brother: "In all things we wish to do what the big father tells us. . . . But we would wish, if he had pity on us, to give us a small spot where we might return in safety. We call our country a safe country; we have no enemy there."

Matthew, a subchief: If the governor had come, we could settle by giving him half our lands, "but it does not do well to do it by letter, for now our chief does not know what to decide." The Kalispels needed gunpowder but they had been told they could not have it. "The big chief wants to starve us to death. . . . We have no horses, no cattle, no pigs, no fields, nothing to live on but powder."

Lansdale replied that peaceful tribes like the Kalispels would not be denied gunpowder for hunting. But he could not alter the terms of the draft. The first day of the council closed indecisively.[27]

The next morning, Lansdale learned from Victor that the tribe had discussed the treaty proposal during the night and a majority resolved to sell nothing without obtaining a reservation on their own land. Lansdale adjourned the council. A short time later, with the advice of Hoecken and Menetrey, he informally persuaded Kalispel headmen to live on the Flathead reservation without signing away their home ground. If nothing else, the agent thus prolonged the division of opinion within the tribe. The Lansdale council showed the Kalispels a government inflexible and unappreciative; it disabused those who thought Stevens their protector, and it strengthened the arguments of those who counseled against moving from the Pend Oreille. Enough of the Kalispels must have talked privately with agent and priests, however, to convince Lansdale, Stevens, and the mission fathers that the tribe would someday move to Montana, a belief that colored the government's future dealings with Victor's beleaguered band.[28]

The Lansdale council, with its overtone of betrayal, also may have provoked some of the Kalispel hotbloods, younger men spoiling for a fracas, to join a defense coalition of nine tribes. Some Kalispels fell in with the quixotic scheme of Polatkin, a Spokane subchief, or a plan of Kamiakin, the Yakima, to exterminate the whites. Everywhere they looked, there seemed to be white men occupying the country once so open. In the rains of late 1856, Colonel Edward J. Steptoe led troops that built an army post at Walla Walla; prospectors looking for gold rushed up the Columbia to The Dalles to strike out northward, and others steamed up the Fraser; a survey party ran a belated boundary line between the United States and Canada, publicly quarreling over ground the Indian tribes regarded as theirs. Liquor flowed wherever the white men appeared.

"The prospects for difficulty with the Indians is [sic] flattering indeed owing to the traffic in ardent spirits," Ben F. Yantis, special agent to the Colvilles, Spokanes, and Coeur d'Alenes, warned the territorial Indian superintendencies. "The chiefs say they can't restrain their young men if it continues." Other agents echoed him. Father Hoecken, now ailing, had written De Smet that Spokanes and Nez Perces sought to spread "hatred" of the whites. Steptoe, trying to abate the liquor traffic by threats and small sorties against traders, cautioned that enforcing Stevens' treaties would "be followed by immediate hostilities." He urged new treaty councils. The army suspected Mormons of supplying Indians with ammunition. Over Stevens' objection that the area would be too large to manage, the Oregon and Washington superintendencies merged in mid-1857. By then Stevens, the treaty-maker, was gone, elected delegate to Congress from Washington Territory. The interior Indians would not see him again, one lesson in the interchangeability of white negotiators.[29]

Steptoe, dismayed by Palouse raids on settlers' cattle in the Walla Walla valley, heard whispers of Indian plots. Perhaps inflammatory letters such as that written by a major of Washington volunteers reached him; in it, the major wrote from Colville that "one needs but a short acquaintance with the tribes to discover that their real sentiment towards the white race is one of hatred."[30]

So Steptoe determined to cow the belligerent Indians with a show of force, using a petition from miners in the Colville area asking for protection as his excuse to move north. On May 6, 1858, Steptoe left Walla Walla with a poorly armed expedition of 152 men and five officers. When his troops crossed the Snake River, which the Indians regarded as their borderline, couriers sped to alert the allied tribes, including the Kalispels. Stevens had promised that friendly chiefs would be notified before troops crossed the river. Among the Coeur d'Alenes, Father Joseph Joset now saw painted warriors gathering in the forest and realized they meant to fight the Americans. He tried to dissuade them from an attack on Steptoe, but could not.[31]

Apparently a heated council among the Kalispels failed to deter their young warriors from joining the Indian war party and, as the painted men galloped off, most of the remaining Kalispels marched from the Pend Oreille toward Canada or headed for the buffalo plains, putting themselves far from the fighting. Some stayed away two years. Those determined to fight lived temporarily with the Coeur d'Alene and Spokane tribes. Kamiakin sent word that he especially wanted the Coeur d'Alenes and Kalispels in the war coalition for their rifles.[32]

The combined Indian force attacked Steptoe near modern Rosalia. About 40 Kalispels were said to have taken part. One Kalispel slipped out of the lines to tell Joset that the soldiers knew a priest accompanied the Indian warriors. Joset was doing his best to stop the assault but while he halted one group of warriors to admonish them, another would dash past him to join the fighting. The priest rode out to talk with Steptoe, who was now retreating; their conversation did little to clarify Steptoe's intent, but Joset assured the colonel that all the chiefs, except the Palouse, desired peace. The chiefs simply could not control their young men.[33]

Steptoe's troop, driven onto a hillock and surrounded, escaped at night to gallop to Walla Walla. The defeat of American soldiers by Indians, seven killed including two officers and six severely wounded, resounded in the national capital. The "Steptoe disaster" went into military annals as "one of the most sad events that ever befell our cavalry." But to the Indians, who seized Steptoe's supply train and a hundred pack animals, this was whole-hog victory. It pumped up those fiery warriors who burned to drive out the whites. And yet, their quarrel clearly was with the army and the government; they mounted no general attack against trading posts or missions, although stray whites were not safe in Indian territory.[34]

The savagery of a war dance at Fort Colville—naked, painted warriors leaping and shouting while an old woman sat in the middle of their circle recounting war deeds and displaying the saddle of a fallen cavalry officer—frightened white men who witnessed it. Scalp dance drums throbbed ominously through the nights. Yet at their old mission, Kalispels provided horses and canoes for the party of Major John Owen, the trader who bought St. Mary's, as he moved fearfully through the country. Other Indians thought Owen should be killed because he wrote "bad things" about them to Washington.[35]

To silence public demand for punishment of hostile Indians, the army stripped men and weapons from its western posts to form two strike forces, sending one under Major Robert Garnett northward from Fort Simcoe (near Yakima) toward the Okanogans and a second, commanded by a stern Vermonter, Colonel George Wright, north from Walla Walla toward the Coeur d'Alenes, with vague intent to envelop the Indians—an awkward pincers more suited to white maneuvers than to fluid Indian tactics. Knowing that a white army would come, the Spokanes invited the Kalispels to join them for defense; the Kalispels debated war for several days and then declined when a shaman forecast that the Spokanes and their allies would be beaten, for he saw peculiar formations in the stars. But some young Kalispels rode off, regardless, to join the Spokanes.[36]

Choked with dust and the ashes of grassland burned by Indians to deny the army forage, Wright's ponderous train of artillery, infantry, and dragoons came upon the main Indian war party ready to fight on September 1 near Four Lakes, a dozen miles southwest of the falls of the Spokane River. The Indians were positioned loosely by tribes with the Coeur d'Alenes, and presumably the Kalispels, near their center. Twice during the ensuing battle a Pend Oreille, Spotted Coyote, believing himself immune to bullets, would ride the length of the battle line unscathed as he dared soldiers to shoot him. As firing began, Wright advanced his infantry skillfully, keeping the Indians moving in front of him, and then suddenly sent dragoons at a gallop, slashing with their sabres. One dragoon ran down Xanewa, a Kalispel leader, jerking him from his horse by his long hair, and another shot the Kalispel sprawling on the ground. Indians scattered into trees and behind hills as the dragoons, their horses winded, drew up after a mile. The four-hour battle was over. Out beyond Wright's tired picket lines, the Indians gathered to reassess their tactics and call for reinforcements. Their losses had not been heavy—perhaps 20 killed and four dozen wounded—but their confidence was shaken. The resolute infantry with long-range rifles and the galloping swordsmen showed the Indians a different face of the white man.[37]

The next morning, Wright marched toward the Spokane River. On the fourth day (September 5), as his soldiers entered a large prairie, they found the Indians drawn for battle again on well-chosen ground, rocky, broken terrain where dragoons could not charge effectively. Warriors set fire to the prairie grasses upwind, rolling billows of smoke over the blue-coated soldiers deployed in skirmish lines but Wright doggedly pushed his infantry through the fire and smoke, fighting over rocky ground, trying to break onto a tableland where he could use his dragoons. The Indians galloped close to shoot, sifted away, galloped in again. Gradually the Indian line fell back until dusk when this battle, like the one four days earlier, ended without a victor. The fight had covered nearly 14 miles, with few casualties on either side. No soldiers were reported killed.

The Indians realized now that they could not overwhelm well-armed infantry of nearly equal numbers; the army should have discovered that traditional tactics would not master Indians. Garnett's wandering troop—the other pincer arm—had played no part; it retired untested to Fort Simcoe. And Wright's force moved too slowly to pursue the mobile Indians. His men, however, had captured nearly a thousand horses. Exhausted, nearly out of supplies, Wright's train spent two days destroying the horses, believing them to belong to the Spokanes. Then the expedition dragged on to the Coeur d'Alene mission without another serious Indian threat.

Wright sent a message to Joset: "Nothing but an unqualified submission to my will can now avail them [the Indians]."[38]
Wright's destruction of the horses impressed the Indians—a man who could coldly discard such great wealth. Although they had not been defeated, the Indians were ready to listen to peacemakers, foremost among them Father Joset. But the allied tribes all refused to hand over any of their people to be punished for the Steptoe attack, and with Joset's assurance that the Indians had stopped fighting, Wright accepted a conditional surrender granting him hostages but no culprits. Coastal newspaper editors hailed his expedition as a military triumph. Actually Wright signed compacts only with the Coeur d'Alenes and Spokanes, although other tribes, including Kalispels, protesting their innocence, sat in on the Spokane council convened by Joset and the chiefs who wanted peace.[39]

With fighting ended, some Kalispels edged back into their Pend Oreille River camps to resume the familiar cycle of digging, fishing, and hunting. As the news of a truce spread, most Kalispels returned to their home country. Still, vengeful renegades hid out among the tribes, unsettling them, for they were frightened by Wright's boast that he would "exterminate" the Palouses if trouble broke out again and by his hanging culpable Indians not covered by his treaties.

To cement the interior peace, the government asked Father De Smet, now serving as chaplain with General W. S. Harney, recently transferred from the Mormon war to command the army in the northwest, to tour the interior tribes who knew him well and to counsel them to respect their peace agreements. Now 60, white-haired, rheumatic, and stout, De Smet set out on horseback October 29, 1858, on a 1,600-mile six-month trek, somewhat apprehensive about the Indians' reaction to his role as government conciliator. He found the interior changing: towns where trading posts had stood, white settlers pushing into tribal lands, Indians exploited and many wasted by liquor. The Jesuit priests and brothers of the missions helped assemble Indians to meet with De Smet—snowbound for weeks among the Coeur d'Alenes—and every where the old missionary got an affectionate welcome. He talked with the chiefs; they all wanted peace, but a few Kettles, Okanogans, and some Kalispels remained bitter and unrelenting.

Father De Smet and the chiefs who went with him to Vancouver in 1859. Left to right, front: Victor, Kalispel; Alexander, Pend Oreille; Adolphe, Flathead; Andrew Seppline, Coeur d'Alene. Rear: Dennis, Colville; Bonaventure, Coeur d'Alene; De Smet; and Francis Xavier, Flathead. (OPA)

He decided to invite the chiefs to accompany him to Vancouver to confer personally with Harney. Ten, including Victor of the Kalispels, agreed to the journey.[40]

As the chiefs assembled, John Owen, the trader and now Flathead agent, told De Smet that he, Owen, had been authorized to bring in the company, and De Smet turned them over to him. Kamiakin, the massive Yakima leader (and in Harney's view, the prize catch of the group), slipped away when he learned that the unreliable Owen had taken charge. The others went to Vancouver where Harney angrily dismissed Owen's claim of authority. Except for Owen's interference, the council between the chiefs and Harney seemed to go well; the Indians professed their willingness to go to reservations, their hopes for peaceful relations, and their innocence in the recent hostilities. At Salem they met the territorial Indian superintendent who tried "to convince them of the madness and folly of war, and secure peace with the United States as their permanent policy." The chiefs toured the growing Oregon towns, saw the military post, and visited the Portland prison where the cells and prisoners' chains impressed them forcibly. (As soon as he returned home, Alexander, the Pend Oreille, ordered the wicked ones among his tribe to step forward, and thereupon whipped them.) Outfitted in white men's clothes, the chiefs dined in private homes as exotic social catches. Each received gifts and a letter from Harney recognizing his tribe as friendly. Victor, the Kalispel, would pass his letter to his sons who showed it, at future councils with whites, to testify that the Kalispels had cooperated, as best they could, with the white men invading their country.[41]

CHAPTER 2

Kalispel Country

T HE country of the Kalispels had been theirs as long as anyone knew. They ranged across it in seasonal migrations and
lived in villages along the lakes and streams that white men
would name the Pend Oreille and Clark Fork rivers and Pend Oreille
and Priest Lakes but their central winter camp, nearly permanent,
lay beside the Pend Oreille River north of an east-west trade route
connecting Indian peoples on the west slopes of the Rockies with
those on the upper Columbia River. Despite their dealings with
many tribes, however, the Kalispels kept a Plateau culture, bor-
rowing fewer Plains traits than did such tribes as the Pend Oreilles,
Flatheads, and others south and east of them.

The trail, topography, and language linked the Kalispels with their
neighbors. They spoke Salish, nearly a universal tongue in the
interior northwest—the speech, with variations, of the Colvilles,
Lakes, Pend Oreilles, Spokanes, Coeur d'Alenes, Nespelems, Sanpoils, Okanogans, Columbias, Wenatchis, Thompsons, Shuswaps,
and more than twenty tribes on the coasts of Washington and British
Columbia. The Kalispel dialect was most like those of the Spokanes,
Flatheads, Pend Oreilles, and Chewelahs, the last simply Kalispels
who had settled in the Colville valley. On the other hand, dialects
among Salish speakers differed enough that a member of one tribe
often could not make himself readily understood to another. Recognizing the similarities in Kalispel and Flathead dialects, when Catholic missionaries produced a pioneering dictionary of Salish, they
titled it, *Dictionary of the Kalispel or Flat-head Indian Language.*[1]

Their linguistic heritage hints that Salish-speaking peoples once lived together, perhaps in the British Columbia interior, until several thousand years before Christ when Athabascans north of them began a southward migration that pushed the Salish out of their accustomed places. Some Salish evidently retreated to the coasts; others, toward the western foothills of the Rockies and the borderlands of the upper Missouri plains; and still others, possibly among them the Kalispels, along the intermontane trenches onto the Columbia Plateau. As they gave ground over a period of six hundred years, these displaced bands carried with them their language, customs, and folk tales, and exchanged ways of hunting, fishing, and making utensils, clothes, and weapons with others they brushed against. Recent archaeological examination of the Kalispels' immediate home ground suggests that Indians may have occupied the Pend Oreille River valley for four thousand years.

A legend ascribed to the Kalispels asserts that they came from the north, dwelt awhile beside Priest Lake and then, after a party ascending Mount Spokane saw in the distance the placid waters of a large lake, moved into the Pend Oreille valley where they discovered their "lake" was really a vast field of blue-flowering camas. There they chose to stay. Their name, Kalispels, derives from a Salish place name, *Kalispelm,* which some say means camas. Their neighbors, the Coeur d'Alenes, called the Kalispel "the camas people"; the Thompsons and Okanogans called them "flat country people," signifying flats near Calispell Lake where camas grew; the Crow term for Kalispels meant "the people who use canoes"; and the Yakimas referred to them as "people of the great fir trees." And white traders and missionaries generally confused the Kalispels with Pend Oreilles, calling them Lower Pend Oreilles, River Flatheads, or simply ignoring distinctions. The Jesuit, Joseph Joset, declared the name Pend Oreille "a French invention without foundation," although Kalispels, like other Plateau peoples, wore earrings. The American explorers, Meriwether Lewis and William Clark, who passed south of the Kalispels, relied on other Indians for information about the Coos-pel-lars, whom they numbered at 1,600.[2]

The mountainous, forested land that the Kalispels occupied was incised by rivers. In theory, one could travel by canoe up the Columbia from the Pacific Ocean to the Pend Oreille, thence to Pend

Oreille Lake, across it, and up the Clark Fork and the Blackfoot nearly to Missoula. In reality, turbulent waters in canyons, shoals, and rapids required portages. The Kalispels used much of this water route between their villages on the Pend Oreille and northwestern Montana, but they shunned the lower Pend Oreille's frothing, narrow canyons and traveled by foot, instead, over well-worn mountain trails westward to Kettle Falls in Colville country, or south through the Purcell trench into Spokane territory. To Priest Lake they followed the Kaniksu trail, starting on the east side of the river opposite Jared. The route to Colville country, the Chewelah trail, apparently started at the camas grounds near Calispell Lake and led along creek drainages past Calispell Peak to Wilson Creek where it dipped down the western slope into the Colville valley. (The trail also seems to have branched into north and south arms; it would be used by trappers and settlers later on, and in 1972 was designated a state historical place, the Calispel Trail.) Another land route, the Kalispel (or Pend Oreille) trail wound east and west along the general courses of the Pend Oreille and Clark Fork rivers, and lesser paths fanned from rivers into hunting and trading grounds or, like those north of Lake Pend Oreille, into berrying heights.[3]

For travel on rivers and lakes, the Kalispels built a swift, light canoe 14 to 16 feet long of white-pine inner bark, ribbed with cedar and sewn with pine roots, a craft easy to maneuver. A canoe required about six days to make; it sat low in the water. Father Joset rode in such canoes with Kalispel paddlers: "One has to sit and keep very quiet on the bottom of a frail thing about two feet wide and half a foot deep; and that the whole day unless . . . there be a leek [sic] and you must go ashore to mend it. . . . On a frame cleverly made of small sticks they stretch the bark of a white pine; every hole is carefully shut with hard pitch, and with that they ride safer on stormy waters, than with our . . . boats."[4]

Kalispels fashioned the ends of their canoes into snouts, low and rounded, the so-called "sturgeon nose," which allowed paddlers better visibility and was more stable in winds than high bows and sterns. The Kalispels were the southernmost builders of bark canoes. Spokanes, for instance, made dugouts. Other tribes also adopted the sturgeon nose, perhaps coached by Iroquois trappers who had migrated from eastern states late in the eighteenth century to settle among interior tribes on beaver streams. Because they taught better techniques and white man's religion, these Iroquois assumed honored places among the interior Salish, and they moved freely among the tribes, sowing notions about white men among Indians who had never encountered one.[5]

The Kalispels used their river highways and overland trails in a ceaseless quest for food and materials for clothing and shelter. Their meetings with other tribes to trade often coincided with mutual fishing or hunting, and while these gatherings offered welcome times for games and contests, their primary purpose was trading for materials better than the Kalispels could find for themselves. Dentalia—sea shells—favored by Pend Oreilles and some Kalispels for ornaments apparently moved by intertribal trading up the Columbia and Fraser rivers as raw materials that Kalispels formed and decorated according to their taste. A few catlinite pipes and obsidian points (arrowheads) suggest exchanges with Plains peoples and those north of the Kalispels. Bitterroot and wild parsnip seem to have come from the Spokanes. But archaeologists have not searched much in Kalispel territory, and their few finds have not shed much light on prehistoric life. A man digging gravel near Usk in 1927 found stone pestles, onyx chisels, and a pipe bowl of redstone. Kalispels could neither explain them nor connect them to an old campsite or burial ground.[6]

Kalispel territory consisted of areas the tribe customarily used for hunting, fishing, and gathering, including some ground they visited only occasionally or shared with other tribes. The tribe sometimes went as a group but more commonly as functional bands, large enough for the task, formed for a hunt or a fishing trip. Consequently, during summer months Kalispels scattered widely over their region. When early snows fell, they collected again in winter camps at sites chosen by their chiefs. They opened their territory to other tribes, expecting the visitors to ask permission to hunt or gather roots there, and Kalispel parties went, asking leave, into the grounds of others, particularly the Spokanes and Colvilles to dig bitterroot and fish for salmon. Like Plateau peoples in general, the Kalispels defined their boundaries by geographic features, rivers and mountains—borders encompassing the places they used.[7]

The places they used took Kalispels on a six-month circuit each

Kalispel men in their sturgeon-nosed canoes on the Pend Oreille River in front of their village, photographed by Curtis c. 1910. (Smithsonian Institution, National Anthropological Archives, No. 83–14082)

year, from camas digging in May and early June to salmon fishing and berrying in July and August, to intensive hunting and fishing in September to prepare for the coming winter. By mid-October, most Kalispels collected in winter camp; they would continue to hunt on snowshoes near the camp, to fish through the ice, and to set snares and traps for small game. Winter hunting expeditions, made up of men and teenage boys, searched for animal tracks and when they found them, circled the prey, usually deer (although caribou, it was said, once abounded north of the Pend Oreille River). The deer might be shot with bow and arrow or clubbed and its carcass cached in a tree. The hunters returned to camp happy and the next morning, the chief sent men to bring in the deer from the caches, then distributed the meat. Some smoked the meat, some boiled it, and others ate it raw. Generally, Kalispels celebrated finding meat in winter, gorging themselves, for they might go hungry for weeks before another successful hunt.[8]

For the winter, Kalispels gathered in one of ten or a dozen winter villages, of which the largest (perhaps 800 residents at one time) was on the Pend Oreille River opposite the present town of Locke, on the east side of the river three or four miles north of, and across from, Cusick, and at the mouth of the Calispell River. Smaller winter sites stood near the outlet of Calispell Lake, near Indian Creek about nine miles north of Newport, near Furport, near Albeni Falls, on the Pend Oreille near its outlet from Lake Pend Oreille, on the Thompson River in Montana above its mouth on the Clark Fork, and near Paradise, Montana, a region considered common ground for several tribes, popular for its moderate snowfall and temperatures.[9]

To fit their mobile life, the Kalispels built portable lodges of woven tule or bark mats attached to poles set to form a cone. The mats could be rolled and the poles trailed behind women (later, behind horses) on the march. In addition to their conical tipi, Kalispels built rectangular lodges, their sides and ends pitched toward center poles, measuring 20 feet or longer. A chief's lodge, used for ceremonies, might be 60 feet. During dances, one could hear the rushes rustle. As a rule, three families (about 20 persons) lived in a 20-foot lodge and up to a dozen families might share a larger one. Lodges were set several inches deep in shallow pits with dirt scooped along the outer edges for insulation. (Old tales portray Kalispels living in deep pit houses roofed with boughs and mats.) Small openings near the pole tops allowed smoke to escape. The lodges held everything, including the ubiquitous half-wild dogs. The Kalispels, like other Indians, tossed the garbage outside; when the debris got too deep, they moved. For warmth, Kalispels wore long tunics of small animal skins sewn together and slept in fur robes. But Kalispels seemed inured to harsh winters. "With a shirt and a buffalo skin," Joset marvelled, one could "brave the severest cold. I have seen a young boy, having nothing on but a small calico shirt, barefoot, stand immobile on ice for more than half an hour, watching the play of other boys." Indians, he added, "won't mind" three or four days without food.[10]

With spring's first warm days, Kalispels prepared to break winter camps but before rolling their tipi mats, they gathered in the chief's lodge to talk over their summer tasks. A chief seems to have suggested summer camp sites, which moved often, and to have known in general where each family would go during the summer. In spring, the Pend Oreille River valley floor yellowed with glacier lilies, their bulbs high in carbohydrates, welcome after a diet mostly of meat during the winter. By the first of June, camas fields flowered and the bulbs firmed, ready for harvest. One by one, women entered the camas fields carrying their special digging sticks, a sort of spoon on a long handle, made of deer antler or hard wood. Sometimes men helped dig, but more often men and boys hunted in nearby hills. Camas grew in meadows beside the Pend

Oreille River from modern Newport north (downriver) to Jared. One favored camas site lay beside Calispell Lake where the camas were plentiful and sweet but small—small, says a Kalispel story, because long ago a young boy caught a salmon that he refused to share with his sister, hiding it in a bandage on his leg, pretending to be hurt. Angered by his selfishness, his sister threw all the large camas toward Idaho and the small camas and hulls into the Pend Oreille valley, and camas in the valley had been small ever since.[11]

Women from the Spokanes, Coeur d'Alenes, Colvilles, and other tribes came often into the Pend Oreille valley to dig camas and their men joined the Kalispel hunters. Such meetings were occasions for contests, trading, and visiting relatives, festivities that went on for several weeks.

When women uprooted camas, they broke off the stalks and packed the bulbs in cedar-bark bags, carrying them to ovens fashioned of rock-lined shallow pits, to be steamed in mounds with layers of firewood, sod, bark, skunk cabbage, and camas stalks for two or three days and then dried in the sun and bagged. Carried to the village, cooked bulbs could be ground in stone mortars as flour, baked with pine moss into black cakes, which then were broken into pieces and stored. Women customarily stored foods on platforms to protect them from mice. A few camas might be bagged raw for winter eating. While they visited, Kalispels and other Indians pulled steaming camas from their ovens, coated them with bear grease or deer marrow, and munched them. A delicacy, camas was also considered healthful. Three dried camas a day, declared a Kalispel, would keep a man alive for a year without hunger pangs. An explorer and trader, David Thompson, would describe camas as having "a pleasant taste, easily masticated," and lasting for years when dried.[12]

After digging camas, the tribe broke into family bands or task groups for the summer. A few Kalispels occasionally trekked to the Spokane River to gather sweet wild onions, to trade for white camas, and to visit and gamble. During the summer, near Calispell Lake women gathered Indian potatoes, a small root dug with a stick and boiled for storage; some dug wild carrots to be mashed and boiled (children pulled them to chew raw), parsnips, cattail shafts, and other roots. Women and children climbed into the mountains for berries, eating the juicy ones on the spot, and collecting the rest in bark baskets soft enough to avoid crushing. Usually one woman sat removing berries from branches while others brought branches to her. This natural pruning seemed to benefit the bushes. Berries with pulp and seeds were sun-dried for later use and some, dried, were formed into cakes smoked over a fire before storing in skin bags. The small foam berries could be cooked and stirred into foam as a confection.[13]

Although they caught chub, squawfish, and trout with bone hooks from canoes in summer and through ice-holes in winter, for large quantities of fish the Kalispels relied mainly on weirs woven of flat balsam anchored to poles in shallow water to steer the fish into underwater baskets of woven willow bark. For canoe and ice fishing, men fashioned a three-pronged hook without barbs, baited with a grasshopper, grub, or trout gizzard, which stuck inside the fish that swallowed it. Weirs varied in design and materials, of course, depending on location and the species of fish to be caught. Smaller weirs belonged to families; the larger and more productive, belonging to the tribe were customarily built at the bidding of a shaman daubed in red paint who chose site and materials. The Kalispels were careful not to insult the kingfisher who, many years before, according to legend, cut off the supply of fish because some Kalispels ridiculed him. Not even supplications to the spirits brought back the fish but the kingfisher relented after receiving his share of the catch. Tribal weirs were supervised by men who took a share of the catch for their work.[14]

Twice a year, once as soon as they had dug camas and again in September before snow dusted their mountains, Kalispel fishing parties traveled by canoe, with portages, to the Salmo River, which flows into the Pend Oreille a few miles above the Columbia. Here were salmon, to be speared in deep holes, caught in a stranding trap (a fence to halt downstream migration), or sometimes, when the run was heavy, simply scooped by hand from shallow water. The salmon, cleaned and cut into strips, were hung in trees to dry and then rolled into packs to be hauled home. Kalispels often (but not regularly) caught salmon at Kettle Falls on the Columbia where they joined Colvilles and other Indians or toiled down to the Spokane for salmon. "It is astonishing the number of salmon which ascend the Columbia yearly and the quantity taken by the Indians," observed a missionary. "It is not uncommon for them to take a thousand a day. . . . Their mode in the Spokane is to make a weir and then spear them. . . . In many places they spear in the night by a firelight." They also used small sweep nets woven of strips of inner bark, pulled by men wading upstream, and scooped fish by hand in shallow pools.[15]

To catch smaller fish, Kalispels suspended woven bark traps from logs laid across a stream, with brush baffles atop the logs. When fish leaped to clear the logs, they struck the baffles and fell back into the traps. Some Kalispel torch-fished with Pend Oreilles on the Clark Fork, building small stone dams to impound char to be speared or clubbed. After some fresh fish were eaten at the fishing site, Kalispel women, like other Salish, cleaned and suspended the rest by poles through the gills to be smoked over the fire.

Kalispels used fishbones to make sewing needles, sharp awls to incise or puncture soft materials like skins, and similar tools.

Kalispels hunted animals and fowl year 'round, with an intensive hunt in August and September to prepare for winter. For small animals, men favored snares or deadfalls, devices that dropped a heavy log or loaded platform on the prey when it tripped a baited trigger. Even young bears could occasionally be killed in a large deadfall; wary older bears usually tore the trap apart to steal the deer-meat bait. Difficult to skin with primitive stone blades, bears were killed only for their meat. Kalispels hung a dead bear over a fire to burn off the fur, then butchered and baked it immediately on hot rocks, because bear meat did not keep well.

Snares were made of sinew loops, slip knots greased with pitch, hung along animal trails and tied to logs or to spring poles to jerk the prey into the air. A diligent Kalispel hunter might set a hundred snares or deadfalls which he visited every other day, knowing other hunters would respect his territory.

Kalispels constructed a stubby bow, about two feet long, using arrows tipped with sharpened stone, perhaps obsidian traded from the Thompsons north of them. The bow shot with good penetrating power at close range for hunting large animals and waterfowl. If a Kalispel shot a duck or goose, he canoed onto the water to retrieve it; he did not train dogs to fetch downed birds although dogs, on occasion, treed bears for him.

Furs of small animals were sewn together for robes and clothing but the deer was perhaps the Kalispels' most useful game; its dried meat kept well and its hide, hair scraped off and pounded soft, could be fashioned into the tunics that men and women wore. Supple deer hide made durable moccasins. In summer, Kalispel hunters with bows and arrows crept up on deer resting from flies in thickets or concealed themselves beside salt licks to shoot deer by moonlight; in winter, when a deer broke through the crusted snow, a man on snowshoes might run up to shoot or club it. Large snares snagged deer walking head-down along trails.

Sometimes large groups hunted deer, the hunters hiding with bows and arrows near a forest clearing, at a cliff, or in a draw, and the drivers, men and women—shouting and beating sticks in a fearful noise—stampeding a herd toward the hunters. Sometimes lines of small fires were set to frighten deer toward the waiting bowmen. Beside the Kaniksu trail, it is said, lay a huge fire pit to smoke numbers of deer driven over a cliff nearby. Swimming deer might be speared or shot with arrows; some were surrounded in swamps. Kalispel men occasionally ran down a deer. One Kalispel, Blind Paul, told white men (perhaps with tongue in cheek) that he had become blind from over-exertion dashing after deer.

Kalispel hunters used a variety of calls to lure fowl and deer to places where they could be killed easily. A provident group hunt might yield ten or a dozen deer.

Obviously Kalispels knew the habits and haunts of animals, fowl, and fish but if anyone had asked them how they learned to catch game or make fire, the Indians would have answered that a spirit—probably Coyote, a popular rascal and teacher in Salish myths—taught their forefathers long before. The Kalispels' belief in natural spirit powers twined through the fabric of their lives; they told mythic tales to explain the unexplainable, as moral lessons, and as simply good stories. Their most important hunts were directed by male shamans who used spirit powers to find animals, incantations and dances for success, and spirit songs, paints, rattles, and other charms to divine the conduct of the hunt. The hunting dance, *sin-*

kakua, brought men together at night around a stiff rawhide on the ground which they beat with sticks as they swayed and sang. Some women, standing behind, also sang, and between songs individual men boasted of the deeds they would do in the coming hunt or told of visions and chanted sacred personal songs.[16]

Hunting tested an individual's spirit power. When a man hunted bear, his wife fasted until he returned so he would not be bitten. Kalispels avoided breaking a bear's bones in butchering or cooking, lest the hunter risk a bite or lose a favored dog on the next hunt. All Kalispels knew the story of the hunter caught in a fire, who put a bear tooth in his mouth, and after being burned to ashes, sprang back to life. Talismans, supplications, and rituals assured the hunter success and protected him. And like other interior tribes, the Kalispels held a winter ceremony for those watched by guardian spirits in which each participant tied an offering to the lodge center-pole during an all-night dance.[17]

After the custom of interior Salish, individual Kalispels sought spirit power as a gift in a spirit or vision quest. As he neared puberty, a young Kalispel male fasted and sweated before venturing alone into the mountains to seek a vision of his personal spiritual guide. He returned only after his guide taught him the special songs and incantations (*sumesh*) that he used for the rest of his life to assure success and ward off evil. Guides usually were animals or birds, and the youth was considered to have acquired some of the characteristics of his spirit protector—the guile of the wolf, strength of the bear, quickness of the deer, and so on. A Kalispel man carried a talisman of his own guide, perhaps a piece of fur or a tooth, in a small bag around his neck.[18]

Young girls sought visions, too, but they were watched over so they would not be harmed. As they climbed into the hills, girls on vision quests offered prayers to conspicuous objects on the way: to an old stump, "May I become as old as you!" Girls were confined in separate lodges at their first menstruation to receive spiritual instruction and learn rituals conducted by an older female relative.[19]

If the Kalispels once practiced other rites as initiation into adulthood, they have been forgotten. But the canny Kalispels, like most Salish, waited for demonstrations of personal spirit power. Occasionally a man or woman showed unusual gifts and would be re-

garded as a shaman. Male shamans might lead a hunt, direct ceremonial dances, and serve as consultants or subchiefs. Both male
and female shamans treated illness, some specializing in specific
ailments, because sickness was considered the work of one with
superior powers that the shaman might overcome. These shaman-
istic rituals with sacred songs, shuffling or leaping dances, painted
bodies, rattles, and potions were termed "medicine" by white
men. Jesuits scorned shamans as "jugglers" for the sleight-of-hand
and tricks shamans sometimes used. But the Kalispel who took too
lightly the spirits lurking around him might dream of *Skaip*, a
powerful wraith who sickened one and imposed tasks to perform
as a cure.[20]

Kalispel folktales told of supernatural beings. For instance, Kalispels declared that no salmon came up the Pend Oreille River because long ago, when Coyote loped through the valley looking for a
wife, the Kalispels refused him one. Coyote spitefully uprooted the
riverbed for a waterfall that salmon could not ascend. Familiar
places evoked stories that linked Kalispels to a mythical past or recalled a significant event. Like other Salish, Kalispels felt a spiritual
essence in peculiar rock formations, singular trees, and other phe-
nomena; they satisfied themselves that river courses, mountains,
and natural oddities were the work of Coyote, monsters, or other
mythical beings who, in their stories, talked and sometimes dressed
as humans.[21]

Around 1730 A.D., by white man's reckoning, Kalispel life
speeded up dramatically with the coming of horses. Journeys that
once took weeks now took days; those of days, hours; and burdens
too heavy for a woman rode easily on a horse. Caravans with
horses might travel thirty miles in one day; mounted men, riding
hard, almost a hundred. From the Pend Oreille to the eastern
gateway of the river trade route was eight days by canoe, nine by
horse.

Horses reached the Kalispels by intertribal trading and thievery
from Spanish outposts in the American southwest. A trade route
through Flathead country had carried a trickle of Spanish trinkets
and utensils northward for perhaps a century before horses appeared on it, handed along (or stolen) from Apaches to Utes to Co-
manches to Shoshonis, these last the funnel for horses into the

northwest. The route and date are speculative, of course, but Kalispels said they traded for their first horses with Pend Oreilles,
their relatives who had mingled with the Flatheads, and passed
them in turn to the Colvilles. Having no word for these marvelous
beasts, Kalispels at first called them big dogs. According to their
memory, Kalispels came upon hoofprints and surmised what the
animal must be before seeing it. When a horse approached them,
their first, ridden by a half-breed, they crowded around it, curious
and unafraid. [22]

If horses speeded the pace and extended the compass of Kalispel life, and that of their neighbors, the animals also apparently
deepened factional discord in the tribe. Kalispels already lived at a
dozen or more winter camps and now some, mainly younger men,
eagerly adopted horses while others held back, slow to change old
ways. They drifted into separate camps. The man with horses
spent his days caring for his horses and fashioning weapons for
horseback hunting and warfare, and his women waited on him.
Even those who detached themselves from horse cults, however,
could not avoid the effect of horses on Indian life—the speed of
travel and the widened range of trade goods. (Nevertheless, some
tribes, such as the Sanpoils, eschewed the horse culture.) [23]

As Kalispels traded for (or stole) more horses, the audacious
mounted adventurers took their women and children to join the
Pend Oreilles, Flatheads, and others for buffalo hunts on the prairies of the Judith basin, clashing there with Blackfeet hunters and
raiders. Until he renounced the hunt, one of their leaders was
Standing Grizzly, Loyola. Buffalo did not range in Kalispel country
because, long ago, Coyote killed the wife that Old Buffalo had given
him, so that Old Buffalo could not finish his journey to the Pend
Oreille. Horse cultists won prestige by stealing horses from other
tribes. Vengeful raiders prowled Kalispel ground but it is said that
Blackfeet ventured there once, to Sandpoint on Lake Pend Oreille,
only to be driven off. Kalispel horse partisans did not desert the
tribe; they stayed, a restive and divisive element. Possibly conflict
over horses was the occasion for one band of Kalispels, under Ambrose, to move permanently to Camas Prairie and Horse Plains in
northwest Montana and another, under Michel, to settle at the outlet to Lake Pend Oreille, and be known as Upper Kalispels. Yet
each band seems to have included buffalo hunters. [24]

Women's roles changed when their men turned to the horse culture; they became less beasts of burden and more servants to their men. A folktale suggests the horseman's attitude toward women: Grouse tricked Coyote into swallowing his eyes, thinking he could regurgitate them, but of course he was blinded. Thereupon, Coyote skinned an old grandmother and stole her eyes and, after a spirit dance, he shed the skin which sang: "If it's a girl, throw her in the river; if it's a boy, keep him to help you." Yet, among the Kalispels, as among all Salish, women were known to sit in tribal assemblies and speak their minds.[25]

That astute observer, the Jesuit Joset, remarked that the buffalo hunter only tended the horses and killed game. "All the work falls upon the woman, to the saddling of the horse for her lord," to butchering, smoking, and hauling the meat and scraping and beating the hides for robes. A century after the Kalispels acquired horses, Joset characterized most of them still as hunters of deer, elk, and bear, "all but buffalo. They are necessarily active and energetic; the labors are more equally divided between the two sexes. . . . The wife depends on her husband for a living, and although not so much of a slave as among buffalo hunters, still she is submissive and affectionate." The sacred nature of the buffalo dance shows clearly in the old tale of a 10-year-old boy who innocently joined the ceremony one night before the hunt. Whoever took part in the dance had to take part in the hunt. Sadly, his mother outfitted him and the boy, on a small horse, rode off with the hunters, who attempted to steal Blackfeet horses. In the ensuing chase, the lad fell, was surrounded by Blackfeet and shot.[26]

The horse changed Kalispel life in other ways. A horseman killed and transported more small game than a hunter on foot, and while the Kalispels' boundaries did not change, with horses they could kill off faster all the game in one area. They moved oftener and gave small game less time to replenish. Harder stone points obtained by trade made better weapons. Skins became so commonplace that Kalispels used them for tipis, discarding woven mats. A Kalispel who did not own horses fell behind the horsemen on hunts. In winter, when snows buried the riverside forage along the Pend Oreille, Kalispel horsemen drove their herds fifty or more miles south to the milder Spokane Prairie and stayed to guard them until spring.[27]

The Kalispels did not embrace the horse culture of the Plains—the war chiefs, war honors, counting coup, and the rituals of horse warfare, although they were said to have learned to scalp from the Flatheads—but they hovered at its fringe, positioned on their east-west trade route between Indians on their east who became dedicated horsemen within a generation and tribes on their west who held onto the old ways. The Colvilles, Okanogans, Sanpoils, Lower Spokanes, Columbias, and other fishing tribes perhaps needed horses less than did hunters, but lure of the horse went beyond convenience. To the young man panting for excitement, the horse offered it aplenty.[28]

A Kalispel man organizing a war party quietly painted his head with white earth and pretended to cry while reciting the names of relatives and friends killed by enemies. Others inclined to fight also painted and cried until their group was large enough to persuade the chief to call a war council. If the tribe voted for war, emissaries hurried to allies seeking their help. At such councils, the chief and his advisors smoked a pipe, following the advice of Coyote to Buffalo long before: "When all the animals become people, and when you're angry with one another, smoking with each other will bring peace in each other's feelings."[29]

No matter how reluctant to change, a Kalispel could not ignore the tokens of a world unimagined that the trade routes showed him. Metal, cloth, and glass carried by horsemen flowed along the trails, and with them, tales of white men. In the century before meeting whites, the Kalispels were a people in passage, divided among themselves, poised between old and new, sniffing the aroma of new times that wafted along the trade routes.

No one knows when Kalispels met their first white men and measured these storied creatures for themselves. Legends hint at free fur trappers and vagrant refugees from coastal ships passing among interior Indians but, if these men came, they left no mark. Some seem to have forecast the advent of missionaries and the Iroquois who settled late in the eighteenth century among Salish peoples taught them Catholic hymns and prayers. A fur trader, Peter Fidler of the Hudson's Bay Company, bartered with Kutenais in 1793; perhaps Kalispels traded, too, but if so they did not come home with rifles, as Kutenais did. In 1800, another, David Thompson of the North West Company, sent two men to trade for furs and to winter with the Kutenais; maybe Kalispels met them. The American explorers, Lewis and Clark, passed south of the Kalispels but in 1807 the traders Finan McDonald and James McMillan spent a winter on the Kootenai River near modern Libby, Montana, and surely some Kalispels met them.

Aside from early shadows and traders, the Kalispels felt the presence of white men, not only in trade items and horses, but in the diseases for which Indians had little resistance. Terrifying smallpox sped from tribe to tribe, outrunning trade goods, and struck the Kalispels perhaps as early as 1760. Twenty years later, in 1782 or 1783, a virulent wave of smallpox decimated Plateau tribes. By one estimate, one half to one third died. Hunters returning home found camps stilled, tipis flapping untended, the occupants dead, partly eaten by starving dogs. Interior Indians raised the grisly toll by their traditional cure—heavy sweating, followed by a plunge into cold river water. Shamans worked no magic to stem smallpox as the pestilence swirled, like a macabre cloud, westward from the Crows. [30]

When white men reached the Kalispels, they came from the north, fur traders crossing the continent by river and mountain pass looking for pelts for world commerce. The fur trader and surveyor, David Thompson, left the first record of a white man's meeting with Kalispels. To him, they did not seem remarkable. Thompson knew the general dispositions of Indian bands from his men and from dealings with Blackfeet before he advanced southward along the Kootenai River valley in September 1809, noting in his diary the terrain, weather, distances, and details of his trades with Indians. Although his compass broke and clouds often hid the sun, Thompson's data were precise enough that scholars could trace his paths. A moralistic Welshman, sometimes peevish from the pain of a badly set broken leg, Thompson nevertheless got along well with Indians, learned their dialects, and mapped their ground—mapped it so well that he would be recognized as the outstanding geographer of his time. [31]

Thompson beached canoes near modern Bonners Ferry and sent Finan McDonald and another man ahead to summon Indians with pack horses from Pend Oreille lake. In his journals, Thompson called them "Saleesh," but some may well have been Kalispels, "a mild intelligent race of men; in whom confidence could be placed." The Indians brought 14 horses to carry the trader's packs to Lake Pend Oreille, where some of the goods were loaded into canoes while the horse-train followed the shoreline to the mouth of the Clark Fork River. There on September 9, 1809, Thompson reached a camp of 54 Saleesh, 23 Skeetshoo [Coeur d'Alenes], and four Kutenais. With the help of Indians, Thompson built Kullyspell House, a trading post, in two log buildings with grass-and-mud thatched roofs on a point extending into the lake. Thompson took pains to make one structure, the warehouse, as dry as possible for trade goods and furs he hoped to barter from Indians.[32]

The lake, a later explorer said, was "closely hemmed by mountains of granite. The extraordinary height of the spring floods is shown by a clearly-marked white line on all the trees and rocks that border the lake, 11 feet above the present level of its waters. . . . Meadowland which skirts the lake . . . must all be deeply overflown in the spring . . . so that the country is perfectly impassable till the water recedes, and allows a passage along the shore."[33]

His post built, Thompson set out to explore the Pend Oreille valley, taking one of his men, an "Indian lad," and four horses, hoping to discover a north-south route for trade to evade Piegans who were angry with him because Thompson sold guns and knives to their adversaries. He followed the broad river with its slow current, banks laced with wild grasses, while abundant wildfowl squawked into the air as the horses passed. Thompson's journal does not mention a trail, but as long as the party stayed on firm ground, the going apparently was easy. After three days, on September 30, where the river widened (De Smet's "bay"), Thompson came upon an Indian camp. Summoned by the Indian lad, six men, two women, and three boys paddled across the river in canoes to give the explorer gifts: two cakes of root bread, twelve pounds of edible roots (camas, no doubt), two dried salmon, and some boiled beaver for which Thompson exchanged tobacco. He endured a welcoming speech from an old man. These Kalispels must have looked like many other Indians to Thompson, for his journal mentions nothing about their dress, lodges, canoes, or manner.[34]

"These poor people informed me there were plenty of Beaver about them and the country," Thompson recalled, "but they had nothing but pointed Sticks to work them, not an axe among them." The next day, leaving his horses with the Indian boy, he went downriver by canoe with a Kalispel guide. The river narrowed, the current swiftened, and snow covered the hills. To his dismay, Thompson learned that his Kalispel had never gone downriver to the narrowest canyons and falls, and concluded properly that his information from a Lake chief, that the river bounded over cataracts before entering the Columbia, must be correct. His impression of the Indians was that they "pride themselves on their industry, and their skill in doing anything, and are as neat in their persons as circumstances will allow." With a different Kalispel guide, Thompson would make one more trip down the Pend Oreille in April of the next year, however, to be sure that it offered him no easy route to the Columbia.[35]

Kullyspell House, closed after two seasons, would be one of the posts frequented by Kalispels as the fur trade rose to its zenith and then fell off in the forty years after David Thompson paddled down the Pend Oreille. The Hudson's Bay Company, which in 1821 absorbed the North West Company, dominated a business at first dependent on Indian trappers and then on company brigades combing the streams for beaver. American traders came to the same posts but eventually staged an annual rendezvous for trappers and Indians far southeast of Kalispel country. The Hudson's Bay maintained a Saleesh (Flathead) post intermittently, operated the old North West post, Spokane House, at the confluence of the Spokane and Little Spokane rivers, until April 1826, and eventually settled on Fort Colville, built 1825–26, the most influential of the company's trading sites in territory familiar to the Kalispels. To all of these, Kalispels carried furs to exchange for iron points, guns, utensils, woolens, steel knives, files, and sharp axes.

From fur traders' accounts, the tribes of the interior northwest came to be known as distinct peoples occupying specific territories. The American government largely took the fur traders' tribal names for Indians and adopted, as well, the practice of picking one Indian as head chief for convenience in dealing with a tribe. To

Standing Grizzly, whom Jesuit missionaries called Loyola, the Bay gave new clothes, showing that the company recognized him as chief of the Kalispels.[36]

In little more than a generation, the traditional base of Indian life vanished. The fur traders equipped Indians with better weapons—guns, iron arrowheads, traps, and steel knives—that allowed hunters to deplete game faster; they goaded the Indians to trap fur-bearing animals well beyond their own needs. Some districts became barren because the cycle of reproduction was destroyed. The traders bought Indian products—leather lodges and clothing, roots, and berries for their men and animal skins, pemmican, horse furnishings, and similar goods for export—thus subtly speeding the pace of native life. Kalispels ranked, for a time, as leading suppliers of horse furnishings to Fort Colville. The traders offered European models of dress, conduct, and outlook that some Indians copied. Women especially preferred cloth to leather attire and, if chiefs wore white men's hats and coats as symbols of authority, other Indians bought them, too, to look important. Thompson remarked on "the great advantages of woollen over leather clothing, the latter when wet sticks to the skin, and is very uncomfortable, requires time to dry," and tended to lose shape.[37]

And the fur commerce unveiled the northwest interior to the American people through books, articles, and letters, bringing missionaries and settlers. Tribes in the pathway of settlement would be swept aside while the Kalispels, off the immigrant roads, would temporarily be passed by, to be encircled by a white civilization that breached their familiar trails and bridled their nomadic habits.

Settlement and changes in fashion from beaver to silk virtually closed out the fur trade although a small market for furs would continue well into the twentieth century when Kalispels sold furs to wholesalers at Sandpoint. While the organized trade lasted, however, Indians gathered at the posts, savoring lively companions, gambling, horse races, and social contacts. Sometimes buffalo-hunting parties left their aged and infirm camped at a post while they rode to the prairies. Hudson's Bay artisans repaired Indians' guns, sharpened their axes, and company factors sometimes fed them, but the Bay did not give Indians liquor. Americans inju-

diciously plied natives with alcohol to encourage trading. During
the fur era, Kalispels circulated among Spokane, Saleesh, and Colville posts: A trader fussed that Kalispels refused to leave Saleesh
post in 1825 until the company closed it for the season; the Bay
hired Kalispels to pasture company horses, to act as couriers, to
move men and goods by canoe, and a Kalispel chief sat in council at
Colville in 1830.[38]

Father Joset called the Kalispels "a disorderly people, addicted
to drinking, to gambling, to sorcery and troublesome to whites,"
people who harbored grudges, but halfbreed trappers settled among
the Kalispels as friendly and took Kalispel women. Most whites
judged Kalispels as rowdy at their worst but usually friendly and
industrious. Kalispels welcomed a few white men among them,
hoping to learn farming, metal working, and other skills, curious
about their spirit powers. Kalispel trappers traded diligently at Colville during spring, summer, and fall months, failing to appear only
when snow blocked their trails; they sold beaver, large numbers of
muskrat, some mink, and even a few bearskins from a territory
bountiful enough that Kutenai trappers had to be warned repeatedly to stay out. Here again, however, Kalispels differed, for a
Hudson's Bay count showed that only one in three Kalispel men
owned guns, and fifty years after the fur trade penetrated their
land, only half of the men owned horses. Clearly not all Kalispels
coveted horses or guns. Many preferred the quieter life of their
ancestors.[39]

A bellicose element among the Kalispels, presumably the horse-
gun-buffalo crowd, picked fights. Thompson tried to shame a
Kalispel and Spokane war party attacking defenseless Okanogans
but managed only to divert about 50 warriors to a foray against
Piegans. To persuade the Kalispels to go home peacefully, a Hudson's Bay man gave gifts to them when they set out to avenge an
alleged murder by Coeur d'Alenes. (The murdered Kalispel, incidentally, sprang back to life, not an uncommon claim among
shamans.) The fur companies, of course, maintained peace for the
sake of their business and safety of their people. Their men not
only mediated Indian disputes but, under its 1821 government license, the company was obligated to give Indians moral instruction, and under an 1823 resolution of its managers, to observe Sun-

days as religious holidays for the edification of whites and Indians. The Bay's pious posture at least piqued Indian curiosity; many natives learned hymns and prayers. But it is doubtful that they understood the white man's religion with its abstractions so different from their covenant with Mother Earth. Joset thought the Kalispel had no words for good, soul, spirit, or hell—and if he meant abstract terms, perhaps he was right. The Kalispels understood what it meant to be good and had a word for that, *xest*.[40]

In their first encounters with white men, the Kalispels foresaw no threat to their territory or their way of life. They obtained better weapons and better tools. South of the Kalispels, however, the Nez Perces, Umatillas, and others watched with sinking hearts the creaking trains of weary immigrants plodding by hundreds toward new homesteads. In little more than a century after the Kalispels traded for horses, their ground was encircled and breached and, however slowly they realized it, the land was theirs no longer.

CHAPTER 3

Promises

G ENERAL Harney's order at the end of October 1858 proclaimed peace in the interior northwest, authorized settlement near military posts, and lifted the army's 1855 ban on
immigration east of the Cascades. Harney had recently met in
council with the chiefs and with Father De Smet; he had every confidence that the tribes who fought Steptoe and Wright would not
make war again. Like Isaac Stevens, Harney wanted the country
opened to fulfill its manifest destiny as farmland and cattle range
for white settlers. His order dismayed the territorial Indian superintendent, J. W. Nesmith, already at odds with the army's handling
of Indians, who warned that its effect would be to "throw open the
entire Indian country . . . to immediate occupancy and settlement," while the Indians were protesting "intrusion of white settlers upon their lands."[1]

On the other hand, Ben F. Yantis, special Indian agent in eastern
Washington, said that "most of the chiefs of the Tribes composing
my district have expressed a desire to have a few Americans settle
among them for the purpose of teaching them farming, as they are
fast becoming convinced that it will not do to depend entirely on
their fisheries for subsistence." A few months earlier, Yantis, estimating the Kalispels at perhaps 250 souls, reported the Indians,
"very friendly disposed toward the miners" on the Pend Oreille
River, remarking that even some Indians were mining.[2]

47

Brevet Major Pinkney Lugenbeel, sent in 1859 to establish a military presence among non-treaty Indians at a camp about 14 miles south of the old Hudson's Bay post at Colville, wrote that during his battalion's march north from the Snake River, the tribes allied against Wright—Palouses, Spokanes, Pend Oreilles [Kalispels], and "some Coeur d'Alenes"—called on him to express their friendship for the white man. The tribes around Lugenbeel's station, Harney Depot, were "well affected," he said, and the "Pend Oreilles, the most numerous tribe near this Depot . . . have always been friendly, sober, and industrious." He requested a shipment of pipes, tobacco, matches, and blankets to pass out as gifts to head men who visited him, suggesting (between the lines) a fairly steady traffic of friendly Indians from tribes now benign.[3]

Thus the consensus from the interior, military and civilian, portrayed the Indians as peaceful and resigned to white immigration. The official letters of the time advocated opening schools for the Indians, giving them farm tools, and settling the vexing uncertainties of land titles.

If no permanent settlers yet invaded the Kalispels' sheltered river valley, towns and farm districts sprang up around them and freight and travelers crossed the traditional Indian trails, intersecting the routes to salmon fishing and buffalo. Yantis warned the superintendent, late in 1857, that the Indians had no winter provisions; they had to hunt buffalo or starve.[4]

A raw village, Pinkney City, clustered near Harney Depot, populated by rough men bent on quick riches as new discoveries of gold rekindled mining excitement. Gold-hunting parties, organized in Portland, streamed northward from The Dalles and Walla Walla. A merchant, William Newman, established a way station (at future Sprague) in the Spokanes' country for travelers and government trains. Cattlemen drove herds over the Okanogans' trail into British Columbia to feed miners and prospectors struck out from the gold diggings on a tributary of the Kettle and at the mouth of the Pend Oreille to look for more gold. They found rich sandbars on the upper Fraser. Miners rushed from Colville and some coastal mills closed as workers left them to dash inland. Shiploads of miners arrived from California.[5]

In the Flatheads' country, where the Kalispels and other tribes

formed buffalo-hunting caravans, John Owen protested that cattlemen and farmers had appropriated land in the river valleys, and
when Congress ratified the Flathead treaty in March 1859, trains
of immigrants appeared, thinking the Flathead country open for
settlement. The next year, Captain John Mullan's crew, nearly a
hundred men with hand tools and wagons, constructing a military
road from Fort Benton on the Missouri to Walla Walla on the Columbia, struck directly through the lands of the Spokanes and the
Coeur d'Alenes.[6]

As incursions increased, reports to the Indian office protested
that white men were corrupting Indians with whiskey. "Miserable
squatters," Lugenbeel called them, sold whiskey from mobile sta-
tions along the Columbia River. Yantis warned of "prospects for difficulty with the Indians . . . owing alone to traffic in ardent spirits
that is carried on here by persons coming up to the mines," and
quoted the chiefs: "They say they cannot restrain their young
men." Settlers wanted to destroy the liquor.[7]

Lacking both treaties and agents, the Kalispel head men went to
Harney Depot. Lugenbeel appealed to the territorial superintendent on their behalf and tried to counsel them, but the territorial
Indian service was snarled by frequent changes in personnel and
uncertainty about the location of agents or their districts. Mail
moved at a snail's pace—news of the Civil War arrived 22 days
after its outbreak. The government's official posture toward Indian
peoples and their lands was still the plan for reservations outlined
by Stevens.

In the national capital, Alfred B. Greenwood, thrust hurriedly
into the post of Commissioner of Indian Affairs in 1859, found Indian policy outmoded and neglected by Congress; he adopted the
plan fashioned largely by his chief clerk, Charles E. Mix, to con-
centrate Indians on small reserves "for a limited period until they
can be fitted to sustain themselves." William P. Dole, who succeeded Greenwood in 1861, advanced this policy of assimilation and
believed that if Indians were going to be farmers, their reservations were already too big. In other words, the permanent reservations that Stevens had promised were being discarded in the
capital.[8]

The government seemed to have no settled policy for tribes

without reserves. The Kalispels, Coeur d'Alenes, and other non-treaty tribes distrusted most whites; they "sneered" at the docile Flatheads who had accepted a treaty, sarcastically asking to see the farms, equipment, schools, and "other fine promises" of the Stevens compact.[9]

Although the territorial legislature in 1861 authorized a company to divert the Pend Oreille into the Spokane River to mine the riverbend for gold—the company never functioned—the Pend Oreille lay far enough north of advancing settlement that the Kalispels remained relatively undisturbed at home. With the start of the Civil War, the Indian service's already meager resources dwindled. Much of the administration of interior Indians had fallen unofficially to the army, which tried to shield Indians from flagrant white abuses, but now the regular troops marched away to war. Two companies of the Second California Volunteers moved into Fort Colville [Harney Depot] as a peace-keeping force, isolated, in unaccustomed cold, resentful, and drinking whiskey liberally. Some men were said to be criminals who chose the Volunteers rather than prison. The highlight of the Volunteers' service was a memorable ball in February 1863 attended by perhaps four hundred guests, including eight score Indian and halfbreed women. A boundary commissioner, summing up, predicted, "Whiskey and civilization are doing their work quickly and surely. . . . In 20 years time, they [the Indians] will be a matter of history." His view was widely shared, even by those most sympathetic toward Indian peoples.[10]

For perhaps a decade before the Civil War, Congress had been scrapping its earlier concept of tribes as sovereign, rejecting proposed treaties that embodied native land titles and treating Indians, instead, as wards. (In 1871 Congress would stop making treaties with tribes.) Commissioner Dole, and congressmen who opposed this change, tried to preserve Indian titles by agreements with Indian tribes that contained careful descriptions of Indian lands, but the Senate regularly attached disclaimers to these contracts, denying that Congress recognized any native claims to title.[11]

While the government thus changed its attitude toward Indians, prospecting and mining continued in the northwest, little slowed by war. Prospectors had ascended the Pend Oreille as far as Kalispel fishing sites at the mouth of the Salmo in 1858, finding only a little flaked gold, then rushed southward in 1860–61 with the news of discoveries near Pierce City in Nez Perce country. The legislature, trying to establish roads and mail routes in this chaotic interior region, estimated that five thousand or more men engaged in mining. Back the miners rushed in 1863–64, to Wild Horse Creek in the east Kootenay district of British Columbia, veterans from California, Colorado, and Nevada. To reach gold placers at Last Chance Gulch [Helena] in Montana, freight and mail carriers followed the Columbia, crossed overland to Lake Pend Oreille, navigated the lake and the Clark Fork, and took trails to the gold camps. With freight lines and towns to serve the miners, enough settlers populated eastern Washington by 1858 that the legislature created Stevens County, stretching roughly from the Cascades to the Bitterroots.

Five years later, on March 3, 1863, Congress sliced off Idaho Territory; in May 1862 it had yielded to demands for open lands to settle by passing the Homestead Act, and in 1864 chartered the Northern Pacific Railroad to follow generally the route surveyed by Isaac Stevens, subsidizing the railroad company with grants of alternate sections of land along its route.

In the expanding commerce and government of white settlement, Indians struggled to find their place. On Fool's Prairie [Chewelah] in the Colville valley, uprooted Kalispels and other Indians cultivated "small patches" aggregating perhaps a thousand acres, raising chiefly wheat and potatoes and continuing to hunt and fish. (These were Chewelahs, Kalispels who had married Colvilles and had moved to a place between the tribes.) A few Kalispels joined Chief Moses' band on the Columbia River. But a large number of displaced natives, estimated variously at 1,000 to 1,500, Kalispels among them, milled through the river valleys of northeastern Washington and northern Idaho, trying to hold to shreds of their nomadic life, driving their horse herds with them, "renegades . . . who have no treaty relations to the United States," declared a Commissioner of Indian Affairs. "They subsist mainly on fish, and have no desire to cultivate the ground."[12]

The 1866 legislature memorialized Congress to make treaties with these wandering Indians, asserting that "the security of life and property is in constant jeopardy from . . . roving tribes."

Pinkney City emerged as a bed of Indian corruption with "as many prostitute Indian women and drunken Indians as soldiers and citizens." Desperadoes driven out of Lewiston, Idaho, scurried there. By 1862, Pinkney City had six licensed saloons and a brewery. Victor complained that a white man carried whiskey into the Pend Oreille valley to trade for horses.[13]

The Colville agent, William Park Winans, soon would be accused of countenancing prostitution and drunkenness and of diverting Indian goods to his own use, charges he stoutly denied. To be sure, Colville was a particularly awkward agency—an agency without a reservation, managing Indians without treaties, a gathering place for vagrants, and a distribution point for supplies and gifts for Indians. Moreover, agents and priests were no longer so quick to speak out against whites, now that there were so many of them. "The white does not sympathize with the savage," Joset wrote to a fellow Jesuit, "and if we should limit our ministrations to the latter, we would be sure to share the antipathy of which he is the object."[14]

The main body of Kalispels, estimated at between 403 and 420, remained in the Pend Oreille valley, living on both sides of the river. Near the old mission, timothy hay gone wild spread over 1,200 acres. Kalispels cut it for their horses. A dozen or so Kalispel farms, totaling perhaps 385 fenced acres (not all tilled), produced wheat, oats, potatoes, peas, corn, and garden seeds, according to the reports Winans sent to the commissioner, and Kalispels owned among them 13 plows, 6 cradles, and 14 hoes. They packed some wheat to Colville to be ground into flour. The Kalispels continued to dig camas in May and June and to join other tribes for salmon fishing at Kettle Falls. Winans remarked that "the advanced state of civilization that exists among them is due, in great measure, to the Catholic fathers who . . . planted in their minds the desire to better their condition. They seem well disposed toward whites," none of whom had yet settled in the valley.[15]

Winans, counting the Kalispels and other tribes in anticipation of the Northern Pacific Railroad, distributed gifts supplied by the territorial government. To the Kalispels, he said, he gave 150 pounds of bacon, 400 pounds of flour, 24 boxes of matches, 25 pounds of sugar, 5 of soap, 10 of tobacco, and 5 of tea in a three-month period. (He neither saw nor supplied Michel's band at the foot of Pend Oreille lake.) Victor instructed his people to give Winans true information about their families, and he asked Winans again for farm implements when the agent suggested what the government might give. "The blankets and calico given my people only make them lazy," the chief lamented, "for if they can get such things without paying for them, they will not work." And he added, "I want a school established among my people." The isolated Kalispels remained Catholic. Father Paschal Tosi, a sturdy, stern Jesuit serving the Upper Spokanes, now came once a year to spend a month among the Kalispels where Winans saw him "instructing the children in their religious exercises, they were very attentive, and it was truly a very pleasant relief to the savage surroundings to see the Father seated under a tree, the children seated around him on the ground repeating the Catechism and singing Sacred Songs."[16]

The impending construction of the Northern Pacific presaged abrupt, wholesale changes: immigrants, farms, substantial towns, roads, commerce, and government. The railroad would close a fading Indian era. Irked by the railroad's false starts, Congress decreed that track-laying must commence in 1870. The railroad issued mortgage bonds, filed a map of its proposed route (to be changed) with the General Land Office, and let contracts for building at both ends of the line. Congress had granted the railroad much of the land claimed by non-treaty tribes in eastern Washington and northern Idaho, and now the Indians must be gotten out of the way. By executive order on April 9, 1872, a new reservation was set aside for Kalispels, Spokanes, Colvilles, Sanpoils, and Coeur d'Alenes. The Coeur d'Alenes had never settled on the reserve defined in an executive order in 1867.

The reservation extended from the mouth of the Spokane on the Columbia north to the Canadian border, ran east along the border to the Pend Oreille River and then south along the river to the Idaho line, and from there southwesterly, following the Little Spokane to the Spokane. For the Kalispels, the reserve meant giving up their land north and east of the Pend Oreille, their traditional winter camps and favored hunting and fishing sites.[17]

Neither Indians nor whites had been polled for opinions on this preserve. White settlers protested noisily. "On the reservation there are now nearly one hundred farms and between five and six hundred settlers . . . induced by invitation of Gen'l Harney to settle up the country," Winans told the territorial superintendent, and although most were squatters, they would have to be removed from "homes which they have made in good faith under assurance of government protection."[18]

Winans called the tribes into council near Antoine Plante's place (on a creek about a mile and a half north of the Spokane River) on June 21, 1872, to tell them about their reservation. The Spokanes scolded the government for building roads and choosing a reservation without consulting them, and a Sanpoil denounced the proposal: "We are men, not to be branded and driven like Cattle. The land is ours and instead of the whites giving it to us, we have given them what they now occupy." Yet, realizing that it was inevitable, the Indians generally agreed to a reservation expanded to take in their homelands. Simon [Semo], a Kalispel subchief, asked that the border be moved to the mountains east of the Pend Oreille River, as Winans understood him, approximately the Idaho line.[19]

An inspector general at Fort Colville reported the Indians distressed, preferring to "take their chances" among white settlers, muttering that they "had better be killed where they are than to starve on the reservation." Winans, meanwhile, warned that these same Indians, expecting Fort Colville to be closed, had gathered in May 1870 to plot a war of extermination against the whites when the troops withdrew (approximately 60 soldiers remained at the fort) but the inspector general thought the Indians peaceable, making no threats.[20]

The tribes had neither moved to nor agreed to the preserve when a second Executive Order on July 2, 1872—three months after the first—abruptly changed the boundaries: to the Columbia on the east and south, the Okanogan River on the west, and the Canadian border on the north. This reserve, the Colville, would strip the Kalispels of all the territory they claimed. The territorial superintendent characterized this reservation as "mostly a conglomeration of barren, rocky mountains," and predicted gloomily "that if the non-treaty Indian tribes in this Territory . . . are forced on it to remain, . . . the greater portion of them would probably soon be starved to death."[21]

In the sudden changes of reservation boundaries, Winans played the scapegoat, accused of lying to the Indians about the land and actively opposing the first reserve because white settlers wanted the area. A special commissioner charged that "when the order setting off the first reserve reached Winans . . . he concealed the fact from them [Indians] until he could and did manipulate the change." The accusation seems unfounded in view of Winans' role in the council of June 21, and Winans indignantly wrote Selucius Garfielde, territorial delegate in Congress, that he had never recommended the reservation east of the Columbia; he had merely asked Senator Henry W. Corbett of Oregon to keep the army at Fort Colville.[22]

Garfielde, it would seem, yielded to citizen demands that the reservation be changed; he had been known "to vary his politics according to the winds of fortune," and in 1873 would be rewarded with appointment as collector of customs for Puget Sound. The furor ended Winans' term as agent; he was succeeded by John A. Simms, nominated by Catholics, and whispers soon spread that Simms "and the Jesuits put up a job to steal the Colville Valley for the Indians and by false statements secured an Executive Order making it an Indian Reservation."[23]

Now the interior northwest roiled with uncertainty. A Kalispel chief was quoted: "If they attempt to move us, there will be blood in this country. . . . In another year you would have had all the Indians farming if you had helped us with tools to work with. Now you want us to leave our farms and we don't propose to do it." New settlers scouted townsites and farmlands, speculating on the railroad's route, claiming land without regard for Indian title. "The present unsettled condition of affairs is very embarrassing to both Indians and whites, and greatly retards the work of civilizing and Christianizing the Indians," said Simms.[24]

Few non-treaty Indians lived on the reservation; hundreds continued to rove in seasonal hunting, digging, and fishing caravans, and others rode to the buffalo plains on trails intersected by immigrant routes and fenced for farms. They found the buffalo disappearing and the plains perilous with horse-stealing and fighting between competing tribes; they toiled home again, angry, frustrated, and bruised. Two government observers predicted that within five years the Indians could no longer depend on the buffalo for food. Bands of Indians camped restlessly at the Colville agency, begging for medicines and blankets, waiting for news, then trailing off to harvest neglected fields or to hunt.[25]

Once more the Indian office dispatched special commissioners to investigate the condition of Indians in Idaho and adjacent areas. Hearing that three commissioners were inspecting the Nez Perces, the Washington Superintendent of Indian Affairs, R. H. Milroy, intercepted them at Lewiston and persuaded one member, J. P. C. Shanks, a congressman from Indiana, to go with him by wagon to the Colville agency. Shanks, whose name the commission informally bore, met in council near Kettle Falls on August 12, 1873, with Kalispels, Spokanes, Colvilles, Lakes, Okanogans, and Sanpoils to hear their views. The commissioners, incidentally, had reached a tentative contract with the Coeur d'Alenes for a change in reservation more in keeping with the Coeur d'Alenes' wishes.

Shanks' impressions of his meeting near Kettle Falls were appended to his commission's report to the Indian office. He declared that placing Indians on the Colville reservation would "either annihilate them or make them a perpetual tax on the government," and recommended instead that "these Indians be permitted to remain where now situated" on a permanent reserve covering most of northeastern Washington east of the Okanogan and north of the Spokane rivers. (In another report, Shanks would point out that "the continued practice of our Government in making treaties with Indians, and decisions of the Supreme Court of the United States, have ripened this title of occupancy at will into a title of occupancy with power to hold until willing to sell.")[26]

By now, the interior Indians' early hope of sharing their country with white men and learning from them had been dashed repeatedly. Embittered, the Indians saw clearly that they were to be pushed out of the way. Shanks' report confirmed that the Indians were peaceable and industrious, a few farmed, and some worked for white men who had bought their farms; the whites "have encroached on the Indians very much and are continuing to do so," and unscrupulous whites, among whom Shanks named Winans, wanted to herd the Indians to an area "where they would not reside themselves." Shanks concluded, "It would be expensive, dishonorable, and wicked to drive these people away from their homes, where they have lived from time immemorial, to give place to cunning men who have supplanted them, and procured the action of the Government against them."

The chiefs had complained to Shanks of liquor, prostitution of Indian women, and abandoned children of unmarried white men and Indian women. A Colville, Antoine, looking directly at squaw men watching the council, said, "White men, I am talking to you of your actions; I am raising your children on my poor food, my roots and berries and fish and rotten salmon (rotten salmon being those found dead along the river) and when I have raised them these white men demand them and take them."[27]

As with recommendations of earlier negotiators, Congress never acted on those of the Shanks commission. The report touched on two perplexing questions: the law as applied to Indians, and religion. Shanks mentioned religious competition in his report of the Kettle Falls council, calling "the contest between the Catholic and Protestant churches, one of the most troublesome questions in the way of the Government controlling Indian affairs."[28]

The Jesuits had served as negotiators, counselors, and teachers as well as confessors and ministers to the Indians, and Catholic tribes listened to them. By threatening to close their missions, the Jesuits swayed both whites and Indians. At the Colville agency, when a grand jury criticized the priests' practice of marrying Indians without a county license, the missionaries declared that "if such a rule was enforced here they would abandon their mission and leave, as war would certainly follow, for which they wished in no way to be responsible." The licenses were not required.[29]

The Shanks commission recommended new legislation to clarify Indians' liabilities for debts, service as witnesses in trials, and similar matters, and to extend criminal law to them. The Commissioner of Indian Affairs also urged laws for Indians, pointing out that the Intercourse Act of 1834 remained the principal statute applying to Indian peoples and that, despite the government's purpose of civilizing Indians, there was no legal way for an Indian to become a citizen. "No officer of the Government has authority by law for punishing an Indian for crime, or restraining him in any degree," the commissioner said. "The only means of enforcing law and order among the tribes is found in the use of the bayonet . . . or such arbitrary force as the agent may have at his command."[30]

Portrayal of the Kalispels in the Shanks report, brief as it was, indicated a peaceful people willing to cede large areas for a guaranteed reserve in their homeland. In official Washington, however, the Kalispels continued to be destined for the Flathead or Colville reservation. Yet another commission, a civil and military one whose members included General Oliver O. Howard, in 1876 would recommend "judicious consolidation" of existing reservations, perhaps separating Catholic from Protestant Indians, declaring the government's "plain duty" to "treat Indians as its wards, and exercise over them the necessary and wholesome authority." Although this commission intended to meet with Kalispels, Coeur d'Alenes, Spokanes, Colvilles, and Kutenais, its members decided that the season was too late, and instead relied on the views of a merchant on the Columbia River, Marcus Oppenheimer, to recommend that these tribes be consolidated on an existing reservation.[31]

Among the tribes that the Shanks commission and the civil and military commission met was Chief Joseph's band of non-treaty Nez Perces roaming the Imnaha and Wallowa sections of northeastern Oregon which the Indians refused to leave. Both commissions reported Joseph influenced by itinerant shamans—"dreamers," the whites called them—who preached that Indian dead would rise to drive white men from their lands. Sometime earlier, a shaman from Canada circulated among the tribes near Colville, declaring that he had been dead six days and had visited heaven where he saw two dead chiefs who had scandalized Catholic Indians. He had been laughed out of the camps but other shamans played on the longing of Indians for release from whites.[32]

Now Smohalla, the aging shaman and Wanapum chief, preached among the restless Indians around Colville, rattling his amulets and singing his sacred songs, a short, thick-set, bald man, nearly hunchbacked, whose magic was considered strong. Chief Moses once had tried to kill him, and many believed that Smohalla had risen after his murder, prophesying that white people would soon vanish, leaving the natives again in solitary possession of the country. As his disciples proselytized in every Indian village, tinkling bells and drum beats stirred the Indian camps.[33]

Smohalla, the Wanapum shaman, and his priests, according to the caption provided by an unidentified photographer. Smohalla won followers along the Columbia River and in the Colville area. (Thomas Teakle collection, Spokane Public Library)

When Joseph and his Nez Perces took arms to resist moving to a reservation, whites feared that the tribes would unite again in a general war. Some fled their farms to cower in crude forts. The Jesuit priests visited the tribes to learn the Indians' mood and counsel peace. Wiry Father Joseph Cataldo, the Coeur d'Alenes' missionary, soon extracted "promises of neutrality" from the Kalispels, Spokanes, Colvilles, and Coeur d'Alenes. The hotbloods of 1858 were now nearly 20 years older and the Indians realized the numerical superiority of white men. Joset wrote the Colville agent, Simms, "Almost daily false reports are started to scare the settlers. . . . I am writing in every direction to quiet the [white] people." And Father Gregory Gazzoli, of the Colville mission,

Kalispels, Coeur d'Alenes, and Spokanes on a ceremonial occasion. The Kalispel, Charles Smeelt, is at far right; next to him, wearing a hat, Stooychen, a Coeur d'Alene from Worley, Idaho; and in the center, wearing hat, Sam Boyd, a Spokane from Wellpinit. The others are not identified. (Kalispel tribal collection)

scoured Indians camps with a face like wrath, "to prevent any of
their people from joining the belligerent Nez Perces," and then
wrote his bishop that "in general the Indians are now more disposed to follow a civilized career than their ancient life." He complained of sensational news reports, and blamed the Nez Perce war
partly on white cupidity and miscalculation by General Howard at a
council with Joseph where "a great show of armed soldiers, had a
very bad effect on all the Indians . . . who considered it an appeal
to war."[34]

Cataldo, Joset, and Gazzoli also participated in the council in August 1877 near Spokane Bridge where Colonel Frank Wheaton,
who had ridden north from the campaign against marauding Ban-
nacks, met with the chiefs of northeastern Washington and northern Idaho tribes. A report of the council identified Victor and the
subchief, Simon, as representing the Kalispels but also noted 60
Colville Kalispels without a chief. As they rode to the conference,
the Kalispels could not have missed seeing farms in what had been
open country, cattle on the prairies, log bridges on the Spokane
River above and below the falls, settlers' cabins, and a store near
the upriver ferry. Fences laced the prairies above the river, closing
off springs and bottom land, and a tiny settlement of shacks stood
near the river falls. Some Spokanes carried mail to farms and small
towns.

At the meeting, Wheaton, following Howard's example, foolishly
appeared with 500 soldiers, which "so over-awed and inspired them
[Indians] with the conviction that they were to be forced from the
land of their birth—a land that they have never ceded—that in-
activity, despondency and sullenness have since been the prevailing
condition among them," said an Indian inspector.[35]

Wheaton signed peace agreements with eight tribes: Victor's
Kalispels, the Palouses, Coeur d'Alenes, Okanogans, Spokanes,
Kettles, Sanpoils, and Lakes, gave them presents of beef, flour,
and tobacco, and talked about the government's plans for them. Although they understood clearly that Wheaton's contracts pledged
them not to join Joseph, the Indians apparently were confused and
intimidated by the colonel's statement to them. Victor and Simon,
"of the Colville band of Pend Oreilles," put their marks on an ap-
pendix agreeing to move to the Colville or Flathead reservation.

They left the council sadly with the notion that Wheaton proposed to herd them into corrals.[36]

As promised, the Kalispels and their allies stayed out of Joseph's war, except to shelter refugee Nez Perces fleeing from the fighting. Nevertheless, because settlers feared an Indian uprising, troops remained at Fort Colville. But the army's fruitless attempt to keep the Nez Perces from getting ammunition by denying it to all interior Indians deprived the Kalispels and other hunters of shells for killing game. Victor, the Kalispel chief, appealed to Agent Simms who wrote the commissioner on behalf of the Indians, explaining that the order "prohibiting the sale of ammunition to them is particularly hard on them at this time, as their catch of fish last summer was almost a total failure, besides there were but few berries and roots." Victor's letter accompanying this appeal pointed out that the Kalispels "have never troubled the whites nor intend to trouble them;" hunting was their only subsistence; the tribe had no land to cultivate and no tools. Simms testified, "The facts in his letter I know to be substantially true." (Seven years earlier, Winans said that Kalispels tilled most of 385 acres.) Victor also asked that his people not be punished for the "misdeeds" of other tribes. The army loosened its ban on shells for peaceful Indians.[37]

Father Alexander Diomedi portrayed the Kalispels as peaceable but neglected, spending their time in "gambling, sorcery, and adultery" when he visited them at their camas grounds. About 80 lodges of various tribes had gathered to dig camas a mile west of the Pend Oreille river. Kalispels pitched twenty lodges on the west, and twenty more on the east side of the river. Victor, now an old man, came by canoe to see the priest. Diomedi scolded the chief for encouraging gambling to amuse his people, and ordered Victor to stop it; he railed at the young men for adultery and shamanism, confiscating two "charms or instruments . . . parts of the animal under whose form the devil appears to them in their dreams . . . curiously wrought, and powerful instruments of crime."[38]

Diomedi rang a bell for morning and evening prayers, preached twice daily, and twice a day taught catechism to the children. He watched the boys, in one of their favorite games, shoot with bows and arrows at a rag-wrapped rolling wooden hoop, "many . . . so dexterous as to pierce its edge or its centre and stop it altogether."

After dinner, the young men raced horses for three or four hours; they "look very wild, being nearly naked, with faces painted red. Before starting they yell hideously; then they set out and run their horses almost to death. While racing, their yelling increases and they practice several manoeuvres, picking up from the ground sticks or other objects while at full speed." The women worked constantly, digging camas or tanning skins.

Diomedi felt that the Kalispels on the river responded well to his ministry—all but one eventually took communion—and before leaving he chided the chiefs for their lack of authority. "Don't you know that the young people laugh at us," the chiefs told him, "and say we are good for nothing, and pay no heed?" Diomedi appointed fifteen sturdy Kalispel men as "soldiers" under the chiefs' command. "The young men did not relish this," he observed, "but they had to bear it." He induced the Kalispels to begin building a 20- by 30-foot log church and priest's cabin. [39]

Meanwhile, Victor was called to Horse Plains (Montana) by Peter Ronan, the Flathead agent, to straighten out tiffs between settlers and Kalispels there, "a few uncontrollable spirits—young men who would pick a quarrel and involve his people in troubles," Simon called them, adding, "They were watched and punished on every occasion." Ronan and the Kalispel head men agreed to talk over the situation after Christmas at St. Ignatius. [40]

There Victor hinted that his people might accept Horse Plains for their reservation. "Tell the Great Father in Washington we like the country around Horse Plains and I think our people would like to have their reservation in that country," the chief told Ronan. "I do not say this for sure, but I think so." Ronan suggested to the commissioner that Horse Plains be attached to the Flathead reserve, but it was not. About 30 Kalispel men, chiefly hunters and their relatives, considering it Indian country, lived on Horse Plains because it was nearer game; they had committed a number of petty nuisances against six white families and the whites had retaliated. Simon lived at Horse Plains for the winter "to punish any Indian who did wrong." Ronan admonished both Indians and whites to live peaceably there, and in his report to the commissioner, he asked, incidentally, if he were now in charge of the Kalispels. [41]

The settlers at Horse Plains expected the railroad to build there

soon but the Northern Pacific, bankrupted in the panic of 1873, had
stopped construction. An Indian agent, A. J. Cain, warned General
Howard that "the immigrants and miners . . . do not regard the
Indians as possessing any rights they are bound to respect in locat-
ing upon lands." He predicted that a large military force would be
required to preserve the reservation system as settlers poured
into the country with the railroad. Settlers all along the anticipated
route waited impatiently for the road, but five more years passed
before construction resumed. For a time, Northern Pacific surveyors considered crossing Montana and Idaho by Lolo pass which
would have routed the main line through southeastern Washington
(and conceivably elevated Walla Walla or Lewiston to the central
city of the interior) but instead chose a northerly route through the
Flathead reservation, down the valleys of the Missoula and Clark
Fork rivers to Lake Pend Oreille, where a long bridge crossed the
outlet at Sandpoint, and thence southwesterly past Spokane Falls
into the Columbia plain.[42]

Passing through an area the Kalispels regarded as theirs, the
railroad acquired hundreds of square miles by congressional land
grants. The railroad promoted settlement and by 1879 had begun
selling tracts of its grant lands. Until 1898, moreover, the Secretary of the Interior accepted the railroad's choices of land before
surveys and plats were filed in local land offices, permissiveness
that would result in massive contention over land titles.[43]

In the fall of 1881 Joset went with a railroad geologist to Kalispel
country as interpreter. The man wanted to hire Indians to haul gold
by trail and canoe from his claim on the Clark Fork 80 miles to the
railroad but they refused to accompany the *suyapi* (American)
without their chief's permission, and after talking to the chief, they
declined for fear of losing their horses in the winter snows. The
geologist, angered, called them lazy, "the worst Indians he ever
saw," and stormed off. That was a common white response to Indians who did not do what the whites wanted. Joset wrote a fellow
Jesuit about the changes the railroad worked in the region; he saw
Chinese and white graders toiling along the line, and rude towns
springing up, "besides the railroad company's buildings . . . a
store, a restaurant, a number of temporary shanties, and about a
dozen saloons; the population . . . mostly . . . idlers, tramps,
gamblers, and drunkards."[44]

Of the Kalispels, Joset observed, "These Indians have always been friendly to the Whites. . . . At the same time, they are afraid of Americans, and seeing their country invaded, they are sorry and keep apart." Finding "poor stray Indians" begging around railroad camps, Joset told them to go home and start farms. He offered mass at a trader's post on the Clark Fork, well attended by Indians, before returning to Colville. On reflection, he thought that in this "great rush of immigration . . . the Indian, now in a minority, must make haste to profit by the kindness of the government, who allows him to take his homestead, or very soon he will not have where to put up his wigwam."

The Northern Pacific reached Spokane Falls from the west in July 1881, and connected its western and eastern sections at Gold Creek, Montana, in September 1883, at last completing a railroad across the northern tier of western states. The railroad, territories, and towns advertised for settlers. Spokane Falls would grow to nearly twenty thousand residents by 1890, with seven transit companies, largely sponsored by real estate promoters. Within eight months of the ceremony at Gold Creek celebrating completion of the line, the Kalispels resorted to turning away whites who came to settle in their valley, warning them not to return. But when nine heavily armed settlers moved in, attracted by the wild hay on the river flats, the Indians let them stay.[45]

Other settlers soon came but rather than assail them the Kalispels appealed to the new Colville agent, Sidney D. Waters, asking "whether they will be protected in their natural right to their homes." Now feeble, Victor came to see Waters on the arm of his son, Masseslow. Waters told the commissioner, after talking with Victor, that the Kalispels, "wildest of all Indians attached to this agency . . . do not desire any whites to come into the country who will try to take away their land." Victor had resisted sending Kalispel children to the agency school because he did "not want their children to learn the language of their enemies." The Kalispels had seen the Spokanes humbled, Waters added, "yet are willing to let the whites come into their country, provided that if they go on a reserve they will be paid for the relinquishment of their country, or when the land is surveyed . . . they shall each head of a family have their allotment."[46]

A political appointee of President Chester Arthur, Waters was removed as agent when Grover Cleveland took office, but he continued to write the Commissioner of Indian Affairs as a citizen, signing himself, "Colville agent—suspended." Waters had settled in Spokane Falls where he became prominent as a contractor and as acting mayor in the difficult times after most of the city burned in 1889. Calling himself "no longer their agent but still their friend," Waters lamented the predicament of Spokanes who hung around Spokane Falls, melancholy, dissolute, and maltreated. The Kalispel lands, he told the commissioner, were "eagerly sought" by settlers, adding that the tribe "will not allow anyone . . . to settle in what they call their country." The Indian office at least read his letter, for Charles A. Larabee, an office employee, asked on the letter-file jacket for "estimates for money to remove Indians."⁴⁷

On the other hand, a new Colville agent described the Kalispels as "yet undisturbed in the peaceful possession of their country"— the camas fields and winter campsite on the Pend Oreille—but pointed out that "the land has been surveyed and will soon be open to settlement. It contains some very fine hay meadows." As a matter of fact, surveys had stopped south of the Kalispels for the time being. The Kalispels "farm in a small way," the agent added, but spent most of their time hunting and raising horses. He, too, urged that the Indian lands be allotted as individual tracts or that the tribe be moved to a reservation, predicting ominously, "Unless this is done, there will be trouble." A year later, the agent reported "the Calispels . . . still living in the Calispel valley . . . still refuse to permit whites to settle there." He discounted rumors that Kalispels murdered white prospectors in the mountains, explaining that "a company of cavalry has been stationed in that country since early spring, but have found no need of active service"—troops from Fort Spokane, near the confluence of the Spokane and Columbia rivers, garrisoned in 1880 to intimidate interior Indians. And again, a warning: "Sooner or later, serious troubles must arise, as the whites are determined to settle in the Calispel valley."⁴⁸

Waters wrote again as a businessman, calling the commissioner's attention to "lamentable conditions among the Spokanes and Calispels." Half-clad, dirty Indians loiter on city streets, he complained. "Only last week some drunken Indians from Calispel rode down through the settlements of Wild Rose and the Little Spokane spreading terror," until volunteer soldiers from Spokane Falls and two companies of regulars from Fort Coeur d'Alene corraled them, "quieting apprehension of the settlers."[49]

His letter closed, "No sickly sentiment must stand in the way of their removal for the people of eastern Washington will not stand any such nonsense." Here Waters referred to the flourishing evangelical movement for Indian rights that had gathered strength since the Civil War. Indian rights advocates took Americans to task for their brutal treatment of Indian peoples. Catching the spirit, Congress in 1867 had voted an Indian commission which called for a reformed Indian service, rid of political hacks and cheating agents, and for military protection of Indians on their own lands. One immediate result was assigning army officers as Indian agents and supervisors of the delivery of goods to tribes, which helped employ surplus officers after the war. President Ulysses S. Grant encouraged religious sects to nominate reservation agents, and such eastern reformers as the Mohonk Conference (named for its meeting site) cried that Indians must be given their rights as individuals to enable each to work out his own salavation.[50]

The Office of Indian Affairs under Commissioner Ezra A. Hayt and his successors continued to seek consolidation of Indian tribes to reduce the number and size of reserves and to advocate turning Indians into citizen landowners. (In addition to opening land for settlement with this policy, Hayt saw possible savings in federal expenditures for Indians.) Scandals in Hayt's administration, however, were said to have shocked Congress into seeing the need for a general reform of Indian affairs. One of the major remedies would be the General Allotment Act of 1887 (familiarly known as the Dawes Act for its sponsor, Senator Henry L. Dawes of Massachusetts), which provided for breaking Indian land into parcels (allotments) for individual Indians, the sale of surplus (unallotted) lands, and citizenship for Indians born in the United States. The Dawes Act would serve as a cornerstone of U.S. Indian policy for 40 years and, to such promoters of individual Indian rights as the Mohonk Conference, would seem "a pulverizing engine for breaking up the tribal mass."[51]

Surely the Kalispels heard little or nothing about these groundswells in federal policy, although they would be affected by them, and the idea of reducing reservations would have struck them as needless, for their territory had shrunk with settlement and commerce. A gold rush into the Coeur d'Alene mountains in 1883–84, virtually coinciding with the completion of the Northern Pacific track, and the subsequent discovery of lead-silver ores, brought hordes of adventurers, as well as merchants and attorneys, into forested country the Coeur d'Alenes once claimed. Prospectors spread in all directions hunting precious metals. Two miles east of Fool's Prairie (Chewelah), silver and lead were discovered at Embry Camp in 1883, and the Old Dominion mine, one of the early producers of northeastern Washington, was claimed in 1885 six miles east of Colville. By the late 1880s, Lake Pend Oreille would be ringed with mining claims. The old Kalispel territory now held railroads, mines, towns, highways, and an advancing farm frontier. In the peculiar view of settlers, Kalispels were trespassers on land they once roamed freely.

And as we have seen, the Kalispels had been scattered by closing of their mission, by warfare, and by their preferred lifestyles— a few joined Chief Moses on the Columbia, others farmed in the Colville valley near Chewelah, twenty or more lodges stood on Horse Plains, Michel's band nested on Lake Pend Oreille, and patriarchal Victor's, nomadic hunters, fishers, and diggers, wintered on the Pend Oreille River. Michel's people and the Chewelahs adopted white men's clothing; other Kalispels wore combinations of white dress and native costumes, generally replacing leather tunics and fur robes with cottons, woolens, and blankets. In its relations with all of these Kalispels, the government regarded Victor as head chief although, in fact, his son, Masseslow, had assumed many of the old man's functions.

To carry out a policy of consolidating tribes and reducing reservations, Congress in 1886 formed a Northwest Indian Commission, charged with writing new agreements, moving tribes, and reducing the lands held by Indians in Minnesota, Dakota, Idaho, Washington, Oregon, and Montana. Comprised of a one-time Confederate infantry colonel and former congressman, John V. Wright of Tennessee, Jared W. Daniels, a 27-year veteran of Indian bargaining, and H. W. Andrews of the Department of the Interior, the commission reached Spokane Falls in February 1887, intending to deal with

Masseslow, chief of the Kalispels, with the badges of his office: top hat, pipe, and crucifix. His brother Jim stands beside him. Date and photographer unknown. (Thomas Teakle collection, Spokane Public Library)

the Kalispels among others. Like so many negotiators before them, the commissioners turned to the Jesuits. Father Leopold Van Gorp, who knew the interior Indians well from his years at St. Ignatius mission, was in Spokane at the new Gonzaga College, scheduled to open in the fall.

Fearful that they would be stranded by snowfalls if they ventured into the Pend Oreille valley, the commission sent a messenger to Victor asking him to meet them at Sandpoint and, while they waited for his reply, discussed the Indians with hard-headed Van Gorp. Undoubtedly the Jesuit gave the commissioners a matter-of-fact analysis of the Indian situation, and from him and from their messenger, the commissioners were "led to believe that we will be able to make a satisfactory agreement with the Indians . . . for their removal either to the Coeur d'Alene or Jocko reservation," they advised the Commissioner of Indian Affairs. The Spokane Falls *Morning Review* reflected the temper of whites: "Those who have been so long annoyed by the presence of lazy, loafing Spokanes," it said, hope they'll be moved to the Flathead, farthest from the city.[52]

But when the commission moved to Sandpoint, neither Victor nor Masseslow appeared. Instead, a handful of Indians came, saying the Kalispels were hunting in the mountains. Piqued, the three commissioners sent men to find the Kalispel chiefs; they had come ready for a quick parley, with Michel Revais as interpreter, the Flathead agent, Ronan, Father Van Gorp, and two Flathead chieftains, these last presumably to invite the Kalispels to the Jocko reservation. The council was delayed until April 21 when messengers brought in Victor, although the Kalispels explained that Victor had recently given the chieftainship to his son, Masseslow, whom the commissioners heard was "an obstinate, untamed, and contrary chief." About forty Kalispel men accompanied Masseslow when he finally rode into Sandpoint, but only 31 would take part in the meetings.[53]

The older Kalispels had been warned that the commissioners called them to Sandpoint simply to get them off their land for a few days so white men could seize it. Consequently, the Kalispels at Sandpoint were suspicious and restless, mostly younger men; some bought whiskey, reeled drunkenly through the streets, and scuffled among themselves and with whites; these Kalispels, the commissioners thought, "are naturally vicious and combative, and when under the influence of intoxicants are absolutely dangerous neighbors." Michel, from Pend Oreille Lake, was mild, by contrast, cut his hair short, and wore white men's dress.

If Victor was no longer head chief, his influence remained strong and his son adhered to his father's views. The bargaining took a turn familiar in Indian councils—a government commission without authority to modify its program, and Indians, wary and distrustful, unwilling to give up what remained theirs. The government's proposal was the standard contract: if the Kalispels moved to the Flathead reservation, the government would build them saw and grist mills, 40 family homes, break and fence farmland for them, provide animals and implements, and hire men to teach them milling, carpentry, smithing, and other skills, and pay their chief, all costing $37,865. For his part, Victor explained that his people were hunters and fishers and needed their land to sustain them. They had lived a long time on the Pend Oreille and while they would cede their larger country, he said, "Our land is not for sale."[54]

For a while, Michel (Sitting Grizzly Bear) remained silent, perhaps in deference to Victor, but finally he spoke in favor of the government's proposal and two of his head men, Pierre and Joseph, echoed him. In the end, Michel agreed to the contract and signed it "for himself and his band of Pend Oreilles, numbering over 25 men." Pierre also signed. Van Gorp witnessed their signatures. Victor, Masseslow, and their followers refused. Louis Lee, a white man from Rathdrum well acquainted with the Kalispels, observing the council, pulled Masseslow aside to advise him to go to the Flathead reservation; the interpreter, Revais, told the commissioners that if they left a copy of their contract with Ronan, he was sure Masseslow would sign it eventually. Lee believed that many of the river Kalispels would have moved to the reservation "if they were not afraid of their chiefs and young braves."[55]

Appended to the contract is a curious footnote by Michel Revais which reads, "The foregoing agreement was carefully read in open council and by me correctly interpreted" but the words "in open council" have been scratched out.

And so the Northwest Indian Commission reported to the Indian office in Washington that the larger part of the Kalispels had agreed to their terms, and that all that lingered in the old homeland were uncivilized renegades. For years afterward, Flathead agents would remind the Indian office of the Sandpoint treaty, which Congress never ratified, asking that the Kalispels under Michel who had moved to the Jocko reservation be given the benefits promised at Sandpoint in 1887. They never were.[56]

CHAPTER 4

Settlement Along the Pend Oreille

MOST of the Kalispels' home country—the part that became Pend Oreille County in 1911—is mountainous and forested with only narrow flatlands along the Pend Oreille River and near Calispell Lake level enough for farming, but this lies at elevations 2,000 to 2,500 feet above sea level where the growing season is short, chill country with 162 to 180 days a year below freezing. The valley averages 70.4 inches of snowfall a year. Oldtimers recall winters with five feet of snow choking the lowlands and the river blocked with ice.

The country seemed inhospitable to all but the hardiest looking for farmland. Consequently the Pend Oreille valley did not begin to fill with settlers until the Great Northern railway proposed to build through northeastern Washington. James J. Hill's organization of the Great Northern on the shoulders of the Manitoba Railroad in October 1889 convinced people that Hill was serious about extending his railroad from Minneapolis to Puget Sound. They speculated on its route, as settlers 20 years before had rushed to grab land to farm or sell on the line of the Northern Pacific.

Before the railroad came, the wild timothy along the Pend Oreille had attracted some stockmen who brought small herds, mostly Durhams, into the Cusick area early in the 1880s and drove their animals, fifty or so at a time, to Spokane Falls for sale. A few settlers took land. One homestead patent had been issued in June 1882 and others in February and April 1884, but up to 1890 only 20 patents covering 2,913 acres would be approved by the government land office, all near Newport, south of Kalispel ground.[1] Albeni Poirier, for whom Albeni Falls was named, cut a nine-mile road from his place by the river to Blanchard Valley where a road ran to Rathdrum. In 1887 Spokane Falls merchants furnished the food for a five-man crew to improve a bumpy, winding wagon road from Rathdrum to the Pend Oreille valley by way of King Hill and Sacheen Lake. (When the food ran low, the crew left boulders in the roadway.) At the creek that bears his name, Edwin Winchester erected a small sawmill to make lumber for settlers, and the steamers *Bertha* and *Torpedo* ran from Albeni Falls downriver to the mining camps at Metaline, replacing rafts poled along the stream. A road hacked through the forests in 1886 connected Colville with Metaline, and on October 18, 1889, the Spokane Falls & Northern Railroad linked Colville with Spokane Falls. The army regularly sent mounted patrols from Fort Sherman [Coeur d'Alene] and Fort Spokane into the Pend Oreille valley, ostensibly for training, to cow the Kalispels. Nearly every year, the commissioner of Indian affairs put a paragraph in his report saying the Kalispels were being crowded out of their valley and unless the government acted, trouble must occur between Indians and whites. Not much came of the commissioner's warnings because most whites found the Kalispels obliging and friendly, peddling berries and venison door to door and doing odd jobs.[2]

Nevertheless, wariness marked relations between whites and Indians in the valley. During an outbreak of smallpox in 1890, settler John Jared patrolled the river, rifle crooked under an arm, to keep infected Indians from crossing. Settlers wrote to the Indian office and their congressman, swinging like weathervanes in an errant wind, crying one moment for the Kalispels' removal as menaces and pleading, another time, for their removal for the Indians' welfare. The Commissioner of Indian Affairs, adverting to Congress' failure to ratify the Northwest Indian Commission contract, advised Representative C. S. Vorhees of Washington that "if said agreement fails of ratification, I do not see any present prospects of securing their [Kalispels'] removal." Settlers telegraphed that Kalispels burned eight square miles of hayland and threatened lives, bringing an infantry company galloping into the valley but the

Kalispels were peaceful, no haystacks had been singed, and no one threatened, and the troopers trotted placidly back to Fort Spokane.[3]

"The Calispel Indians are farming in a small way in the Calispel valley, but the country is becoming settled very rapidly by white people, and the Indians will soon be compelled to move on," observed the Commissioner of Indian Affairs in 1890. "They are not as degraded a class of Indians as the Upper Spokanes, owing to the fact that they are farther from civilization and are not surrounded by the bad element." The Upper Spokanes, waiting three years for ratification of their contract with the Northwest Indian Commission, were "leading lives of shame and degradation around . . . Spokane Falls."[4]

Construction of the Great Northern brought civilization and the bad element nearly into Kalispel country. Using Indian guides, surveyors crossed the area seeking routes to mountain passes and, in Indian canoes, navigated the Kootenai River, determining that the railroad should follow the river into Washington. A frontier village, Newport, partly in Washington and partly in Idaho, sprouted on the Pend Oreille where the Great Northern crossed the state line. One surveying engineer called this "terrible country;" his thermometer dropped to 44 degrees below zero. As construction workers followed, mobile towns bloomed with "saloons gaily lit . . . filled to the doors with wild men and wild women, yelling, singing, dancing and cursing, with glasses lifted high." Some camps were so lawless that train crews locked cars passing through them. The track, laid east and west from the hamlet of Kootenai, Idaho, reached Kalispell, Montana, on January 1, 1892, Spokane Falls by June 1, and a year later opened for traffic to Puget Sound.[5]

From the railroad spread shock waves of settlers and speculators grasping for land, mines, waterfalls, townsites, and any other opportunity. Anticipating a land rush, the government contracted for surveys of townships containing the best farmland in 1891 and 1892, and during those years the land office issued homestead patents for approximately 8,280 acres in Kalispel home country. Already two hundred or more settlers lived in the Pend Oreille valley and a steamer, the *Dora*, ran three times a week between Newport and points downriver, delivering freight and mail, and stopping at any ranch on signal.[6]

Again those familiar phrases. "The Kalispel tribe are scattered over land lying in the Kalispel Valley and along the Pend Oreille River," reported the Colville agent. "They cannot remain long on the land they occupy as whites are fast settling up that part of the country, and the game which was once so plentiful is growing more scarce each year." The Kalispels were better off than the Kutenais near Bonners Ferry. Many of them "were driven from their homes at the point of a shotgun."[7]

Settlement northward from the Great Northern into the Pend Oreille valley might have continued at a rapid pace had not a national depression spread like a pall over the country in 1893, stifling migration for three to four years. Few families had money to move, build homes, fences, or buy equipment; anchored by privation, they stayed where they were, waiting for better days. Homestead entries in Kalispel territory fell to 19 in 1893, 16 the next year, and 15 in 1895, the low point. And any settlers who looked over the valley in 1894, a historic high water year, found the riverside lands under ten to twelve feet of water.[8]

Meanwhile, as the government surveyed northeastern Washington, the Northern Pacific claimed odd sections as land grant: 479,218 acres patented for the railroad company in Kalispel country in October 1894 and an additional 1,451,875 acres in 1895, not all, of course, in the river valley. The railroad offered these lands for sale but in the depression, few buyers appeared.[9]

Some whites tried to discredit the Kalispels. Masselow, now a stooped, aging chieftain, was arrested on a burglary charge so vague that the judge released him; he was immediately arrested again on the same charge, but with the intervention of the Colville agent was released a second time "on account of the old chief's good reputation, as vouched for by persons who have known him for many years," said the agent.[10]

Others spoke up for the Kalispels. Representing themselves as counsel for the tribe, John Mullan (the road builder, now become a Catholic attorney in the national capital) and Joseph K. McCammon, who had negotiated (among other agreements) the contract allowing the Northern Pacific to cross Flathead land, submitted a draft bill to the Indian office for ratifying the Northwest Indian Commission's compact with the Kalispels. They called for "equity for these Indians." Ratification, which never came, would have helped Michel's band on the Jocko.[11]

Among the few whites continuing to acquire land during the depression were the LeClerc brothers, migrants from Canada. Napoleon LeClerc, who came into the valley in 1887 to settle near the bend of the river on the east bank (across from Jared), offered to buy adjacent Indian land in the spring of 1894. He wanted Masseslow to sign away Indian claims to the land in return for a cow and calf, a mowing machine, a hay rake, and a wagon. Masseslow turned him down because he and others pastured cattle and horses and cut hay there. LeClerc then tried to take the land by intimidation; he filed a homestead claim, ripped out Indian fences, stopped a Kalispel from putting a log cabin on the ground, built his own fences, and threatened Indians with arrest if they camped on the land. As much as any single incident, LeClerc's high-handed tactics alerted the government to the pressure on the Kalispels in their valley.[12]

The commissioner directed the army officer serving as acting Colville agent, Captain John W. Bubb, to look into the Kalispels' confrontation with whites. Bubb felt that he was on trial; he had attempted to negotiate a revised north boundary for the Coeur d'Alene reservation, and counseled the Lower Spokanes to cede part of their reserve. His predecessors as Colville agents publicly accused him of provoking their dismissals and, as Bubb complained, "seem to be using all means in their power to thwart the influence I hope to acquire and prove my capacity for managing Indian affairs." The former agents gossiped that Bubb was anti-Catholic. A farm boy who enlisted for the Civil War and, after it, made the army his life, Bubb looked on his service to the Catholic Kalispels as a chance to prove himself. He had a wife and seven children at the agency and to support them engaged in petty tyrannies—kickbacks and false vouchers. At fifty-one, a little stout, Bubb, however, would be precise and scrupulous in his dealings with Indians and whites along the Pend Oreille. Until the commissioner sent him to the Kalispels, Bubb remarked, he had not realized that these Indians fell within his jurisdiction.[13]

After conferring with Masseslow and seven other Kalispels who rode to see him at Colville, Bubb told the commissioner, "I am of

Masseslow, near Newport, c. 1890. The unknown photographer evidently intended to show Masseslow as a sovereign of the forest. (Thomas Teakle collection, Spokane Public Library)

the opinion that a determined effort is being made to freeze them out and the Indians do not understand the situation." He found that the land register at Spokane had accepted homestead applications from the Pend Oreille valley because "there is no evidence in [his] office of Indian occupation."[14]

Bubb translated a letter from the commissioner to the Kalispels reminding them that, as non-reservation Indians, they were subject to state and local laws. To this, Masseslow retorted that the Kalispels were "called to account for things that white people . . . are never troubled about," and insisted that Indians of other tribes, passing through the valley on their way to hunt and fish in Kutenai country, committed the mischief that he and his people were blamed for.

Many settlers got along well with Kalispels. John Brown's daughter recalled, years later, that Masseslow showed up at the Brown cabin promptly at 10:50 every Thursday morning to smoke and eat dinner, and that when their house burned, Kalispels gave the Browns new blankets, cooking utensils, and new moccasins for their little girl. But competition for land in the valley caused conflict. Tales circulated that Indians with guns stopped whites from fencing land. Settlers continually accused Indians of stealing from them, and after the 1894 flood, when many lost goods, petitioned Congressman John L. Wilson for removal of these "government pets." Many whites thought the Kalispels had agreed to a contract in 1887, as the Commissioner of Indian Affairs mistakenly advised Wilson. Contradictory reports reached Washington and the commissioner concluded that, at least, the Kalispels should have the ground they occupied. He instructed Bubb to survey and list the lands claimed by Kalispels.[15]

During August 1895 Bubb spent several weeks with the main body of Kalispels, surveying their land claims and writing their legal descriptions. (He did not see a few families upriver.) Three claims lay on the west side of the river; the remainder, on the east, on the tribe's traditional winter campsites. "The very high water of 1894 washed away the Indians' houses (or huts), such as they had, and pretty much all their fences, leaving but little to indicate their individual claims," Bubb reported. "Being in a state of uncertainty about their lands, has made them slow to rebuild." High water marks still whitened trees along the river. "I find pretty much all the settlers in the valley, who have honestly settled upon land, are well disposed toward the Indians," Bubb continued, "but those who are trying to swindle them out of their lands are only too willing to attribute all kinds of misdemeanors to them and throw every possible obstacle in the way of their peaceable residence in the valley." The agent named no whites, but observed that law-abiding settlers recognized Indian right to "the land these Indians claim, and have occupied for years."[16]

The Kalispels told Bubb that Victor, in his last hours, had called them together and urged them "all to remain on the East side of the river and be buried there." This they resolved to do. Reasonably sure of his survey lines because some government survey stakes from 1891 and 1892 remained in place, Bubb sent copies of his list to the Indian office and to the land office at Spokane. The Commissioner of Indian Affairs referred his copy to the General Land Office.

"The entries made, by whites, are all in violation of existing instructions to local land officers, as there is every evidence of Indian occupation, which must have been the case at the time the filings were offered at the Land Office in Spokane," Bubb said urging that these claims be investigated. "I am of the opinion that if an investigation is ordered, some of the whites will let their cases go by default, as they told me they knew it was Indian country, but . . . thought they would file and take their chances."[17]

After Bubb's survey, the Spokane land office turned down applications from settlers for land occupied by Kalispels and the General Land Office contested a few white claims to Indian ground. If the captain thus preserved the Kalispels' space for them, he also tacitly ceded the remainder of their accustomed territory. Future government officers would point out that the Kalispels' title to the Pend Oreille valley had never been extinguished, but from 1895 the land office honored applications for tracts not assigned to Indians, and by presidential proclamation on March 1, 1898, a Priest River forest reserve closed to settlement thousands of acres the Kalispels regarded as theirs. Few Kalispels, as a matter of fact, lived solely on the tracts Bubb mapped for them; they camped and hunted on land platted for any member of the tribe; unlike whites, few put up fences or barns, but preferred to live together in mobile

Kalispel women, Louise Andrews, left, and Lucy Seymour, riding on Kalispel ground in 1907. The reservation, contrary to the lettering on this postcard, was not formally established until 1914. (Kalispel tribal collection)

villages, maintaining their tribal ties, and using the land in the old way, as tribal ground. Gradually they leased some of the arable acreage to whites for farming.[18]

The Northern Pacific's title to more than half of the ground platted for Kalispels remained in doubt for another decade, balanced on legal niceties, but the railroad made no overt attempt to push Kalispels off the odd sections it claimed for its land grant. "While their [Kalispels'] occupancy of odd-numbered sections in conflict with the grant to the railway may be technically illegal," declared a Secretary of the Interior, "yet by every moral right and in absolute justice the title belongs solely to the Kalispels." The General Land Office asked the Northern Pacific to give up the ground occupied by Kalispels shortly after Bubb surveyed Indian claims, but the railway declined because the interior department lacked authority to allow alternative choices—lieu land. Not until 1906 would the Northern Pacific, assured by Congress that it could select other ground, release its hold on 2,711 acres occupied by Kalispels.[19]

With the return of prosperous times, a seasonal fleet of plain, cramped steamboats plied the Pend Oreille northward from Newport. Eventually a dozen of various sizes ran the river. By 1900 settlers filled the land south and west of the town, and scattered farms appeared on the hills for 50 miles downriver. The nucleus of a community huddled around Joe Cusick's farm. The Great Northern Express Company opened an office in a log-cabin store there. The years 1896 to 1910 bulged with immigrants moving to the West, hundreds a day crowding Spokane before scattering into the countryside. Newport, incorporated in 1903, would grow to 1,194 residents by 1910, its post office in Idaho and railroad station in Washington; it would not be that large again until 1950. Spokane growing from 36,848 persons in 1900 to 104,402 by 1910, was the billowing hub of transport and wholesaling in the inland northwest.[20]

Steamboating days on the Pend Oreille were brief, but for a few years men like George H. Jones, founder of Usk, the Cusick brothers, and Napoleon LeClerc held prestigious places as steamer captains—not romantic figures but widely known men of substance. The Cusicks operated the *Red Cloud* and the *Volunteer*, the latter a stern-wheeler with two decks, its storm-tattered roofs patched with castoff tin, called "Old Booze" for its saloon on the upper

Kalispel man and woman with the Pend Oreille River and Indian Village in the background, pictured in 1910 by Frank Palmer, a Spokane photographer. (Eastern Washington State Historical Society)

deck. LeClerc captained the *Metaline* with tubular boiler and triple expansion engine near midship, a 25-passenger launch that ran from Newport to Metaline, bouncing through the shoals of Box Canyon. LeClerc was also the largest land owner in the area, one of the few homesteaders, with John Brown, on the east side of the river. North of Kalispel ground, LeClerc bought 412.65 acres from the Northern Pacific between 1901 and 1904; three homestead claims, one for himself and two for his brothers, brought the LeClerc holdings to approximately 890 acres with three miles of frontage on the river. The LeClercs lived in a two-story whipsawed log house beside a large meadow; they kept a huge garden and 80 cows, making butter for market; their home "famous locally as a seat of hospitality."[21]

During summer months, steamboat proprietors offered excursions from Newport to Box Canyon as a merry diversion from the hard life of ranching in cold country along a river that overflowed nearly every year. Tourists liked to stop at the Kalispels' summer camp with its decorated tipis and quaint inhabitants; steamboat captains advertised the Indians as a tour attraction, and Kalispel women traded briskly in trinkets and beadwork. Thus, as the Kalispels mellowed, they became for some whites curiosities, unpredictable, an aboriginal enclave in a growing white community.[22]

If the river was the artery of civilization and recreation to settlers and tourists, many believed that its most beneficial use would be to open the Metaline mines. Congressmen from Washington and Idaho offered bills to improve the Pend Oreille for navigation, and a one-time engineer wrote his congressman that the Metaline would be "as good a camp as the Coeur d'Alenes if the river could be opened to permit economic navigation," declaring that removing a few large boulders and stone reefs would allow steamers to reach the mining district easily.[23]

Even though the government cleared obstacles from the river, neither farming nor mining would transform the Pend Oreille country as would lumbering. By the late nineties, midwestern lumber companies, running out of trees to cut in the Great Lakes region, sent estimators and cruisers into the Pacific Northwest to measure its forests before a massive westward migration of the industry. Spokane's mills and the two dozen or more along the Spokane Falls & Northern were cutting the most accessible timber northward from Spokane; after 1895 mills rose south of Newport along the Great Northern line.

Midwestern lumber companies, foremost among them the Humbird and Rutledge firms, Weyerhaeuser satellites, bought stumpage and mills in northern Idaho, intending to saw for national markets. Again the remoteness of the Pend Oreille valley, and the flow of its river northward away from rail transportation, slowed movement into it. But the Northern Pacific aggressively hawked its timberlands, and in 1902 a Wisconsin company, Bradley, bought 100,000 acres of railroad land in the hills above the valley on both sides of the Pend Oreille from Newport downriver. Settlers along the river already did a brisk business in cedar poles, cut indiscriminately from their own and public lands, to be barged upriver to the railroad at Newport.[24]

Into the Pend Oreille district came F. A. Blackwell, 50, a squarish, pushing, self-made lumberman from Pennsylvania who had been in the business since age 17, backed by Pennsylvania associates, William H. Howard and Allen P. Perley, partners in logging the western foothills of the Appalachians near Williamsport. Blackwell's first northwest venture was an electric railroad between Coeur d'Alene's expanding lumber mills and Spokane, the Coeur d'Alene & Spokane Railway, Ltd. Not 24 months later, however, Blackwell merged with the electric Spokane & Inland Empire, which used Blackwell's line as a branch to serve mills and its resorts at Coeur d'Alene, Liberty, and Hayden lakes.[25]

For his Pennsylvania associates, Blackwell began to buy timberlands, but Howard died and Perley proved more interested in Pennsylvania. Blackwell, now well acquainted with the interior northwest and its leading businessmen, projected a railroad northward from Coeur d'Alene into the isolated forests of northeastern Washington, along the mountain trough to Newport and by the Pend Oreille River grade to the Metaline mines. He would drive rails into a virtual forest wilderness of western pine, with lesser stands of fir, larch, hemlock, spruce, and cedar. To a lumberman, here sparkled the end of the rainbow.[26]

Blackwell's railroad would open for lumbering, and perhaps for industry and mining, the last isolated hunting grounds of the Kalispels. He organized two companies, the Panhandle Lumber early in 1906, made up of Pennsylvania speculators and associates in his Coeur d'Alene railroad, and the Idaho & Washington Northern Railroad in 1907 with Pennsylvania and Illinois stockholders. For his lumber company, Blackwell bought the Bradley tracts along the Pend Oreille valley. The railroad raised five million dollars for construction and equipment with a mortgage to the Illinois Trust and Savings, Chicago, and because railroads were building busily in the northwest, Blackwell recruited his own surveying and construction crews (including a number of new-immigrant Bulgarians) rather than using contractors. Perhaps for this reason he seemed secretive; to residents of the area, his railroad seemed to bloom suddenly. Only eight months passed between the first surveys and November 24, 1907, when the I&WN inaugurated freight and passenger service between Spokane and Newport, entering Spokane by a connection with the Spokane International, D. C. Corbin's road through northern Idaho to the Canadian Pacific.[27]

An early map of Blackwell's proposed right of way north of Newport, published in *Railway Age Gazette* and the *Newport Miner,* showed the tracks crossing the Pend Oreille above Newport to the east bank and down the river directly through the land claims Captain Bubb had staked for Kalispel Indians. If this had been the chosen route, Blackwell changed his mind; his directors met in the spring of 1909 to approve extending the Idaho & Washington Northern along the west bank of the river, crossing to the east side at Box Canyon. Near Usk, the route crossed the three west-side claims of Amos Nick, Isabel Abrahamson, and Mary Andrews and, as compensation, the railroad paid the Kalispel owners $653.10.[28]

Blackwell also acquired control of the Pend Oreille River Navigation Company which had consolidated steamer lines on the river and through his Panhandle Investment, intended to develop farm and townsites along his rail line. Panhandle bought the sites of Usk and Ione, turning over promotion and sales to Fred B. Grinnell, a Spokane real estate man who also boosted townsites and orchard tracts for the Spokane & Inland Empire. Panhandle Lumber built sawmills at Spirit Lake, Idaho, and Ione, where Blackwell became an organizer and director of the town banks.[29]

Through a fellow Pennsylvania lumberman, Harry C. Trexler, Blackwell also persuaded the Lehigh Valley Cement Company of Allentown, Pennsylvania, to underwrite a cement factory at Metaline Falls, where a pioneer cement company eight years earlier had operated briefly. He acquired the Sullivan Creek water and limestone rights of Lewis P. Larsen, who promoted mines in the area, and in October 1909 began building a power station for the factory at Sullivan Creek on the east side of the Pend Oreille. The Inland Portland Cement company started producing in April 1911, a dozen connected buildings with workers' housing nearby, grinding in solitude beside the stately forests of northeastern Washington.[30]

The Kalispels seemed indifferent to these changes. None could read, and few spoke more than halting phrases in English. They were accustomed to commercial bustle among white men. They had not been visited by an Indian agent since Bubb's survey in 1895. Another of those federal delegations, the Crow, Flathead, Northern Cheyenne, Uintah, and Yakima Commission had passed them by in 1897, although the Commissioner of Indian Affairs suggested that, if the commission persuaded the Kalispels to negotiate, the terms of an agreement with them could be inserted into a contract with the Flatheads. Neither did the commissioner see "any harm" in the commission's informally trying to entice the Kalispels to move to the Flathead reservation. Two members of this inept delegation talked with Michel, the Kalispel chieftain who had moved to the Jocko. He indignantly refused their request to negotiate or cede land, saying sarcastically that the 1887 Northwest commission "talked just as fair, just as honest, and made the same promises you do. Twenty-five families signed the treaty, and we left our homes in the Calispel valley and moved to the Flathead reservation, and where are the things you promised us?"[31]

But controversy over Northern Pacific claims in the Pend Oreille valley brought the Kalispels back into the view of the Indian office, like misty specimens swimming under a microscope. Bubb had been replaced as Colville agent by a retired army captain, John McAdam Webster, who, he explained, was not aware that the Kalispels belonged in his jurisdiction. A veteran of 27 years of military duty on the frontier, Webster nurtured a lasting sympathy for Indians. Never robust (he had been forced by illness to drop out of West Point for six months and had retired from the army as disabled), Webster was in a hospital when the Commissioner of Indian Affairs wrote to ask him what to do with the Kalispels. As soon as he read the letter, Webster trotted off to see the Kalispels—their first visit from an agent in ten years—and wrote a strong defense that prompted the attorney general, in his attempts to settle the railroad claim, to withdraw his recommendation that the Kalispels be forced onto the Coeur d'Alene or Flathead reservation. Webster also wrote Masseslow a letter the chief could show to whites, declaring the Kalispels' land held in trust for them by the government. Shortly after, Congress allowed the railroad to select other lands in lieu of their claims to Kalispel ground.[32]

The Indian office had considered drafting a presidential order designating the Kalispel claims a reservation but decided instead simply to allot the ground to individual Kalispels. Allotment, authorized by the Dawes Act of 1887, was intended to break down communal living in tribes, to which the Kalispels clung. Whenever anyone asked them, which was not often, the Kalispels said they wanted their land protected from whites, a school, and someone to teach them to farm. Webster counted 98 adult Kalispels; he found that 23 adults, one-fifth of the tribe, had died since 1895. [33]

In the fall of 1908, almost a year after Blackwell's railroad reached Newport, the commissioner directed Webster to start the allotment procedure for the Kalispels. The Indians, at the time, were confined by county quarantine for a mild outbreak of smallpox among them and an agency employee burned one log house and all the tipis in their tourist camp to prevent the infection from spreading. Other houses were fumigated and Kalispels, themselves, burned bedding and clothing. No whites caught the pox, Webster remarked, and "there was no real cause for the hullabaloo" the whites raised.

Webster was in a Chicago hospital with an ulcer attack, and the commissioner's order to allot lay on his desk until the following April. In the meantime, Napoleon LeClerc, incensed by a land office ruling against his appeal for the Kalispel land denied him in 1894, circulated a petition up and down the river demanding that the Kalispels be removed. The petition, said the *Newport Miner,* was "quite generally signed by the residents of the valley and Newport," adding that "the move is a good one . . . for the protection of the Indians and the development of the valley." The editor opined that the Kalispels were "an extremely worthless set of redskins . . . squatting on some of the most valuable land in the valley . . . nearly always afflicted with smallpox or some other disease," who passed their time gambling. After someone conveyed this opinion to the tribe, the Kalispels held a lasting grudge against the *Miner.* At the same time, a justice of the peace circulated a petition for a jail at Cusick for "hoboes and bad men following in the wake of railroad construction" as the Idaho & Washington Northern extended its tracks toward Ione. [34]

With LeClerc's petition in hand, Representative Wesley L. Jones pressed the Indian office to make a decision on the Kalispels. Webster wrote a report designed to placate the congressman and relieve the commissioner. "These Indians are about as well off as, and are more happy and contented than, most of their white neighbors," he asserted. The captain derided "land grabbers" among the whites, saying that the Kalispels "have always had the respect of most of the decent settlers in this vicinity; the merchants are willing and glad to extend credit to many of them, knowing they are as trustworthy in that respect as their white patrons; they are self-supporting and raise enough crops to supply their necessities, supplementing them by hunting, fishing, trapping, bead work on moccasins, gloves, etc.," and most had log cabins on their land but preferred to live in tipis during the summer.[35]

In reality, the Kalispels grubbed in poverty, their old trails and hunting grounds blocked by settlements, barred by language and schooling from all but the simplest roles in white commerce; they earned a little money doing odd jobs, selling beaded moccasins and trinkets in their riverside tipi camp erected solely to amuse tourists, and taking part in the "Indian village" at Spokane's annual fair. Once a year most of the Kalispels rode in a horse caravan to De Smet on the Coeur d'Alene reservation to attend a Catholic mass. As for farming, river floods often washed out their meager plantings.[36]

"Old blind Masalaw," as Webster called the Kalispel chief, appeared at Miles (the Colville agency) frequently to plead for a school and a church for his people. "The Kalispels are a simple, peaceable, and law-abiding people . . . so long neglected and left to shift for themselves that, five years ago, they nearly lost their lands to the Northern Pacific," Webster told the commissioner. "Masalaw and his tribe have a strong desire for a school, having been denied all educational advantages since the abandonment of the Catholic mission among them more than 60 years ago. They also want a church, being very devout worshippers." Webster suggested a school for the Kalispels like those on the Spokane and Colville reservations, while a visiting inspector reported that Cusick, across the river from the Kalispels, had only a one-room school without space for Indians. For a few months, agent and commissioner exchanged letters about a school until the commissioner explained that the Indian office had spent all its money and Webster agreed that the Kalispels could probably wait another year.[37]

The commissioner sent a special allotting agent, Clair Hunt, to settle finally the land dispute with Napoleon LeClerc. Hunt, a former mining surveyor who had allotted the Spokanes and was allotting the Colvilles, badgered the commissioner for more work. In his review of LeClerc's claim, Hunt probably came as close as any-

A postcard picture of unidentified Kalispels in the Indian camp beside the Pend Oreille River. Photographer and date unknown. (Hazel Hunter album, Kalispel tribal collection)

one to describing the early days of settlement and, in the end, he ruled against LeClerc, who then appealed to Senator Miles Poindexter. (Hunt also took pictures to sell as postcards.) As Hunt explained, in early days the Kalispels "occupied their land in a tribal, communal manner, having no separate ownership of land. Inasmuch as no individual Indian was especially injured [by settlers' claims], they made no complaint until such a large amount of their lands were taken . . . [that] they found the whole tribe restricted." A pioneer settler, John Brown, confirmed Hunt's version: When Captain Bubb came, he said, the Indians "claimed all the land, pastured horses and cattle in common and camped on any portion they fancied." Under Bubb's direction, however, the Kalispels tried to divide the land into individual ownerships by fencing and building cabins. LeClerc told Hunt that settlers generally gave money to Masseslow so the Kalispels would leave them alone on their homestead claims.[38]

Hunt resurveyed Bubb's plats, recorded the genealogy of each claimant, and classified the land by use. Perhaps two dozen Kalispels from Bubb's time had died and more had been born. Now Hunt found twice as many Indians as land available and reported this unhappy conclusion: "There is only enough land to allocate 40 acres of agricultural land or 80 acres of grazing land" to each Kalispel, less than the allotments authorized by federal law which allowed 160 acres to each head of a household and 80 acres to each adult single person.[39]

Hunt suggested, however, that Kalispels could receive full allotments by moving to the Colville reservation or by taking some of the forest reserve in the Pend Oreille valley. The Kalispels would not move, and the government did not offer them forest land. The Indians, Webster commented, "cling tenaciously to their mother land, and prefer to take allotments of one half the usual size rather than go elsewhere. . . . It would be nothing less than a crime to move them." Hunt also thought that 40 acres might be enough if Kalispel farms could be protected by a river dike, and the commissioner asked W. B. Hill, the Indian service irrigation engineer, to look at this possibility. Hill, who did not reach the Pend Oreille until a year later, counseled against diking, saying the Kalispel land was not valuable enough to warrant the cost. Allotments to the Kalispels had been suspended until Hill reported. In the meantime, Hunt was ordered to appear at Lake Mohonk, the annual conference of Indian advocates, and then to go to Washington to report to the commissioner, in person, about the Kalispels. Hunt considered that "the entire Pend Oreille valley is land to which the Indian title has never been extinguished, and the Kalispel tribe has a moral right to recompense for the land taken by the whites." On his return from Washington, Hunt went to finish allotting the Colvilles.[40]

Hunt's resurvey was treated as allotment although Indian owners did not actually receive titles to their land for years, some in 1925 and others in 1933. One barrier to clear titles lay in a series of proposals for power dams or irrigation projects on the Pend Oreille. In 1906 three Spokane land promoters, David T. Ham and Wilbur S. Yearsley, president and vice-president of the Palouse Land Company, and Ernest A. Torrance, investor, formed the Pend Oreille Development Company to build a hydroelectric dam, obtaining a government powersite withdrawal of more than 2,135 acres in a narrow strip along the river. All but 80 acres had been claimed by settlers and 1,059 acres were Kalispel land. The Indian office delayed giving titles to Indians, thinking that legislation was necessary to allot in powersite areas.

When the company could not raise the capital to build, Ham dropped out. Late in 1911 the government restored the strip for homestead entry but Yearsley organized the International Power & Manufacturing Company with Montana investors, intending to dam Z Canyon, and got from Congress a three-year extension of the earlier firm's rights on the river. This second company did not build, either, but in 1914 conveyed its rights to Hugh L. Cooper, a noted engineer. Proposals for using the Pend Oreille for power or irrigation would appear for half a century more, casting shadows on the titles of riverside land owners.[41]

Delays in land titles, postponement of a school, and continual crowding gnawed at Chief Masseslow. The Dalkena Lumber Company had petitioned to cut timber on Kalispel land in 1909 and, although the government turned it down, lumber companies cut busily all along the river. Perhaps Masseslow had some misgivings about the effect of a new county government, for the 1911 legislature formed Pend Oreille County from Stevens County during a

Below Kalispel villages on the Pend Oreille, the river flowed swiftly through narrow canyons. This is Z Canyon, for some years promoted as a hydroelectric power site. (Frank Palmer photo, Thomas Teakle collection, Spokane Public Library)

bitter battle over legislative reapportionment and everywhere in the valley, men chattered about what the new county would do when it started up in July. Late in June 1911 Masseslow rode down to Gonzaga College in Spokane to appeal to its president, Father Louis Taelman, for a church. Taelman, a brusque, wiry Belgian, now 44, had learned to speak Salish during his five years as a teacher of scholastics at St. Ignatius mission in Montana. The Jesuit readily agreed to visit the Kalispels.[42]

Taelman found the Kalispels in "pitiful" condition, Masseslow surviving on coffee and bread smeared with lard. Not long after the priest's visit, Kalispels were reported killing deer illegally in the Skookum Creek area. "The Indians are in desperate need of food and they can hardly be blamed for their violation of game laws," the *Newport Miner* said, adding that the Kalispels' privation was "another argument for their being placed on a reservation." Yet a government school superintendent disputed tales of Kalispel want, declaring the tribe owned 30 head of cattle and Indian families were cultivating small patches of land. Such conflicting reports, often biased, hampered the Indian office's best efforts to understand the true condition of the tribe. Doubtless Taelman's assessment was close to the truth.[43]

The Jesuit said that he had been called to administer the last rites to a dying Kalispel girl but arrived too late "because the tribe together could not muster the price of a telegram," adding that the Indians "have never had the benefit of a doctor . . . never a school. . . . These people are always destitute and on the verge of starvation." From the dying girl episode emanated one of the pious tales that circulated through Catholic Indian camps: The girl's mother claimed to have seen her dead daughter two times, pleading, "Pray for me," and a third time, "Today, rejoice!" The Indians all knew the story and interpreted it as the soul's release from purgatory.[44]

Taelman, who preferred missions to academics, went to see the Kalispels often enough in 1911 to set his Gonzaga colleagues grumbling that he neglected his duties at the college. On crossing the river by canoe to the Kalispel camp, the priest customarily shook hands all around. Abrupt in manner, he ordered the Indians about like children. He told newspaper reporters that the devout Kali-

Masseslow, chief of the Kalispels, photographed by Edward S. Curtis c. 1910. Curtis photographed Indians in a tent equipped with skylight, intending to convey native dignity. (Smithsonian Institution, National Anthropological Archives, No. 83–14079)

spels still sang well the hymns taught them half a century earlier. Learning that there had been no Christmas service in their camp for 25 years, Taelman agreed to spend the holiday season of 1912 with the Indians, finding on his arrival that the Kalispels had built a 15- by 35-foot church of logs and boards—with building paper tacked on the walls and ceiling to keep out the cold—heated with two small stoves.[45]

A few minutes before midnight mass, tribal policemen stalked through the camp ringing bells, and the Kalispels gathered around Masseslow's tipi to escort the blind old chief, now 85, long hair drooping to his shoulders, to their church by lantern light as they sang "Adeste Fidelis" in Salish. After a circle of young men fired a rifle salute at midnight, the tribe followed Masseslow into the building, men on one side, women on the other. Taelman's mass and homily lasted two hours. Then the Indians shook hands with him and went out to circle a bonfire, chanting, "Let us be glad and rejoice, for this is the day the Lord has made."[46]

As he learned to know the Kalispels better, Taelman traced the family relationships in a two-page list waggishly headed, "History of the Calispel Indians," in which he concluded, "The Calispels are one big family."[47]

Taelman's devotion to his Indians cost the Kalispels their priest, for he was quietly removed as Gonzaga president—while most of the Jesuit community was away on a summer break—and assigned to the Montana Indian missions. Jesuits "whose voices had been heard in Rome . . . admitted Taelman's good qualities," chronicled a Jesuit historian, "but objected to his frequent absences to the Kalispel Indian mission." Taelman would spend the rest of his life ministering to Indians and when he died in 1961 would be hailed as the greatest missionary of his time.[48]

While the Kalispels reveled in the short-lived ministry of Louis Taelman, the government tried to untangle the tribe's knotty land claims. The commissioner again considered setting aside tribal ground by executive order, again opted for allotment, again proposed giving the Kalispels full allotments on the Colville reservation, and again John Webster counseled against moving them. "It would be better . . . to have the land shortage filled from the nearest Forest Reserve rather than to allot any of these Indians on the

Colville Reservation, with the tribes of which they have no affilia-
tion," he wrote the commissioner, "and unless land within easy
reach of them could be added to their present holdings they would
prefer to accept smaller allotments in order to be held together.
But they are justly entitled to full allotments." This would be
Webster's last stand for the Kalispels; in March 1912 he transferred
from the Colville to the new Spokane agency and, although he was
nominally responsible for the Kalispels in his new post, he did not
see much of them. Fred L. Wolf, editor of the *Newport Miner*, was
not sorry to see Webster leave, calling the agent the person "most
responsible" for keeping the Kalispels in the valley. Wolf thought
the captain "knocked the agricultural values of the Calispel valley"
when Webster, commenting on irrigation, remarked publicly that
the "lands were worth more when overflowed than diked."[49]

Doubtless Napoleon LeClerc was partly responsible for the Kalispels' keeping their traditional homeland, for by pressing his claims
through congressmen, he forced the government to resolve the
tribe's status. Now, LeClerc, too, was gone; he and his brothers
sold their ranch for $70,000 in August 1911 to William Merry-
weather, a Spokane real estate man, and left the Pend Oreille.[50]

In the end, stubborn Masseslow prevailed. When the Indian
office at last realized that the Kalispels would not move and that too
little land remained for individual allotments, Secretary of the Interior F. K. Lane drafted an executive order for President Woodrow
Wilson's signature setting aside the Kalispel claims as a reservation. With his draft, Lane sent a memorandum explaining that not
enough land remained to allot each Indian the acreage allowed by
law, and stating the government's intention of building a school for
the Kalispels. On March 23, 1914, Wilson signed the executive
order reserving 4,629.27 acres as a reservation for the Kalispel
Indians. Upon receiving a copy, the register of the Spokane land
office took the trouble to write the General Land Office to explain
that the government's increasing use of the spelling "Kalispel" was
incorrect. The name, he admonished, should be either Calispel or
Calispell.[51]

CHAPTER 5

Learning Through Neglect

NEARLY 25 years would pass between the creation of the Kalispel reservation and the mobilization of the tribe as a corporation under the Indian Reorganization Act. In that quarter century, the American attitude toward Indian peoples changed from an evangelistic fervor for individual salvation that demanded breaking up the tribes to a tolerance of tribal unity and tradition. By World War II, Americans no longer expected Indians to give up their heritage but adopted a bi-cultural outlook that, despite good intentions, seemed to deny young Indians a realistic place in either Indian or white society. Many an Indian found himself too white for Indians, and too Indian for whites. The reservation gave Kalispels a sanctuary where they gingerly experimented with new ways. But much did not change. Old Kalispels clung to old ways, and the young vacillated between ingrained ties to their past and a present they were poorly equipped to challenge.

Throughout those 25 years, the Kalispels contended with a federal bureaucracy that took them into account only incidentally; they would never have their own agency but always be attached to one somewhere else. Sometimes the Kalispels felt neglected; sometimes they were happy to be left alone.

Yet they got their church and school, the church during the ministry of Father Edward M. Griva, a gnarled, stumpy Jesuit missionary. He had been a diocesan priest in Italy before he entered the Jesuit order; he came to the United States in 1894, learned English at the Coeur d'Alene mission, and Salish at St. Ignatius. Griva had been traveling by horse and buggy around the Flathead reservation for six years when he was reassigned to St. Francis Regis at Kettle Falls, to be responsible for the spiritual welfare of more than a dozen untended missions in northeastern Washington.

Nearing middle age, his health failing, the peppery Griva nonetheless traveled incessantly by train or horse, spending a day in one town, two in another, no matter the weather. He preached to the Kalispels for the first time on August 13, 1913, using a vacant house in Cusick as church and a borrowed table as altar, and then celebrated mass in the Indian village. In later visits, he said mass for Indians in the chief's house, and for whites at the Sullivan home where he instructed children and occasionally stayed overnight. Like nearly every other Jesuit, he treated Indians with gruff paternalism and loved them like children. Whenever he could, Griva squeezed in an extra day or two among the Kalispels.[1]

Griva was a builder; in half a century of mission service, he raised money for 16 church structures. Late in 1913 the Jesuit provincial consented to a church for the Kalispels and in February 1914 the Diocese of Seattle approved. Griva thereupon wrote begging letters to prospective donors whose names he took from religious magazines and newspapers and, he said in his memoirs, "a lady about to enter a convent made a big donation" which the priest spent for lumber. (He was building simultaneously at Tonasket and Molson.) The Kalispels, themselves, contributed the labor for a whitewashed frame chapel with double doors and square steeple, and they tore down the church built for Taelman the previous Christmas for some of its lumber. On August 21, 1914, Griva celebrated the first mass in the Kalispels' new church. A bell was installed the following January. Griva counseled his Kalispels to visit the church to pray and sing hymns even when the priest could not be there.[2]

"They were eager for [religious] instruction," Griva wrote in his autobiography. "One thing . . . was making me sad is that they are too near the white people, who were selling them liquor and caused lots of drunkenness among them. No one at that time was living in adultery or concubinage so that all except the too small . . . could receive the sacraments." Of Masseslow and the succeeding chief,

A snapshot of Indian houses as Father Griva found them when he began his mission work among the Kalispels. The priest generally lodged with a white family near Cusick, and was paddled across the river for religious services among the Indians. (Griva collection, OPA)

John Bigsmoke, Griva recalled, "Both were very good Catholics and gave a good example to the Indians."[3]

The first bishop of Spokane, Augustin F. Schinner, dedicated the church on March 8, 1915, as Our Lady of Sorrows. Mounted Indians fired a rifle volley to greet the bishop when he debarked from a rough river crossing by canoe. He confirmed 41 Indians, some white-haired and blind, and six whites. "Two good white ladies" of Cusick sent the bishop his dinner, and then the Indians knelt in two lines for his blessing. Griva remembered the dedication as "the happiest day we ever had in Cusick." Shortly after, he was transferred; he would not see the Kalispels again for nearly four years.[4]

In the meantime, the Indian office shifted the Kalispels to the jurisdiction of the Coeur d'Alene agency and, as it entered a new fiscal year, directed the superintendent, Morton D. Colgrove, to tally the school-age children and recommend the "proper location" for a Kalispel school. Colgrove chose a site on a slope above the river's flood stage about one mile from the Kalispel village, and reported 24 children "in accessible distance." (The adults he recorded as 114: 54 men and 60 women.) A frame schoolhouse, using the same floor plan as a school for Kutenais, was built in 1914, for $3,650. The Indian office regarded such schools as "industrial training" day schools where Indian boys would learn farming and manual skills, and girls, sewing, cooking, and housekeeping. The school contained living quarters for a couple, teacher and housekeeper.[5]

The Kalispel school would be temporary, at best, because the government had already begun sending Indian children to public schools with white children wherever it could find space. The Washington state attorney general accelerated the entry of Indian children into public schools with his opinion that districts could count Indian pupils in claiming their shares of state school monies. Already a fourth of the Colville reservation children attended public schools, where the government paid tuition for them. The Kalispels had been granted a stop-gap—a school until their children went to Usk or Cusick.[6]

Colgrove realized that regular attendance would be a problem. One time when he visited, all but three of the Kalispel families had

The Kalispel schoolhouse, classroom, and living quarters for the teacher and family. After Kalispel students started to attend Cusick schools, the old building served as community hall until, dilapidated and crumbling, it was burned to make room for a new community hall. (Dellwo albums)

moved 19 miles away to clear 80 acres of timber and brush for $800. "The parents must work," he observed. "We probably will never be able to have more than a seven-month term," referring to the fact that some town schools ran nine months. Many rural schools in Washington, however, managed no more than three or four months a year, and the Indian office had stated its clear intention "not . . . to advance much beyond conditions in country day schools as provided for white pupils."[7]

The furnishings had not come and the water pipes had not been connected when the Kalispel school opened in the fall of 1915 with Charles Inman as teacher and his frail wife as housekeeper. Their four young children went to school with the Indians. Built for 30 pupils, the school enrolled 34 but only half attended on an average day. The Inmans bought two enameled basins and two towels, one for boys and another for girls, so the children could wash. Inspectors found Mrs. Inman's housekeeping "careless," but more detrimental was Inman's "difficulty . . . to get his pupils to speak English. . . . None of his pupils . . . [is] able to understand and speak in the English language." Inman did not know Salish. Days passed in which teacher and pupils exchanged only the simplest ideas by pointing and naming objects.[8]

Nevertheless, the school progressed and the Inmans became popular with the Kalispels. The school distributed clothing and shoes to children, and fed them at mid-day. Colgrove wrote the Indian office that "these Indians are sober and quite industrious but very poor; what they receive in the way of a mid-day meal and a limited amount of clothing for the chidlren is a godsend." If not skilled as housekeeper or cook—Colgrove faulted her cooking as "a meal after a fashion"—Mrs. Inman was good-hearted; she sewed skirts and dresses for the girls and visited their homes to care for sick children and sometimes, for ailing adults. Inman found jobs for men of the tribe—17 of them were working by 1918 at $2.50 to $4.50 a day—and with his pupils planted a short-lived garden and built playground equipment.

Inspectors complained that the school's studies were "not along definite lines," but acknowledged that Inman taught "vocabulary, language, and number work . . . along practical lines with reference to the pupils' everyday life." The school might be, as the Indian office classed it, "sub-primary" for students who did not speak English but both curriculum and attendance improved and Colgrove, impressed by the Kalispels' regard for the Inmans, withdrew a recommendation that they be replaced. Obviously the Kalispels learned enough English for simple conversations. The Inmans would stay until 1920, when Mr. and Mrs. R. H. Knox succeeded them. That was the year Congress directed that education be compulsory for Indian children.[9]

By 1920 the economy of Pend Oreille County was static, like most of the inland northwest, deflated from its artificial wartime spurt. The county bridged the river at Usk in 1919–20 with a wooden span on pilings that grew rickety as years passed. Even the most ardent boosters saw that the county's agriculture, much of it "stump farming" on logged-over lands, was marginal; the zinc and lead deposits of the Metaline, low grade with the market skidding; and the principal industry, lumbering, seasonal. As the migration to the northwest waned after 1910, the Idaho & Washington Northern had reduced service, blaming at one time "the depression in the lumber line," and another, "a general policy of retrenchment." Although lumbering produced the area's major payrolls, the companies faced ruin; on the average, profits barely exceeded one percent which would not meet the interest on capital debts. Throughout the inland lumber industry, large companies swallowed small. Even the industrial prince of the Pend Oreille, F. A. Blackwell, wallowed in trouble: the Milwaukee Railroad bought his bankrupt Idaho & Washington Northern at auction in 1916, replacing its green and gilt cars with gaudy Milwaukee orange, and the Menasha stockholders in Blackwell's lumber companies quietly removed his men among the directors.[10]

Metaline Falls, busy but not growing, shipped cement as far as Boise and Missoula; Ione, site of a Panhandle mill, shrank between 1910 and 1920; and so did Newport, declining 10 percent. Part of the shrinkage could be laid to the end of large railroad building projects, and part to the realization that, for the time being, Pend Oreille County was stalled. The high-water mark of the county's lumber industry was 1920: six mills cut steadily that year but, even with the advent of the Diamond and Ohio match companies which bought stumpage briskly in 1920, only two big mills would remain a decade and a half later and lumber production would have fallen 50 percent. [11]

Strapped for funds, the county government collected one-third of its tax revenues from the Great Northern and the Idaho & Washington Northern, which protested the levies. The gingery owner of the *Newport Miner*, Fred Wolf, assured his readers that "the pronounced fall off in demand" for lumber would not seriously curtail operations of the match companies. Had not speculation about hydroelectric plants on the river cast fleeting rays of hope for better times, Pend Oreille County would have been dreary indeed. "The great water power on the Pend Oreille river constitutes our biggest potential asset," Wolf wrote, burnishing the bright lining of hard times, as a local editor should. [12]

Times were perennially hard for the Kalispels, their numbers reduced by deaths from influenza in 1918. They supported themselves by occasional work for white ranchers or lumber companies, supplementing meager incomes by hunting and fishing. Some Kalispel women washed clothes for Usk and Cusick families. A few Indians planted gardens or cut hay on their "tentative allotments" (as an inspector termed them) and perhaps 15 families grazed 300 cattle on the reservation. "The houses on the allotments are poor," an inspector reported, "being log houses mostly of two rooms; some have four rooms containing two in the loft." [13]

Compared to their white neighbors, the Kalispels were impoverished but Superintendent Colgrove saw virtue in their extremity. "The poverty," he remarked, "has not proved an un-mixed evil; they have learned that to live they must work, and through neglect have learned to rely on themselves." [14]

For the most part, the Kalispels maintained their tribal life. "There is a chief who has a staff of five advisors and five policemen who keep order," the Coeur d'Alene superintendent said. "When an Indian gets drunk, he is taken before the Chief, tried, sentenced, or acquitted. . . . If he is found guilty, he is punished by the whipping post. . . . This custom suits them, is not cruel, and the white man has no part in it." [15]

Kalispels generally adopted white clothing, fashioned their tipis from canvas, and despite their schoolmaster's carping, spoke En-

Paul Tom (Piq al gai') wearing a hat of the kind popular with Kalispel men as they adopted white dress. (Kalispel tribal collection)

This faded snapshot shows the Kalispel baseball team, probably in the 1920s, when rivalries were keen among town and Indian teams. Left to right, front row: Gabe Andrews, Antoine Peuse, unknown; second, Willie Tom, Mose Nick, Willie Sam, Joe Andrew, and two unknown; third, Joe Blackbear, far right. (Hazel Hunter album, Kalispel tribal collection)

glish well enough to shop in local stores and do their jobs for white employers. The tribe moved when snows were not too deep: caravans to the Coeur d'Alene reservation, treks to hunt and fish and dig camas—constricted by settlement and game regulations—and performances and parades at the September and October county fairs where they joined other tribes in Indian villages, sideshows for gaping patrons who cheered tipi races, stick games, Indian dances, horse races, and even Indian baby shows. The fairs brought Indians together to trade and gamble, and they were encouraged to seem primitive, wearing native costumes and painted faces. "More demoralizing than beneficial," an Indian inspector branded these shows. "The influence of these gatherings is not conducive to progress in civilization as they tend to degrade the Indians to the level of curiosities." But for 20 years or longer, the "barbarian In-

The occasion has been forgotten, but the photographer evidently intended to depict both aboriginal and, at the time, modern Kalispel dress with ceremonial staff and drum. (Kalispel tribal collection)

An unknown photographer persuaded John Meshell (Ts' way' elsh) to pose with pistol and rifle and beaded vest for a postcard. Such finery would be reserved for ceremonial occasions, not for warfare or the hunt. (Hazel Hunter album, Kalispel tribal collection)

dian" was a staple attraction of fairs and outdoor shows. Lacking the distinctive Plains feathered war bonnets, the Kalispels were perhaps not as conspicuous as Montana Blackfeet—Blackfeet even performed at the dedication of Spokane's Davenport Hotel—but they appeared for one dollar a day regularly in the Indian village at the Spokane and other fairs.[16]

And like other tribes, the Kalispels organized their own public frolic, an annual August powwow on the reservation with games, races, and dances—the delight of some and despair of others. The Coeur d'Alene superintendent growled that "the principal feature seems to be . . . gambling," and belittled the powwow as "some wild west stunts." He sent his police from the Coeur d'Alene reservation "to maintain order." An anonymous pencilled letter, purporting to speak for the Kalispel tribe, asserted the powwow "the last few years has been a failure because the chief, John Big Smoke, has been taking it over himself and taking all the money which . . . should have been used to pay for peace officers so there won't be so much bootlegging around. . . . The last few years bootleggers has been selling their whiskey freely." The Indians would "like to get a committee" to run the powwow, and the writer wanted the superintendent to tell Bigsmoke to step aside. Like Kalispel appearances at fairs, the powwow would be controversial among Indians and whites for years, regarded by some as great fun and others, a binge. But it would continue.[17]

The primitive, subservient Indian exhibited at county fairs was out of step with the government's efforts to turn each Indian into an independent American citizen, "competent and capable of managing his or her affairs," in the language of the Burke Act of 1906 which empowered the Secretary of the Interior to grant land patents to "competent" Indians who would then be on their own. (The Burke Act amended the Dawes Act of 1887, which stipulated that Indian lands should be held in trust for 25 years.) No one knew precisely how to judge "competence," although reservation agents tended to assume that Indians with white blood were more competent than fullbloods.[18]

Competence implied education, of course, and as one way to better education, the government required teachers to submit written lesson plans. Charles Inman at the Kalispel school sent the superintendent a calendar with the customary patriotic holidays,

Louis Malewolf, left, and Eneas Michel, Kalispel men photographed at the U.S. Indian Congress in Omaha in 1898. (Smithsonian Institution, National Anthropological Archives, No. 3027)

Most Indians who attended the Omaha congress wore native costumes. This unidentified Kalispel girl wears earrings of the kind that prompted French trappers to name her people Pend Oreilles. (Smithsonian Institution, National Anthropological Archives, No. 83.14078)

Omaha congress photographers tended to idealize Indian subjects, as in this thoughtful portrait of a blanketed Kalispel man holding a symbolic feather. (Smithsonian Institution, National Anthropological Archives, No. 14080)

a "Humane Treatment of Animals Day" on March 12, and a daily class schedule from 9 A.M. to 4 P.M. of reading, numbers, writing or drawing, and language, with an "industrial period" each afternoon, although the school had little industrial equipment. The superintendent considered Inman's calendar "unsatisfactory," and Inman's successor, Knox, who was not trained as a teacher, wrote his on a blackboard. As might be expected, it had been erased when an inspector called, but the teacher mailed an elaborate outline that seemed acceptable. As a matter of fact, only teacher and pupils knew what went on in the Kalispel school. The Indian office, indeed, had considered closing it when Inman resigned but kept the school open because Kalispel children had no other place to go.[19]

Competence was still government policy when President Wilson's Commissioner of Indian Affairs, Cato Sells, who had been a small-town Texas banker, in April 1917 proclaimed that "every Indian, as soon as he has been determined to be competent . . . shall be given full control of his property," and no longer be a ward of the government. Sells assumed, as did most whites, that Indians would be farmers or cattlemen; he collected data on livestock herds among Indians, and then demanded "radical and speedy" improvement, declaring that "primarily the opportunity for advancement among Indians is largely agricultural and stock raising." He ordered reservation superintendents to push hard for better herds and herding practices. The Coeur d'Alene superintendent observed, however, that Indians preferred working together; they did not like farming or herding because these were lonely occupations.[20]

The Kalispels, of course, legally held no individual property and got scant notice from the government. Agency farmers rarely visited; requests for farm tools had been ignored so often that Kalispel chiefs stopped asking. The government said time and again that it intended to allot land to the Kalispels, as the Commissioner of Indian Affairs told an inquiring citizen in 1916: "The lands are soon to be reallotted to individual members of the tribe," estimating that 114 Indians lived on the reservation, 94 of them enrolled in the tribe. But Kalispel land rested in a sort of legal twilight, reserved but not awarded, and in the meantime, the Kalispels lost a piece of it—Indian Island at a bend in the river about seven miles downstream from Newport.[21]

Before white settlers arrived, three Indian men had cut wild hay on Indian Island, regarding it as theirs, and handing it down to their heirs. One built a house and barn on the riverbank north of the island but they fell down within a few years. One surviving heir, Joseph Andrews, finally claimed it all; he and his wife Mary buried three of their children on the island; they resisted attempts to take the place from them. For nearly 10 years, white settlers applied to buy or lease the island until in 1923, on the application of Lyle Everett of Newport, the widow Mary agreed to relinquish it in return for a reservation allotment. It may have been the only formal relinquishment of Kalispel land. [22]

In its unresolved status, Kalispel reservation land was closed to ordinary uses. The Panhandle Lumber Company was refused permission to build a temporary wagon road across it to reach private stumpage. Dalkena Lumber applied to harvest reservation timber, estimating it worth perhaps $32,800; the request was turned down because a "Kalispel allotment schedule had never been approved." An application for an irrigation ditch was rejected for the same rea-

The Pend Oreille River occasionally froze during winter months. The posts (right, center) are pilings for Diamond Match Company log-storage booms near the reservation. (Kalispel tribal collection)

son (and because the land office lost the request). Diamond Match, however, was granted the right to attach a logging boom to the reservation riverbank in 1921; the company proposed to store 15 million board feet of white pine logs in the river. While the Coeur d'Alene profited from the sale of its timber, and logging on reservations became commonplace enough that the Indian office in 1920 issued general rules for the sale of Indian timber, the Kalispel trees stood untouchable.[23]

The long delay in turning over individual tracts to Kalispels reflected the government's dilemma about providing for heirs of allottees. Under law, an Indian's heirs inherited equal interests in his land—which meant that, as generations passed, each individual's share grew smaller. Because each living owner held an equal share, all had to agree on the use or disposition of the land. Families split in land disputes. The 40-acre tracts platted in 1909 by Clair Hunt had been too small for economic farming in the first place, and as older Kalispels died and their children claimed shares, the owners of individual allotments multiplied. From time to time, the tribe enrolled children as new members. In one of his frequent letters to the commissioner about Kalispel lands, a Coeur d'Alene superintendent, H. D. Lawshe, put his finger on the problem: "Possibly the delay [in allotting] has been caused through there being claims of a number of children whose parents or guardians have made application to have them adopted [into the tribe] and allotted."[24]

Sufficient land for heirs was a national problem and, because of it, a new American policy was taking shape, rising both from the realization that the Dawes Act had been impractical and the conviction that Indians ought to be freed from government supervision with full citizenship. Allotment to many tribes had often been followed by the sale or lease of Indian lands or parceling shrinking tracts for heirs, leaving individual Indians without an economic base.

As they strove to solve land problems, Indians turned slowly to the courts and legislatures, with a new awareness that they might win redress with lawsuits and lobbies. As early as 1911 the Yakimas hired a Spokane attorney to carry their land claims before Congress. Soon after, a guardian sued in federal court to regain control of his Indian ward's land. Indians formed short-lived political alliances: the Indian Tribes of America, organized in Yakima, and at

Toppenish, the Brotherhood of North America Indians. When Commissioner Sells proposed giving Indians their land and letting them "work out their destiny," northwest Indians dispatched a Yakima chieftain to lobby against an abrupt end to federal stewardship.[25] Congress confirmed citizenship for native-born Indians in 1924 but many states dodged the Indian franchise. The Washington attorney general held that an Indian who voted must pay taxes and otherwise qualify under the state constitution.[26]

About 1924 the Colvilles, Okanogans, Sanpoils and associated tribes engaged the Spokane attorney and historian, William Stanley Lewis, to lobby a bill through Congress that would allow them to sue the government for lost land in the U.S. Court of Claims. (Under an act passed in 1863, Indian tribes, like foreign nations, required congressional authority to sue the United States.) Most likely the Colvilles chose Lewis because he had interviewed Indians for historical articles and was a member (and perhaps organizer) of a small Indian advocacy group in Spokane. Few lawyers solicited Indian clients in those years, remarked one attorney, "in the light of the highly specialized nature of the litigation and the small likelihood of recovery." An erect, slender, aloof man, neither socially nor politically prominent, Lewis sympathized with Indians as a result of his historical inquiries and, at any rate, his law practice does not appear to have been flourishing. Once involved with Indian causes, he seems to have given them most of his time.[27]

New to politics, Lewis approached Representative Samuel B. Hill of Washington to introduce a bill for the Colvilles, and asked a leading Republican, U.S. Marshal David T. Ham (the same man who proposed developing power on the Pend Oreille), to put him in touch with Senator Wesley Jones. Hill was something of a local hero; he had nursed a bill through Congress to pay Stevens County $44,309 and Ferry, $71,458 in lieu of local taxes on allotted Indian lands. Hill and Jones both introduced bills for the Colvilles and Hill's passed with little comment. The interior department seemed neutral, but the Bureau of the Budget opposed unexpected federal expenditures and, with this in mind, President Calvin Coolidge vetoed the measure.[28]

Lewis was now working rapidly, as a trustee of the National Indian Congress scheduled for Spokane late in 1925, to assist in inviting Indian delegates and arrange a program. He found time to persuade Jones and Hill to introduce their bills again in the next session. A house committee limited any attorney's fee to 10 percent of the tribe's award, and in any event not more than $25,000, and stipulated that the Indians could not recover more than $1.25 an acre from any lands lost through relinquishment, settlement, or other means. Any funds awarded would be deposited in the U.S. Treasury. With these qualifications, Jones' bill passed near the end of the session. Because a hundred or more tribes had by now sought authority to sue the government, the Bureau of Indian Affairs drew guidelines for bills involving tribal suits, specifying that they must cite treaties and acts of Congress related to land claims. Even though the Colville bill conformed, the interior department and budget bureau opposed it, and during a brief debate, a congressman growled that "attorneys dig up these matters and arouse in Indians the feeling that they have something coming," arguing that the bills were drawn "in such wide-open language . . . that I believe Congress ought to proceed with more care." Coolidge pocket-vetoed the Colville bill by declining to sign it in the 10-day period set out in the Constitution. [29]

Lewis audaciously filed a land-claim suit with the U.S. Court of Claims in March 1927, arguing that the adjournment of Congress had prevented Coolidge from returning a vetoed bill, and therefore the measure had technically passed, the first challenge to pocket vetoes since Thomas Jefferson's presidency. The U.S. attorney general demurred, carrying the case to the Supreme Court. In 1929 the court ruled against the Colville litigation, relying on the attorney general's review of federal archives showing that, in the history of the nation, no bill which a president failed to return in 10 days had become law. [30]

In the meantime, Kalispels, with two hundred or more Indians from other tribes, had taken part in the National Indian Congress at Spokane from October 30 through November 5, 1925. Staged by civic boosters and the Great Northern Railway largely as publicity for Spokane, the Congress proved frustrating to the Indian delegates; they pitched tipis at Glover Field, a city athletic arena, and on the parkway of Riverside Avenue, where thousands of gawkers stared; they wore large convention buttons, staged a beauty pag-

An Indian beauty contest at Gonzaga stadium during the 1925 National Indian Congress in Spokane selected Alice Garry to tour the nation as an Indian princess. Here, contestants stand on or beside a flatbed truck as man with megaphone announces the winners. (Thomas Teakle collection, Spokane Public Library)

eant, mock war games, races, and native dances at Gonzaga Stadium, and rode in costume in a parade through the center of the city. William Lewis also paraded and judged several contests. Haskell Institute defeated Gonzaga in football, 10–9. When it was over, H. B. Peairs, Haskell's superintendent, prudently praised the idea of an Indian congress but observed that white people did all the talking. Indian leaders were patently unhappy with their roles as exhibits.[31]

Nevertheless, approximately one thousand Indians from 28 northwest tribes attended a 1926 National Indian Congress in Spokane. Lewis had spent four months in Washington, D.C., lobbying for the Colvilles (who chided him for expensive dinners at the Willard

Hotel) and was, therefore, not much involved with this second congress but a newspaper quoted him: "Among the Colvilles, W. S. Lewis found so much poverty, he said, that it set him wondering why we ignore an impoverished race at our door to send money to Turkey." The visit of the Columbia River Historical Expedition, 20 writers traveling on the Great Northern, made the second congress nearly as much a carnival as the first but an Indian committee voiced a number of resolutions, including those urging that the government "hold in force" a congressional act making Indians citizens, that the government honor the Yakimas' wish to maintain their tribal rights and keep their lands in trust, that Flathead lands be put in condition to farm, and that the Colvilles be permitted to present their case in the Court of Claims.[32]

Spokane would not convene another Indian congress, but possibly during the 1926 meeting, the Kalispels approached, or were approached by, William Lewis. Probably the Spokane, Ignace Garry, whose first wife, Josephine Revais, was a Kalispel, talked to Lewis about the Kalispels. He had met Lewis when the attorney was writing his book about Garry's great-grandfather, Spokane Garry, chief of the Upper and Middle Spokanes. Garry, rising in Indian politics, was directing Kalispel business affairs during the midtwenties. Lewis convinced Jones and Hill to offer bills in the 70th Congress authorizing the Lower Spokane and Kalispel tribes to sue the government in the Court of Claims. (The Supreme Court had not yet rejected his suit on behalf of the Colvilles.) The stipulations limiting attorney's fees and recovery by the tribes were the same as those in the Colville bills. When a congressional committee on Indian affairs reported favorably on Hill's bill for the Lower Spokanes and Kalispels, asserting that "through oversight and neglect of the government the original possessory rights were never extinguished," the *Newport Miner* headlined an article, "Calispel Indians May Become Wealthy Tribe."[33]

Noting that the 68th Congress had authorized western Washington tribes to sue, Hill declared, during debate on the Kalispel bill, "These Indians . . . because of the fact that they were peaceable and gave the government no trouble, were simply neglected and they have never been able to succeed in getting a hearing from the United States government. . . . I believe this government should give them their day in court." The interior department was "noncommittal," but the Bureau of the Budget again opposed Indian claims as contrary to the President's fiscal program. Congress passed Jones's bill, identical with Hill's, but on May 18, 1928, Coolidge vetoed it with a tart, brief message: the claims would amount to $9.1 million representing 6,500,000 acres at $1.25 and hunting and fishing rights at $1 million which, in the president's view, "were not based on any treaty" and lacked "unmistakeable merit." There would be no suit by the Kalispels until the government established an Indian Claims Commission 18 years later.[34]

A few months after Coolidge's veto, when Kalispels performed at yet another local fair, a newspaper reporter talked with Baptiste Bigsmoke who had been elected chief of the Kalispels in 1926 after his father's death. "We thought Uncle Sam was the Great White Father . . . but he is only a step-father who boots his red children around without cause," the newspaper quoted Bigsmoke as saying through an interpreter. And one of his father's advisors, Aneas Meshell, chimed in, "It was all right for years. . . . Now, white men warn Indians not to hunt or fish off the reservation. The next thing Indians fear, white men will forbid them to gather huckleberries in the mountains."[35]

Shortly after the supreme court denied the Colvilles access to the Court of Claims, the Indian bureau turned down funds to continue Lewis's contract with the Colvilles. The attorney closed his Spokane law practice and retired to Los Angeles. He was said to have spent $10,000 of his own money lobbying for the Kalispels, the Colvilles, and other northwest tribes.[36]

While they waited to become a wealthy tribe, to use the *Miner's* phrase, not much changed for the Kalispels. A few men worked seasonally in logging camps or sawmills; eight found work as woodcutters; Kalispels continued to dig, and to hunt and fish without county licenses, clashing with whites. (As soon as Pend Oreille County was established, the commissioners had adopted laws requiring a one-dollar hunting license and restricting seasons.) When an Indian was fined $50 for possessing a deer hide out of season, however, the U.S. attorney at Spokane intervened to have his case dismissed. Two Kalispel families farmed 40 acres each; six raised cattle on a thousand acres; and two leased their land for pasture.

Mrs. Yellow Eagle (Mary Masseslow), right, and her daughter, with beadwork patterns at their feet. Kalispels sold beaded moccasins, bags, and other items to tourists. (Thomas Teakle collection, Spokane Public Library)

An unidentified Kalispel woman and children in a scene typical of reservation life in the first half of the twentieth century. In aboriginal times, the tipi would have been made of rushes or skins and the clothing of leather. (Kalispel tribal collection)

Two or three Kalispels cut and sold wild hay. Some chopped firewood on their land for sale. Bands of men and women peddled trinkets and fish at the Sandpoint railroad station where passengers tossed them apples and oranges from car windows. The aggregate income of 84 adult Kalispels on the reservation did not reach $6,000 a year. The Coeur d'Alene superintendent felt that the Kalispels did "not apply themselves consistently to work and appear to exist on rather short rations. . . . At every opportunity, they arrange to have some celebration when gambling can be carried on." He opposed letting county or state lawmen police liquor among the Kalispels, however, because "with the attitude of the whites . . . the Indians would not always be treated fair." [37]

Celebrations relieved the tedium of cramped lives. The Kalispels traveled often to hunt and fish or to go to Indian and county fairs, moving on horseback along public highways, jaunty caravans with men dressed in sombreros, plaid shirts and jeans, and women, hair concealed by bandanas, in bright colored dresses. When Pend Oreille County law officers attempted to curb liquor at Kalispel powwows, they were turned off the reservation by Indian police from the Coeur d'Alene agency. An Usk man who helped organize the 1926 powwow wrote Bigsmoke, "I see some drinking around your celebration grounds. . . . You have declared on your honor that you would prohibit drinking. . . . Let your people know they must obey." Bigsmoke called a council to pass the word. Indians from 10 tribes rode to Cusick for the Kalispel frolic, and the Kalispels, in their turn, made the rounds of fairs organized by Flatheads, Umatillas, Nez Perces, Coeur d'Alenes, Colvilles, and others. The 1927 Kalispel powwow nearly lost its star rodeo performer. Charlie Saluskin of the Yakimas was arrested by county deputies for liquor possession but he paid a $50 fine in time to ride. "Quiet games of chance," the *Newport Miner* called them,

A confirmation class at the old Kalispel church built by Father Griva, before its removal in 1948 to higher ground. Bishop Charles D. White of Spokane and Father Taelman stand at the church door. (Hazel Hunter album, Kalispel tribal collection)

Tribal elders at the Kalispel church, c. 1935. Left to right, Charlie Nick, Bazil Andrews, Paul Tom, and Pe'el Joseph. (Kalispel tribal collection)

also occupied powwow participants and spectators. The *Okanogan Independent* reported that men and women played separate stick games, the women for a pot of blankets, scarves, and trinkets, while the men's involved "queer chanting and tapping" by players that held spectators for hours with "peculiar fascination."[38]

Most of the Kalispels lived in two-room frame houses clustered on a knoll beside the Pend Oreille River and, although their village flooded in high water, they refused to move. During the summer, nearly all pitched tipis which could be cooled by rolling up the sides. A Jesuit priest from Gonzaga University celebrated mass on the reservation once a month but the Kalispels rarely saw anyone from the Indian service. Sometimes a year passed without a visit from the Coeur d'Alene superintendent.[39]

For perhaps 30 years, the Kalispels believed that cattle-raising would be their economic base. The director of agriculture for the

Indian bureau surveyed the reservation, concluding that 250 to 300 head could be grazed there, not a large herd but a business for the Kalispels. Quite a few white ranchers in the Pend Oreille valley were trying to establish dairy herds; they, too, were looking for a way to stay in the valley.[40]

One quick source of income might be to sell the timber on the reservation, but the old problem of allotments stood in the way. Indian trees could not be cut without the owner's consent, and under the law, none of the Kalispels yet owned a share of the reservation. As early as 1920, new selections of 40-acre allotments had begun for older Kalispels and for 41 born since Clair Hunt had laid out their land in 1909. Two years passed, however, and some still had not chosen ground. A government forester guessed that reservation timber might bring $50,000 to $60,000, pointing out that all of it lay within one and one-half miles of the river, easy to reach and haul. Depression notwithstanding, lumber and match companies continued to compete for stumpage. The Commissioner of Indian Affairs asked the Coeur d'Alene superintendent to talk to the Kalispels about selling, but the superintendent did not have travel money for a trip to Usk. He suggested that if the Kalispels could be allotted, the day-school teacher might "ascertain the wishes of the Indians" and take the powers of attorney of those who wanted to sell the timber on their tracts.[41]

After five years, enough Indians had chosen ground that titles could be issued to half the tribe. The first batch of Kalispel patents was dated August 5, 1925; the second, February 21, 1933. Nearly all specified tracts of 40 acres but a few were bigger: the riverside allotments of Bazil Andrews, 60.8 acres, and John Bigsmoke, 48.15 acres, the land contested by Napoleon LeClerc a quarter of a century earlier.[42]

With an allotment schedule in hand, a sale of timber could proceed. (By cooperative agreement, incidentally, the Kaniksu National Forest provided fire protection.) The Dalkena Lumber Company had cruised the reservation, estimating 18,045,000 board feet on 2,231 acres, and Kalispels, remarked the superintendent, were "clamoring for their money to buy automobiles, pay living expenses, and meet old bills." One allottee, Joseph Ignace, petitioned to log his allotment but the superintendent, suspecting that Ignace simply intended to sell to a white man, refused, declaring the Kalispel timber should be "sold to the best advantage of all the Indians." On the Coeur d'Alene reservation, some Indians had sold stumpage too cheaply or their stands had been butchered by careless loggers; Lawsche did not intend to let the Kalispels sell one by one.[43]

The Indian bureau went ahead with the timber sale reluctantly for, as its valuation engineer said, "The time is not at all opportune, from a lumbering standpoint, because of the depressed condition of the market. However, the Indian owners are practically all quite anxious to dispose of their timber and are badly in need of the funds and it is believed advisable, therefore, that the unit be placed on the market during the year 1928." In his letter approving the sale, the commissioner asked the superintendent not to prepare a contract "on mimeograph paper," cheap paper the agency had been using to save money. When bids were compared, Panhandle Lumber Company won a four-year contract to log the Kalispel reservation, the so-called "Pend Oreille unit," and started, late in the year, by building two camps of loggers' huts with arched roofs. Under the agreement, Indian allottees would be paid at the end of each year for timber cut from their ground, based on board feet, species, and the price per thousand feet (averaging under $4) set out in the contract.[44]

The Panhandle contract was not the bonanza that Kalispels had expected. Fires in other Panhandle forests pulled the company's crews off the reservation in 1930 and the market was so wretched that cutting suspended in 1931. Logging sputtered, speeding or slowing with an erratic market, until Panhandle, granted a series of extensions, finished cutting and clearing slash near the end of 1938, six years after expiration of the original agreement.

Obviously some Kalispels owned better timber than others. Consequently, annual payments ranged from a low of $51 to a high of $2,800, but the owner who received $2,800 probably got no more, for his timber was gone. The Panhandle company harvested 26.8 million board feet—one third more than estimated, of which 21.5 million were yellow pine—and in 10 years paid the Kalispels $90,446.67. The superintendent put the funds in trust accounts, requiring each Indian to tell what he intended to do with his money before doling it out. Few bought automobiles; several paid off debts; and four improved or built houses.[45]

The Panhandle contract also produced small payments for the school, $1,641, and for the tribe, itself, $2,141. Fortunately, a good residual stand of immature timber remained.[46]

Not long after Panhandle started Kalispel logging, the federal Indian office granted Pend Oreille County a right of way for a road, north and south the length of the reservation, an extension of the old Ashpaugh road established in 1903. When Pend Oreille County was carved out of Stevens County, the dirt road, little more than a bumpy wagon trail, reached almost to the LeClerc ranch and so, as county commissioners adopted a map showing the road, they called it "LeClerc road," perhaps the last name Kalispels would have chosen for a thoroughfare through their ground. In 1930, the county engineer prepared to improve the road as a county highway, paying $25 an acre to each Kalispel allottee whose land the route crossed.[47]

In granting right of way, writing a logging contract, and other business, the government acted for the Kalispels, presuming that the tribe could not conduct its own affairs. Meanwhile, an expanding flow of business and official correspondence called for tribal consensus, requiring someone among the Kalispels to read, interpret, and respond. The Coeur d'Alene, Ignace Garry, handled Kalispel business as one of the few adults on the reservation who could read and write. A short, round-faced, earnest man, an eloquent speaker, Garry dipped deferentially into the contrary waters of white man's law and politics, realizing that for the time being Indians relied by necessity on white lawyers and congressmen, most of whom looked on Indians as unpredictable children. A few whites, like the publisher of the *Newport Miner*, considered the Kalispels nuisances; he could snap, when assured in 1927 that the reservation was a legal entity, "It had been presumed here that the Indians were . . . simply squatters."[48]

Throughout the twenties, Indians continued to dance at fairs, prolonging the image of a primitive people. Fairs advertised war dances, a "love dance," horse races, and other Indian events, all performed in costume; reporters wrote colorful accounts of Indians gambling at sticks or cards: a man wearing a yellow shirt with

Ignace Garry, Coeur d'Alene, left, and Francis McFarland, Nez Perce, two of the delegates dispatched to invite President Coolidge to the 1925 Indian Congress in Spokane. (Thomas Teakle collection, Spokane Public Library)

purple collar and cuffs, another in a white buckskin jacket glittering with red-bead flowers, one wearing a red silk shirt and black sombrero, another smoking cigarettes in a long holder, and so on. Photographers pictured white men in war bonnets being inducted into Indian tribes as publicity stunts—the president of the national hotel men's association, for instance, christened Chief Many Wigwams by the Coeur d'Alenes in 1928, posing beside a feathered Ignace Garry.[49]

During his rise as an Indian leader, Garry had been one of three Indians sent to Washington, D.C., in 1925 to invite President Coolidge to the National Indian Congress. Naturally, the delegates wore fringed buckskin costumes and feathered bonnets. Coolidge turned them down. Garry's daughter, Alice, named Princess America at the congress, toured the country in costume.

Both Coeur d'Alenes and Kalispels accepted Garry as a spokes-

Lucy Garry, Ignace Garry's second wife, at left, with her aunt and uncle, Coeur d'Alenes from Worley, Idaho. The Garrys eventually elected to enroll as Coeur d'Alenes. (Kalispel tribal collection)

man; although he was an enrolled Coeur d'Alene, a man of stature who would become a tribal policeman, tribal judge, ceremonial chanter and drummer, and eventually chief, Garry took his family to the Kalispel reservation every summer and Christmas. A son and daughter held allotments as enrolled Kalispels. Among white men, Ignace was respected as the great-grandson of old Chief Garry, who died in 1892, disillusioned and neglected, in a tipi in Indian Canyon outside Spokane. As a child of four, Ignace had been among the mourning relatives.[50]

Ignace was also a grandson of Antoine Hayden (for whom Hayden Lake, Idaho, was named), a half-breed Kalispel, but when his grandmother, Spokane Garry's granddaughter Nellie, took Ignace to live with her she registered him at the Cove school, near Fairfield, as Ignace Garry rather than Ignace Hayden, and he kept the name. As a man, he farmed in Lovell valley, on the Coeur d'Alene reservation, and his son, Joseph, occupied Nellie's allotment there. Ignace perceived that an Indian striving for political influence needed a white man's education and although he completed only the third grade, he insisted that his children go to college. Ignace was so proud of his daughter, Celina, when she graduated from Tekoa High that he drove 60 miles roundtrip to Moscow to buy a rose to present her in the graduates' procession.

If Spokane's 1925 and 1926 Indian congresses had publicized the city, as intended, they had also exposed the dilemma that faced Garry and other Indians. The Indian chiefs tried to refuse to permit their people to be displayed any longer as primitive curiosities and declared their dissatisfaction with "white domination at their Congress." Yet Garry and other Indian politicians wore native costumes, however reluctantly, when they mixed with white businessmen and politicians, and they were treated largely as showpieces, living waxworks. A costumed Kalispel chief attended the dedication of a monument marking the Battle of Spokane Plains, Wright's campaign, in 1926.

Even while they counseled their people against exploitation at fairs, the chiefs realized that the fairs kept Indians before the white public, brought in a little money, and could be good fun, chances for relatives to get together. The delineation of an appropriate Indian role was agonizingly emerging, and the chiefs resented stereotyping, like that of Commissioner Charles H. Burke, who remarked that "the old Indian in many cases is a child and really incapable to handle his own affairs. . . . Their [Indians'] future salvation lies in staying home and doing their work, rather than attendance at rodeos and following their natural nomadic instincts." Perhaps older Indians, like older Kalispels, could not read or write but they understood their condition. The tribal chiefs formed a committee to "bring to the annual sessions [of the congress] the real problems of Indians," but there would be no sessions after 1926. It is fair to conclude that 1926 brought to a head the discontent of interior northwest Indians and hardened their determination to control their affairs without forfeiting their heritage.[51]

The northwest Indians' resolve fed, as well, on national awareness of Indian problems. Although he would not attend Indian congresses, Coolidge endorsed a private commission financed by John D. Rockefeller, Jr., to inquire into the economic and social conditions among reservation Indians. The commission, headed by Lewis Meriam, reported in 1928 that "an overwhelming majority of

Kalispel elders, left to right, Alec Andrews, Lucy Seymour, and Charlie Seymour. Alec and Lucy were brother and sister. (Kalispel tribal collection)

The Andrews family, leading Kalispels, about 1930. Louis Andrews, far right with hat, would become a tribal chairman and spokesman. (Kalispel tribal collection)

the Indians are poor, even extremely poor, and they are not adjusted to the . . . system of the dominant white civilization." Most Indian schools, the sobering report went on, taught Indian children little of value to them; it urged educating Indians in the public schools.

The Meriam report received such wide attention, as magazines took up its theme with caustic articles, that the Bureau of Indian Affairs, to absolve itself of abusing Indians, ordered a "thorough survey . . . of all our Indian reservations by citizens' committees" who were to send their findings directly to senators, representatives, and congressional committees. To investigate the Kalispels, the Coeur d'Alene superintendent enlisted Charles Howell and Jack Kerr, Cusick, and O. L. Click, Usk. Apparently they reported, as intended, that the government was not mistreating the Kalispels.[52]

John Collier, a former social organizer who had been working to regenerate New York immigrant communities, after World War I devoted himself to the cause of American Indians, seeing in the Indian communal spirit a potential model for reforming society at large. In 1933, the Secretary of the Interior, Harold Ickes, appointed Collier as Commissioner of Indian Affairs. In his first annual report, Collier called for "reorienting Indian land policy." As a starting point, he wrote, "the immediate problem is not that of absorbing the Indians into the white population, but first of all lifting them out of material and spiritual dependency and hopelessness. . . . The place to begin this process is on the land; for if the Indian cannot pursue the relatively simple and primitive arts of agriculture, grazing, and forestry, there seems little prospect that he can be fitted for the more exacting technology of urban industry."[53]

Collier drafted a home-rule bill for Indians that Secretary Ickes pressed Congress to enact, and to undergird the campaign among congressmen, the Commissioner of Indian Affairs called on his agencies to collect data on Indian lands. When the measure passed, the commissioner could praise their "splendid cooperation" which "helped to convince Congress." Steered by Senator Burton Wheeler of Montana and Representative Edgar Howard of Nebraska, the bill's amendments diluted Collier's intent; it lost, for instance, a mandatory transfer of allotted land to tribal ownership and a special Indian court. On the other hand, the bill ruled out future allotments and set up funds for loans to Indian tribes and government purchases of land for them. It passed as the Indian Reorganization Act of 1934, the so-called Wheeler-Howard Act, repudiating the land allotments of the Dawes Act, extending to Indians the authority to form limited tribal governments and corporations, and granting them "certain rights of home rule." On paper, the government had reversed the policies of a century past.[54]

CHAPTER 6

Organizing

F OR the Kalispel tribe, the Indian Reorganization Act (IRA) stands as the beginning of modern times. Under it, they toiled for a generation to develop an administrative system without chiefs and find ways of supporting themselves. Rivalries for morsels of power sprang up within the tribe, disagreements and apathy slowed them, but the act was like the pinnacle of a mountain pass: The Kalispels had climbed long and hard and now, despite the journey ahead, they could see from the summit where they were going.

When the reorganization act became law on June 18, 1934, the United States was suffocating from the effects of depression. Kalispels' seasonal jobs with lumber companies slipped away and logging moved farther from the reservation. On November 25, 1933—the Thanksgiving season—Pend Oreille County commissioners diverted $10,000 for road projects to create jobs under federal and state emergency relief programs. Less than a year later, in one of a series of similar appropriations, the commissioners set aside $5,000 for outright assistance to families without shelter or food. Indians could apply. Hard times seem an unlikely starting point for building their inadequate land base into economic independence, or for beginning a long journey out of the past, but that is where the Kalispels commenced.[1]

About two months after passage of the reorganization act, the Commissioner of Indian Affairs asked each agency to send him "a feasible long-term land acquisition program" that would "consider the future needs of an increasing Indian population" as part of a national plan for natural resources. Six years earlier, when the commissioner asked for five-year industrial plans for Indian tribes, the Coeur d'Alene agency submitted none for the Kalispels, explaining that they had sold their timber to Panhandle and expected to go into cattle breeding. Although there were only 16 cows and heifers and 12 steers on the reservation then, the Indian office's agricultural director had forecast a cattle enterprise of 250 to 300 animals, remarking that a "number of scrub horses will have to be disposed of" to make room for cattle.[2]

Now, in terms of prospective land acquisition, the government's plan for the Kalispels said:

In order to make these Indians self-supporting, it is proposed to set them up in the beef cattle business. Of the 1,824 acres of bottom land, about 900 acres have in the past been used for the production of wild hay. . . . Of this land, about 300 acres would be adaptable for alfalfa and 600 acres could be cropped to rye or oat hay, no irrigation being required. . . . This amount of hay would carry 900 head of cattle or 45 head per family through the winter season. . . . To provide this tribe with the necessary grazing area, it is proposed to purchase 3,560 acres of logged-off grazing lands, which lie between the Reservation and the Kaniksu National Forest. This land is somewhat open, contains some meadow lands and contains very little small timber.[3]

For 30 years, the Kalispels would hold to the goal of a beef-cattle business but the 3,560 acres were never purchased for them and large herds never started. From the government's point of view, grave questions of budget and feasibility haunted the cattle business, and for the Kalispels, the cattle business seemed to shimmer always just out of reach, a dream. A half hundred head came onto the reservation under a depression relief project called the "ID program" (ID for the interior department brand) when, late in 1934, the Department of the Interior bought, from the Agricultural Adjustment Administration, $800,000 worth of purebred cattle to distribute among reservation Indians throughout the country on the basis of each Indian family's prospects of feeding animals through a winter. "The only ones who got cattle were those who could provide hay," recalled a Kalispel. "The ID program helped only a few—

but for them, it worked well." Another: "The ID program put a few
people on their feet." The government transferred 47 heifers and
two bulls from the Yakima to the Kalispel reservation, distributing
the animals among six families.[4]

Nine Kalispel men formed a short-lived cooperative livestock
association, mainly to lobby for more animals, more rangeland, and
a carload of ID cattle from other reservations. During the summer,
they pastured their cattle together and in the winter, tended them
individually.[5]

Meanwhile, the Kalispels faced their crucial step out of the past:
incorporation under the Indian Reorganization Act. The act was
permissive, allowing each tribe to incorporate or not, as it chose.
The Coeur d'Alene agency sent a team—A. G. Wilson, the superintendent, and two Nez Perce men—to explain the act to Indians
on reservations in its jurisdiction.

(The Coeur d'Alene had merged with the Lapwai agency in 1933
and on July 1, 1937, would be renamed the North Idaho agency,
officed first at Moscow and then at Lapwai, responsible for the Nez
Perce, Coeur d'Alene, Kutenai, and Kalispel reservations. With
this realignment, the Kalispels would be 185 miles from Lapwai
and the Kutenais, 230 miles, small tribes too distant for close
supervision.)

In a meeting of the Kalispel tribe at their schoolhouse, the
agency team (which visited once rather than twice as intended)
outlined the reorganization act, answered questions, and tried to
guess what it might mean for Indians. Of course, the Kalispels had
learned that the Coeur d'Alenes were divided, thinking the act
would reduce federal concern for Indian welfare. Old discords
among the Kalispels whispered again, aged Indians suspicious of
government overtures for change, while younger men, Flatheads
and Spokanes married to Kalispel women, saw in reorganization
the tribe's first opportunity to manage its own affairs. The young
activists probably centered around John Abrahamson, Baptiste
Bigsmoke, the chief, and Clarence Campbell, Spokanes; Joseph
Andrews and Frank Nenema, Flatheads; and Solomon Bluff and
Moses Nick, fullblooded Kalispels; all sent their children to school
and had had some schooling themselves; theirs were the large and
influential families on the Kalispel reservation. When a major ques-

Lucy and Charlie Seymour, left and center, at a tribal council with John Abrahamson, right. Abrahamson often translated English into Salish for older members of the tribe attending meetings. (Kalispel tribal collection)

tion arose in earlier days, the chief assembled the respected men of the tribe to smoke and deliberate; now, advocates of the act trudged cabin to cabin to discuss it, trying to still the doubts of elders. On November 17, 1934, the Kalispels voted at the schoolhouse: 29 favored reorganizing, two opposed, and seven would not vote. The Kalispels were the only tribe in the Lapwai jurisdiction to vote for incorporation under the Indian Reorganization Act. Their friends, the Spokanes and the Colvilles, ballotted against it.[6]

When news of their vote reached Washington, D.C., the Kalispels received a congratulatory letter—no doubt a form letter, but addressed to "the Indians of the Kalispel Reservation"—from Commissioner John Collier. "The eyes of the nation have been on you to see what Indians would do with such an opportunity," Collier wrote, adding, "I congratulate you on the wisdom shown" in voting

Two Kalispel men in a playful mood: left, Clarence Campbell, and Frank Nenema. Campbell, a Spokane, and Nenema, a Flathead, were leaders during tribal incorporation and judgment-fund planning. (Hazel Hunter album, Kalispel tribal collection)

to reorganize. He predicted that the act would "bring to Indian people of the Nation a new day."[7]

The Kalispels' next task would be to compose a constitution, by-laws, and a corporate charter setting out their purposes, administrative system, legal powers, and rules for membership, all necessary for a tribe to borrow from a revolving fund set up by the reorganization act. Until this time, the tribe accommodated anyone who cared to reside among them, chose chiefs by acclaim from the sons of preceding chiefs, and were ruled by the chiefs and advisors.

George LaVatta, an Indian field agent of a reorganization unit, actually wrote the Kalispel documents, attempting to reflect the wishes of the Indians, submitted them to attorneys in the Bureau of Indian Affairs, and eventually to Felix S. Cohen, assistant solicitor of the Department of the Interior. Re-drafts passed through the superintendent back to the Kalispels for their review, each level changing words and phrases until the papers seemed to say what the Indians wanted and meet requirements of the law. Cohen, dismayed by trade-offs among interior department experts unwilling to give up supervisory powers while talking glibly of Indian autonomy, would become general counsel for the Association on American Indian Affairs and champion Indian causes until his death in 1953. The Commissioner of Indian Affairs, however, defined the term "Indian" for all tribes as any present member of a tribe or descendants, regardless of the degree of blood, or a person of one-half Indian blood living on or off a reservation.[8]

Progress toward a charter, under this system, was slow, and for the tribes, an unfamiliar process. The Kalispels struggled to fashion a statement of tribal purposes for incorporation. "On account of the lack of opportunities and resources on the present Kalispel reservation," LaVatta observed almost three years after the Kalispels voted for reorganization, "considerable time and effort has been expended in trying to arrive at some definite conclusions as to just how the Kalispell [sic] Indians would benefit once organization is completed." For a beef cattle business, the Kalispels lacked both land and money. "If suitable additional land could be secured for these Indians," the field agent went on, "it would permit an opportunity for them to engage in stock-raising, which vocation they are adapted to and interested in. With sufficient credit and proper supervision and guidance, stock-raising would ensure them an economic livelihood."[9]

Concern for their land, not cattle, dominated the constitution and charter the Kalispels produced after almost four years of negotiation. These documents were in lawyers' language, framed largely by LaVatta. The constitution preserved the rights of each individual and heirs to allotted land but provided for each to sell land to the community—the tribe—and for the purchase of land with tribal funds, and for trades of land for pensions by aged Indians.

For a membership corporation, the Kalispel Indian Community of the Kalispel Reservation, the charter set out general corporate powers allowing the community to "engage in any business that will further the economic well-being of the members." One article prohibited sale or mortgage of communal lands; another provided for termination of federal supervision at the tribe's discretion. The notion of termination, inserted by federal lawyers, would alarm the Kalispels and other tribes before long; it would be a new battleground.[10]

All persons named in a tribal census taken in April 1934, and their descendants, were members of the community. The governing body was a council made up of all qualified voters: enrolled members over 21 who maintained legal residence on the reservation for one year prior to an election. To manage business, lands, and finances, the charter specified a business council of chairman, vice chairman, secretary, and treasurer, and it limited corporate indebtedness to $3,000. The ancient office of chief was thus swept away and the business council became the operative managers, although Baptiste Bigsmoke continued in a ceremonial role as chief until his death in 1957, when no successor would be elected.[11]

The constitution and by-laws were approved by the Secretary of the Interior on March 24, 1938, and the corporate charter adopted by vote of the Kalispels on May 28. The Kalispels were one of 181 tribes to vote for reorganization, one of only 93 to draw constitutions, and of 73, charters. If they had hoped reorganization would encourage immediate federal loans or land purchases for them, the Kalispels were disappointed. Because the Wheeler–Howard Act passed on almost the last day of the congressional session, no funds were appropriated in that session, and when Congress saw

Baptiste and Lucy Bigsmoke and children. The last chief of the Ka-
lispels, Baptiste was one of those active in incorporating the tribe under
the Indian Reorganization Act. (Hazel Hunter album, Kalispel tribal
collection)

the lack of enthusiasm among the majority of American Indians, it subsequently cut the act's proposed funds for tribal loans and land purchases. Most tribes rejected what the Kalispels accepted: a constitution patterned on white rather than tribal customs.[12]

By incorporating, the Kalispels by no means cut themselves free of the federal bureaucracy. Their powers of self-government were limited by federal law. Each action of the business council required approval of the agency superintendent and, in some cases, of the Commissioner of Indian Affairs. Paperwork sifted into the new Kalispel corporation, some incomprehensible to men unfamiliar with federal terms or lacking a file of federal regulations. The business council met in homes; the tribal council in the schoolhouse; they had no desks or file cases. Nevertheless, some of the men, like Clarence Campbell (a Spokane) and Frank Nenema (a Flathead), carried on the tribe's business as well as they could, with occasional advice from the agency staff. And gradually they began to rely on the counsel of Ignace Garry's son, Joe, a clerk at the Lapwai agency.

Joseph R. Garry had been educated at the De Smet mission school on the Coeur d'Alene reservation and the Jesuits' Gonzaga High in Spokane, but when he applied for admission to Haskell Institute in 1930 he called himself a Kalispel. Haskell, then and thereafter, misspelled his name as Geary. He completed the Haskell business courses, took further business training at Butler University, Indianapolis, and beginning in 1936 clerked in the federal Indian bureau in Washington. Three years there, another as a clerk in the North Idaho agency, and a year or more in the office of California Congressman John H. Tolan, father of a nun at De Smet, taught Garry a lasting skepticism of federal precepts and showed him politics behind the public mask. When he left Lapwai, a newspaper, noting that Garry was the great-great-grandson of Spokane Garry, remarked that "other Indians relied on him for interpreting and advice." Joe Garry at 30 was making his mark, a Kalispel who knew his way in the labyrinths of government and politics.[13]

Although the Kalispels believed that, in Garry, they had a colleague in government, during reorganization days their appalling problems were depression and starvation, for there was little work for Indians (or for anyone else, for that matter) and they could no longer hunt and fish across the broad land that supported them in bygone times. They still dug camas every spring, preserving the roots in the old way, and some Kalispel women now canned fruits and vegetables when they could get them. As long ago as 1929, a so-called Business Committee of the Lower Kalispell Indians [sic] had complained to the commissioner that the agency superintendent refused to give them money earned from timber sales, saying, "Most of our people need food and clothing . . . [and] cannot make a living on our lands." The superintendent, of course, had been instructed by the bureau to release Kalispel money only for permanent improvements, such as houses, and real emergencies. Perhaps his refusal to heed Kalispel appeals cemented the tribe's resolve, when the IRA passed, to vote in favor of reorganization.[14]

Now in the thirties the agency estimated that 25 Kalispels supported themselves by selling beadwork, which brought an aggregate of $250 a year; 10 sold firewood, making $500 among them; and 25 farmed with a combined income of $1,500 a year. Granting the probable inaccuracy of round figures compiled by the agency, these amounts yielded an average annual income for 87 adult Kalispels of $25.86. Things did not get better during the depression. During 1931 the government had issued $210 worth of rations to disabled Kalispels. When an Indian girl went to a Newport hospital, the agency needed a special appropriation of $51 to pay her bill. Money was scarce for everyone.[15]

Some fleeting relief resulted from road work supported by federal, state, and Indian bureau emergency funds. In 1929 when the legislature called for county highway plans, Pend Oreille County had listed the LeClerc road high among its priorities and the next year took bids for improving the road virtually the length of the reservation, eight miles north from the decaying Usk bridge. Off and on between 1930 and 1938, limited relief monies paid for small projects. Indian road funds had to be spent mainly to employ Indians at 30 cents an hour (white men received 55) and the agency withheld a portion of each man's wages to be doled out during the jobless winter months. During 1934, apparently the only depression year of significant construction, 41 Kalispel men, nearly every able-bodied man on the reservation, earned $386 among them for clearing timber and removing debris for four and one-half miles along the LeClerc right of way, and an additional $1,466 from Civil Works Administration funds for other road jobs.[16]

Chief Bigsmoke wrote to the Commissioner of Indian Affairs, appealing for more work. "As you are aware, my people have no tribal funds and are badly in need of employment," he said, in a letter typed with all capital letters, but no more jobs could be had because the bureau and the agency were out of money. Whoever wrote Bigsmoke's letter, incidentally, spelled the tribe's name "Calispel."[17]

The notion of a beef cattle business continued to beckon the Kalispels. Extension workers, required to submit yearly reports, in bureaucratic fashion set out goals each year for the tribe, and throughout the depression years, merely repeated the goals from one year to the next. A soil survey in 1936 showed irrigation and fertilizer would be necessary to grow profitable crops on Kalispel land but, regardless, the extension goals stood: each family would plant a half-acre garden, acquire and feed a team of horses, two milk cows, and 20 cattle. Obviously the goals lay far beyond the most optimistic grasp of a people whose average family income rose to $140 a year by 1939 and who owned 19 cabins to house 26 families. One family earned $115 that year selling hogs; three sold chickens for $50; and the tribe's butter sales amounted to $60. A few Kalispels planted small gardens of potatoes, corn, cucumbers, carrots, and beets for their own use.[18]

Goals aside, a Kalispel cattle business seemed out of the question by 1937 although the Indian bureau, lacking an alternative proposal, would exchange polite letters about it with agents and Indians for the next 25 years. Until 1963, no one would tell the Kalispels they were never going to be cattle barons. Under a depression relief program, the Resettlement Administration, the Northeast Washington Scattered Settlers Project in Stevens and Pend Oreille counties bought the marginal lands where white farm families were failing and moved perhaps 150 from unproductive to better land between 1935 and 1938. Resettlement, although it did not affect the Kalispels directly, erected a barrier to an Indian cattle business because, if the government had to resettle white farmers, ran the logic, who would believe the Kalispels could do better? A credit agent in the Indian bureau raised these doubts in

his letter of May 1, 1937: "It is my information that the Resettlement Administration is moving white farmers out of this [Kalispel]
vicinity and settling them on better land farther west. . . . Do the
Indians really want to raise beef cattle? Is such a cooperative or
group activity the one best solution to their economic problems?"[19]
Even if a cattle business required more land, none was available.
The Kaniksu National Forest was extended westward to the Pend
Oreille River in 1938, taking in 1,360 acres once proposed for Kalispel grazing land, and 1,280 acres still belonged to the state and to
Diamond Match Company, leaving no more than 920 acres for sale,
not good land. "The suitability of this range for cattle . . . is seriously questioned," ran a field agent's report. "The area has been
logged over, contains in large part a dense growth of brush and
grass and the grass is largely cheat and pine grass which is very
poor feed." This agent suggested the Kalispels raise sheep. Just
five months earlier, the Kalispel Indian Community had forwarded
a resolution to the Indian bureau, pointing out that "our allotments
of only 40 acres each are much too small to produce an income for
the support of a family, especially since the production of hay and
livestock are the only sources of income that can be realized from
agricultural activities in this part of the country." Signed by
Antoine Peuse, council chairman, and Frank Nick, secretary, the
Kalispel resolution asked for "every consideration possible" for
more land. But there would be no more land. The Kalispel cattle
proposal, in the shadow of resettlement and poor grazing land, had
expired long before anyone admitted it was dead.[20]
     While a handful of Kalispels endeavored to organize the tribe and
discover a business for it, interior Washington state changed. In
July 1933 the Federal Emergency Administration of Public Works
set aside $61 million to begin construction of Grand Coulee Dam
and, thus heartened, Spokane's housing industry spurted in 1936
and stayed strong. Hamlets near the dam and in the intended irrigation districts started to grow, although construction towns faded
in a few years. By the end of the thirties, as the United States em-
barked on a military buildup, Spokane, determined not to be left
out of defense spending as in World War I, captured air bases, aluminum plants, supply depots, and other war-related industries.
Oddly, even with Farragut Naval Training Station on Lake Pend

Oreille, northeastern Washington had only a flurry of business; mostly it slept on, unruffled by gusts of federal spending for dam, irrigation, and war. Cusick, incorporated in 1927 with perhaps 380 residents, counted 360 two decades later; Newport increased about 200 persons every 10 years between 1930 and 1960. The Kalispel reservation seemed untouched by boom or war, except for the few who entered armed services, among whom was Celina, Joe Garry's sister. Logging camps had moved too far from the reservation to hire Indian commuters, and most of the major mills had closed in a surfeit of overproduction during the depression years.

KALISPELS SERVING THE UNITED STATES

WORLD WAR I		
Louis Seymour	Louis Andrews	John Ignace
	Louis Pierre Bluff	Leo Peuse
WORLD WAR II	Andy Bigsmoke	
Hy Nick	Leo Peuse	VIET NAM
(Abraham)	Tony Revais	John Nick
Samuel Meshell	Pete Abrahamson	
Dan Bigsmoke	Joe Abrahamson	CIVILIAN
Ignace Nick		CONSERVATION
Abel Andrew	KOREAN WAR	CORPS
Ray Pierre	Phillip Isadore	PARTICIPANTS
Thomas Ignace	Patrick Isadore	Pete Abrahamson
Pete Bigsmoke	Ignace Bluff	Joe Abrahamson
Louis Peuse	Eneas Nenema	Ignace Nick

The Kalispels' condition changed little during the forties. For example, the income of 12 families herding 126 cattle amounted to $2,897 in 1944, augmented by $595 from the Agricultural Adjustment Administration. One Kalispel received AAA largess of $10 for a garden. In their extension worker's report for that year, the Kalispels asked the government to buy them two bulls, and each year through 1948 repeated the request. Three years later, in 1947, 12 families still herded cattle; it was their best year, for they sold animals worth $11,160. One family reported an income of more than

$1,000. But in 1948, floods prevented spring planting and cattle sales fell to $7,680 distributed among 10 families. For most white residents of Washington, 1947 and 1948 were peacetime years of a bountiful economy, thousands of new houses rising, and jobs for everyone.[21]

Kalispels remember the thirties and forties as times when "half the people on the reservation were on welfare," but in fact welfare assistance among them was limited to dependent children and elderly. With no regular relief program of its own, the North Idaho agency encouraged Indians to look to local relief agencies, and spent no more than $1,350 in agency funds, largely for groceries and clothing for destitute Kutenais. The need for Indian relief was so large, however, that local Works Progress Administration projects could not employ all who applied—but that, until wartime, was true of white applicants, too—and no funds were allocated to North Idaho for Indian defense training. Nevertheless, the North Idaho superintendent felt that local welfare agencies met Indians' needs and "treated them the same as other citizens." Five Kalispels received an average of $20 a month as old-age assistance and one family, $18 a month for aid to a dependent child. The number of Kalispels on relief varied only slightly each year. Apparently they were exasperating clients, as a Pend Oreille County welfare administrator found: "It is impossible to formulate monthly budgets for any of these people as they do not seem to have any idea of their expenses." The welfare reports of the forties suggest that ablebodied Kalispels took care of themselves. Four were denied assistance after the North Idaho agency looked into their applications. Kalispels asked for welfare in substantial numbers—"a number of Indians are applying for assistance," the county advised the agency—but few actually appeared on welfare rolls.

Indian missions had fallen on hard times, too. As the Jesuit provincial mulled over a revised mission policy, old Father Taelman spoke from 42 years with the Indians, mourning that "our missions today are but a remnant or wreck of a glorious past. This process has been visibly going on for 3 or 4 decades." He attributed the receding mission field partly to diluted Indian blood, "morally inferior" Indians "more difficult to control" due to their close contact with whites. Lack of finances had closed missions and schools. The

Celebration in 1944 of the hundredth anniversary of the founding of St. Ignatius mission involved a religious pilgrimage to Manresa Cave. Left to right: Father Taelman, unknown girl, Louise Sample (a white visitor), Alice Ignace, unknown lady and girl (behind horse), Father Griva, Willie Andrews, Martina Sherwood, and Mary Andrews. (OPA)

Jesuits, Taelman urged, should promote religious education with vacation schools and "more frequent visits to the homes and parents of children." And he pointed to the "sad fact" that priests no longer learned the Salish language. [22]

Still, a brief kindling of the old fervor accompanied the one hundredth anniversary of the founding of St. Ignatius mission in the Pend Oreille valley. Taelman took charge of the three-day observance, July 2, 3, and 4, 1944, attended by priests and Indian delegations from a dozen tribes. Bishop Charles White of Spokane led a procession from the Kalispel church to Manresa Cave, followed by young Indian men and women, gaily costumed, on horseback, and nearly a hundred honking autos—the county engineer had patched potholes in the road for the event; at the cave, Father William L. Davis, Jesuit historian, recounted the story of De Smet and founding of the mission and Taelman recited the Apostles' Creed in Salish. The bishop celebrated a solemn high mass. Even Father Griva, 80, was there to celebrate mass on July 3 and sermonize in

Salish. Indians and guests sat in huge circles on the ground for a venison feast prepared by Mrs. Antoine Isadore in memory of Alec Ignace, a tribal leader who had died the year before.[23]

The anniversary rites were merely an interlude in the Kalispels' struggle to organize. Meanwhile, wartime changes eroded the federal Indian policy under which they had voted themselves a constitution and a charter. Congress had been conducting field inspections of Indian reservations since 1928 and by the outbreak of the war felt that John Collier's conduct of the office (now bureau) ran counter to congressional aims. Congress threatened to repeal the Indian Reorganization Act; it repudiated Collier, also opposed by powerful Indian coalitions, and he resigned in 1945. In hearings on the nomination of a successor, William A. Brophy, Congress clearly called for a return to the policy of Indian assimilation. Thus the foundation shifted on which the Kalispels were building their organization.[24]

During Brophy's time as commissioner, Congress dominated the course of Indian relations. It reorganized the bureau into five geographical districts intended to work more closely with Indians, as Brophy explained: "We must constantly strive to have greater participation by the Indians in the initiation, formulation, and execution of our policy and work." A Portland Area office took jursidiction over northwest agencies, including the North Idaho. One more layer of administration. And Congress created an Indian Claims Commission as a tribunal for tribal land claims against the United States, expecting that the commission would wind up its work in 10 years, but would enlarge and renew it for 32 years, until September 30, 1978, when pending suits returned to the Court of Claims.[25]

Federal policy shifts favored ambitious Indian politicians, among them Joe Garry, home from his service with an army rifle company, raising cattle on his grandmother's allotment on the Coeur d'Alene reservation. His father, Ignace, had been elected chief of the Coeur d'Alenes. To Joe Garry, the Coeur d'Alenes, Kalispels, and other tribes turned for advice on dealing with the government. Slender, taller than Ignace, well-spoken Joe wore business suits, cut his hair short, and moved easily among politicians and civil servants who took him for a prototype of the new Indian. Garry's rapid rise as a spokesman for northwest interior Indians, interrupted

Joseph R. Garry, who rose to national prominence in Indian politics, acted as a trusted Kalispel adviser. Here Garry takes part in Kalispel ceremonies at the community center. (Hazel Hunter album, Kalispel tribal collection)

briefly by service as a combat engineer in Korea, lifted him to national prominence: Seven tribes, including the Kalispel, sent him to Washington to demand better reservation services; by 1951 he was serving the first of eight terms as president of the Affiliated Tribes of the Northwest; 1952, president (seven terms) of the National Congress of American Indians; in 1954 named "American Indian" of the year. White politicians learned that one dealt with Joe Garry to deal with northwest Indians; they courted him, flattered him, and wrangled with him as Garry strove for an Indian voice in federal policy, one of a savvy, resolute corps of new Indian leaders.[26]

Near the middle of 1950, Garry called on a noted Spokane Catholic attorney, Nicodemus D. Wernette, in company with—doubtless steered there by—Father Cornelius E. Byrne, Jesuit missionary to the Coeur d'Alenes since 1934. Garry wanted advice on the tax liability of Coeur d'Alenes but a young attorney to whom Wernette assigned his query wrote an opinion Garry would not accept. He then turned to Kenneth R. L. Simmons, a dynamic veteran lawyer in Billings, Montana, who had contracted with the Coeur d'Alenes in 1949 to prosecute their suit against the government before the Indian Claims Commission. Later that year, with Garry as intermediary, the florid Simmons signed up the Kalispels and Spokanes for claims cases.

Simmons' contract with the Kalispels, approved by the Indian bureau on September 11, 1950, was amended to specify that the Washington, D.C., law firm of Wilkinson, Boyden & Cragun would be associated with him, and Simmons' erstwhile partner, Donald C. Gormley, moved to the Wilkinson office. The Wilkinson firm had won a publicized $31.7 million award for the Utes and was moving into a preeminent position in Indian claims litigation. At the same time, however, the Kalispels heeded the counsel of Wernette's new young partner, Robert D. Dellwo. Paired with Garry as go-between, Dellwo represented the Spokanes and Coeur d'Alenes when Louis Andrews, tribal chairman, invited him to come to the Kalispels. Dellwo was not new to Indian problems; he had been hearing about them all his life, born and reared on the Flathead reservation, where his father, Dennis A. Dellwo, had been secretary of the Flathead irrigation district since 1917.[27]

For the Coeur d'Alene and Kalispel suits, Simmons contracted with Gonzaga University for the services of Father William N.

Bischoff, S.J., to compile historical backgrounds on land use. The attorney prepared the Kalispels for their suit at a time when government Indian policy swung back to repression under a new commissioner, Dillon A. Myer, who almost immediately after taking office in 1950 cut off tribal-help monies under the Indian Reorganization Act. Although Myer approved the Kalispels' contract with Simmons, he soon condemned attorneys who solicited Indian clients, calling for federal regulations that would bar "disreputable or unscrupulous lawyers, ambulance-chasers, and fomenters of trouble" from inveigling tribes into contracts at unreasonably high fees.[28]

Myer appalled tribal leaders by publicly calling for an end to federal trusteeship. "If any Indian tribe is convinced that the Bureau of Indian Affairs is a handicap to its advancement," ran one of Myer's policy statements, "I am willing to recommend to the Secretary of Interior that we cooperate in securing legislative authority to terminate the Department's trusteeship responsibility with respect to that tribe." Myer issued a standing offer to help tribes cut their federal ties. He proposed that Indians who remained on reservations manage their affairs without federal assistance, and that Indians who wanted to leave reservations be relocated at government expense. Perhaps in the spirit of hastening Indian independence, Congress lifted the historic prohibition against selling liquor to Indians in mid-1953.[29]

Myer clearly voiced the sentiments of a majority in Congress, although a number of congressmen opposed the direction he was taking. Three years before Myer took office, an acting commissioner recommended to a Senate committee the termination of certain tribes using, as criteria, their degree of acculturation, economic resources, willingness of the tribe to terminate, and willingness of a state government to provide services to Indians like those rendered other citizens. A bureau survey in 1952 summarizing tribes' readiness for termination reported five Kalispel families as self-supporting, four by holding jobs off the reservation. Six families were wholly on welfare, seven partially. The median income of working families was estimated at $2,000 a year, compared to $3,200, the median income of white families in the Pend Oreille valley. Another report cited tribal business activities and enterprises: None. Like other tribes, the Kalispels maintained no current enrollment records.[30]

House Resolution 698 (1952) authorized the Bureau of Indian Affairs to propose termination for specific tribes, although the government played this down as "general framework legislation," not final in details, and House Concurrent Resolution 108 (1953) expressed "a sense of Congress" that Indians "should be freed from Federal supervision and control." By the time Myer resigned (at President Eisenhower's request) in 1953, bills were ready to place Indian reservations under the control of individual states and confer automatic "competency" on Indians at age 21.[31]

The termination and competency bills ignited Garry to call an emergency conference of Indians under auspices of the National Congress of American Indians in February 1954 at Washington, D.C., to "rally an organized protest on a national basis against legislation which, if passed, would endanger the tribal existence" and to demand again an Indian voice in legislation that affected Indians. The conference brought representatives of 43 tribes from 21 states and Alaska to the capital. Although the Kalispels sent no delegate, they considered themselves represented by Garry. Minutes of Kalispel community meetings often mentioned Garry as a Kalispel representative, although Garry now called himself a Coeur d'Alene, and shortly after the conference the Kalispels voted to join the NCAI, endorsing Garry "as a delegate for the Kalispel Tribe to go to the convention and meetings," partly because the tribe had turned over its limited funds to Simmons for claims work and could not pay travel expenses for an alternate delegate.[32]

The conferees passed one resolution opposing "automatic competency" and another asking that "any Indian tribe . . . who may be directly affected by any legislation, . . . be consulted prior to its drafting." They also agreed that a tribe should be terminated only "with the full consent of the Indians" and called for "a broad program of assistance to Indians which will satisfy the letter and spirit of its [the government's] solemn obligations," those treaties and contracts framed a century before.

Despite protests of Indians and their supporters, termination's chief advocate in Congress, Senator Arthur V. Watkins of Utah, a onetime farmer turned lawyer and politican, captivated his colleagues with rhetoric about "taking off the shackles" and making "free men" of Indians. The termination bills met little opposition in Congress which passed the first on June 17, 1954, terminating the Menominees of Wisconsin. Soon Congress would cut off others, including Oregon's Siletz reservation, Grande Ronde community, and smaller bands, the first to sever all ties to the federal government on August 14, 1956. By now, Garry was calling (at the thirteenth NCAI convention) for intertribal action "to hold onto our homelands, our identity, and our precious Indian heritage."[33]

Garry's usefulness as a Kalispel advisor waned as he rose in national Indian affairs. He was mentioned, with many others, as a possible successor to Dillon Myer. The Bureau of Indian Affairs, "unfriendly" to the National Congress of American Indians and its aims, tripped Garry at every chance and challenged his right to speak as a Coeur d'Alene. To hold his political position, Garry relinquished his status as a Kalispel to enroll with the Coeur d'Alenes, his father's people. He would continue to represent the Kalispels on occasion but his old tribe, nettled by what seemed disloyalty in their eyes, thereafter regarded Joe Garry warily.[34]

Photographed for a postcard, three of these Kalispels are Lucy Joseph and her child, Charlie Sherry (Lucy's father), and John Bigsmoke. The man with gun is not Indian. (Kalispel tribal collection)

The five young Kalispels who sat for a studio portrait are, left to right, Joe Blackbear Ignace, Mary Sophie Bigsmoke, Lucy Bigsmoke Peuse, Josephine Bigsmoke Ignace, and Alec Ignace. (Hazel Hunter album, Kalispel tribal collection)

And a new generation of leadership began to take hold. Garry rose in politics, at first, by virtue of both his singular education and his famous ancestor, Spokane Garry. Few Kalispels his age studied beyond the fourth grade, but the old Kalispel school had been transferred to the Cusick district in 1933 and, although conducted on the reservation as the "Indian school" until 1948, its curriculum and services improved. Until the reservation school closed and all children started at Cusick, the district bused Kalispel pupils to Cusick for the fifth and higher grades with the result that, by 1939, roughly one in ten children in the Cusick school were Indian and all school-age Kalispel children attended. In 1940, three Kalispels enrolled in colleges: Anthony Revais at Chemawa, Henry SiJohn at Riverside Junior College, California, and subsequently Gonzaga University where he was noted as an arranger of Indian songs for the glee club, and Celina Garry, in Holy Names College, Spokane. Of the Kalispel generation immediately after Joe Garry's, nearly all completed eight grades and, even though only one or two braved the halls of a white-dominated high school, the level of schooling among young Kalispels dramatically advanced.[35]

To be sure, the schooling was the same for Kalispel as for white pupils and often produced Indian children torn between cultures. The parents of these children, who saw education as a key to progress, emerged as tribal leaders. They seem to have shared three characteristics: education to the fourth or fifth grade, intuitive wisdom, and a love of Kalispel heritage. Perhaps some served from necessity as the Kalispels strove to form a community without a chief: soft-spoken Ray Pierre and Alice Ignace, who wrote much of the business correspondence as council secretary; the reservation's most prosperous farmer, Clarence Campbell, a sturdy Spokane married to Mary Bigsmoke; and stocky Frank Nick, who seemed to have a quip for every occasion. Now a school teacher, Henry SiJohn for a time interpreted official letters and represented the Kalispels at conferences with sympathetic bureau officers and attorneys. And like the Spokanes and Kutenais, the Kalispels turned to Alex Sherwood, a Spokane, who quietly stepped into the Garry role as inter-tribal advisor, a man of chiefly mien whose son, Robert, married a Kalispel. The Sherwoods, educated in the Spokane reservation school at Wellpinit, often acted as interpreters; they spoke superb Salish and fluent English.[36]

Even with the best advisors, however, tribal business moved slowly, requiring someone who understood their problems and issues to go house to house to explain and ask opinions of Kalispels. Clarence Campbell often did this; in his paternal way, he called on older Kalispels to ask about their health and discuss tribal business. (As long as the school lasted, keeping track of individual Indians had been the teacher's unofficial function. Indeed, when Cusick closed the Indian school, the North Idaho superintendent urged that a teacher continue living in the building "to keep medical supplies, and take care of minor medical needs. If she should move out, there wouldn't be anyone living on the reservation who could keep us informed as to the needs of the Kalispels.")

Bureau workers answered questions and helped when they could, but the Kalispels got little official notice. The autocratic William Ensor, appointed North Idaho superintendent, paused at the reservation perhaps twice a year, usually offering prepared resolutions that he wanted the tribe to adopt quickly without question. Ensor disliked Joe Garry, partly because Garry resisted Ensor's authoritarian ways. For his part, Garry once urged the incoming Commissioner of Indian Affairs, Philleo Nash, to fire Ensor. Nash did not.

If Kalispel leaders were only beginning to stand alone, like wobbly colts, the tribe needed little direction, for it conducted little business. Other than suing the United States, only two tribal decisions of moment were necessary in the 20 years after reorganization: one, in 1948, to move the old mission church to higher ground, near the schoolhouse, before floods destroyed it, and the other, in 1954, to grant the Pend Oreille County Public Utility District an easement to overflow Kalispel lands along the river for a flat payment of $1,320 and $75 an acre for erosion damages from the utility's Box Canyon Dam downriver. Joe Garry interpreted for the PUD man who talked to the Kalispel council. Although the PUD paid owners of four allotments, its overflow touched nearly 40.[37]

The Kalispels had little choice but to pin large hopes on a generous award in their land-claim case which, with Kenneth Simmons' death April 13, 1953, passed wholly into the hands of the Wilkinson

During high water on the Pend Oreille, Our Lady of Sorrows Church was flooded. The Kalispels eventually moved it to higher ground, beside LeClerc Road, to prevent its destruction by flood waters. (OPA)

firm and associates. As the attorneys collected evidence for the case, an ethnologist hired by the Department of Justice, Stuart A. Chalfant, spent three or four weeks intermittently among the Kalispels asking about old times with a Spokane, Ignace Camille, as interpreter; he would complain, in testimony, that "someone" advised the Kalispels not to tell him anything.

Since adopting their charter, the Kalispels had lost ground. Their poverty was real; their income, according to the Bureau of Indian Affairs, was "the lowest of any Washington tribe," far below the average rural income for the state, amounting to about $30 a year from tribal funds and $360 from wages. Reservation homes, small frame shacks, lacked pure water and waste disposal, and nearly all needed repairs.

By 1960 there were 145 enrolled Kalispels and the land allotments were so split among heirs that leasing was impractical. To rent out one tract of 607 acres required the approval of 17 owners; but only 16 shared ownership of 2,867 acres of grazing land. "Because of heirship problems and being interspersed with non-Indian lands," said the bureau's survey of the Kalispels, "it is difficult to farm on a paying basis. Because of small income, few families can invest in enough farm equipment to set up a paying operation."[38]

For people in want, the claims case crawled at tortoise pace in an adversarial political climate. The Department of Justice estimated that various tribes claimed 70 percent of the nation's land and that awards might reach $14 billion. Oliver LaFarge, the Indian apologist, retorted that Indians collected less than 2 percent of the compensation they were entitled to. The Indian Claims Commission dragged through a schedule so jammed that it empowered staff lawyers to hear testimony and examine witnesses, naming Leon J. Moran to the Kalispel suit. Depositions for the Kalispels were taken in 1951 and hearings began in Washington, D.C., on January 21, 1952, with Simmons as the tribe's attorney, in the commission's board room, a small conference chamber with low ceilings and sparse furnishings. With Associate Commissioners Louis J. O'Marr and William M. Holt at a table on a dais, the proceedings were informal, an atmosphere, thought one observer, suggesting the commission's surmise that it played "an unimportant and inconspicuous role in public affairs," its secretaries in hallways, clerks and files and visitors' chairs jumbled in a reception room; its decisions not printed, as in a court, but reproduced by mimeograph.[39]

This first hearing considered only the land claims of the Kalispels. If their title could be established, a later one would set the value of lands lost. Allan H. Smith, anthropologist and administrator at Washington State University, offered the most significant testimony from more than 600 pages of field notes taken during the summers of 1936, 1937, and 1938 he spent among the Kalispels. He marked the Kalispels' aboriginal land with red crayon on a Shell road map to show that their ground extended from the Flathead River near Horse Plains, Montana, across northern Idaho north to the Selkirks and south below Pend Oreille lake, and into Washington south of the Pend Oreille River to the crest of the mountains west of the river. This was the old area of the Kalispels, based on accounts of hunting, fishing, gathering, and placenames.[40]

As a graduate student at Yale, Smith said, he chose the Kalispels for field work as "among the least known of poorly known people" between the Cascades and the Rockies and because their culture seemed in danger of dying out. His interpreter with the Kalispels had been Robert Sherwood; they talked many hours with the oldest alert Kalispels who savored old ways. Smith believed the Kalispels a distinct tribe, separated into perhaps three bands, and showed that other tribes regarded them as distinct with a specific territory.

Other expert witnesses, Nancy O. Lurie and Verne F. Ray, noted anthropologists, and even the government's witness, Chalfant, concurred with Smith in the main. The commission's Findings of Fact, issued June 9, 1958, granted the Kalispels the land on Smith's map excepting fringe areas that seemed to have been used by other tribes as much as by Kalispels—common ground. The area amounted to roughly 2,400,000 acres, and the Kalispels began to speculate on the size of a possible award. Some thought it might be as much as four million.

An award would be based on the land's worth at the time of settlement. A Wilkinson attorney, Charles A. Hobbs, sampled the deed records of 29 townships along the rivers in Kalispel territory, a considerable part of it now forest reserves, and the Kalispel lawyers and government agreed that a reasonable date for setting the value would be July 1, 1903. With the commission's approval,

Wilkinson hired a Missoula appraiser, Mont H. Saunderson, and a Portland timber appraiser, Karl D. Henze, to review county and Bureau of Land Management records of land sales between 1901 and 1904 and the history of timber transactions. Ten years had passed since the first depositions were taken. Now the Kalispels waited impatiently for the appraisers to do their work, for legal jockeying, and for their second hearing.[41]

With the valuation hearing set for April 23, 1962, the commission in February stunned attorneys by ruling, in a Crow suit, that tribal judgment funds could not be used to pay witness fees, a decision that would void the Wilkinson contracts for Kalispel witnesses (to say nothing of contracts with witnesses in other suits), and next, flinching from protests, partially reversed itself in a Northern Paiute case. In this uncertain atmosphere, the Wilkinson firm delayed the Kalispels' second hearing; then, shortly before Christmas 1962 concluded with federal attorneys a stipulation to compro-

During the Kalispels' planning for use of their judgment funds, many meetings were held in the church because the community hall—the old schoolhouse—was falling down. Lapwai agency men participated with Kalispels in the meetings. (Kalispel tribal collection)

mise and settle the Kalispel claim "on its merits" for $3 million, 10 percent to be paid as attorneys' fees. [42]

Charles Hobbs flew west for a tribal meeting in the old Kalispel schoolhouse on January 12, 1963, to outline the compromise and ask if the Kalispels would accept it, speaking through Alex Sherwood and Vital Pierre, a Flathead married to a Kalispel. This council, the most momentous since reorganization 29 years earlier, brought out 35 of 67 eligible Kalispel voters, the tribe's largest quorum. Bureau officers from Lapwai and Portland came, including Ensor, and a Lapwai agency man drove his auto through the reservation to pick up Kalispels who otherwise could not attend. Ensor objected to some terms of the proposal, trying to impose his opinions, but the Indians had been meeting among themselves for some weeks to amend their constitution and bring the tribal roll up to date, anticipating payment, and after hearing the attorney's explanation, they voted, 35 to 0, to accept the three million. [43]

Following a brief hearing to be sure that the tribe understood the proposal and voted without coercion, the Indian Claims Commission on March 21 announced the award. "As far as we know," Hobbs wrote Tribal Chairman Louis Andrews, "the Kalispel has obtained the largest judgment on a per capita basis of any tribe in the United States." Two months later, Congress appropriated funds to pay the Kalispels, and on the reservation, a clamor began for an immediate payment of a few hundred dollars to sustain the Indians, who had endured a hard winter without wage work. [44]

But it was not all over. Bills to ratify the judgment stalled in Congress, as the sub-committee on Indian affairs of the Senate Committee on Insular and Interior Affairs decreed that before the government would pay the Kalispels, the tribe should submit a plan for spending the money, that half of the funds should be placed in a private trust (a bank) for future use, and that upon receiving its money, the Kalispel tribe should be terminated. The stipulation of a private trust was Senator Henry M. Jackson's personal requirement, his notion, as a step toward termination. Unlike the Kutenais, the Coeur d'Alenes, and other tribes whose judgment funds had slipped routinely through Congress, the Kalispels were to be an instrument for Congress once more to impose its will on Indians.

CHAPTER 7

The Plan

EXHILARATION from the $3 million judgment of the Indian Claims Commission did not last long. The roof seemed to fall in on the Kalispels almost immediately: the tribe had to write an acceptable plan for spending the award, Congress intended to terminate them, and their long-standing dream of a cattle business evaporated. The Kalispels were no better off than they had been, poor, badly housed, and ill-fed, facing new burdens of management. With the prospect of millions, however, they tossed in rivers of advice.

About a month after Congress appropriated funds for the Kalispel claim, the Wilkinson firm, its work done with the Indian Claims Commission, offered to bow out if the Kalispels wanted an attorney nearer to them. Counseling the tribe had fallen largely to Robert Dellwo, already retained by the Spokanes and the Coeur d'Alenes. Bureau subalterns were said to have told the Kalispels they did not need an attorney for judgment planning but the tribe, feeling the bureau treated them with "benign neglect," in October 1963 voted to sign the first of a series of two-year contracts with Dellwo, Rudolf & Grant of Spokane. Kalispel Chairman Louis Andrews, in the meantime, convened tribal meetings to plan for spending judgment funds, relying on Dellwo, to a lesser extent on Joe Garry, on Alex Sherwood, and a young Coeur d'Alene, Ozzie George. In addition, the domestic peace corps, VISTA, assigned a volunteer, Hiroto Zakoji, to help the Kutenais and the Kalispels.[1]

The Senate's requirement for a plan, however, imposed a task on the Kalispels that was relatively new in Indian relations. Dellwo talked with Indians—Clarence Campbell, for one—and then wrote memos of "random ideas," trial balloons, to bureau officers for their reaction. No one knew precisely what kind of plan the senators expected or the bureau would support, and since the Senate's charge to the Kalispels was intended to test a new direction for judgment funds, Dellwo's conversations with interior committee members, including the chairman, Senator Jackson, offered little guidance. From his experience with the Coeur d'Alenes, Dellwo invented a "family plan" for the Kalispels to distribute money for housing, which the tribe needed desperately, and the Indians grasped this phrase. The family plan was, in Dellwo's words, "a camouflaged per capita distribution," intended to satisfy the senators and avoid the Colvilles' mistake of giving each individual too much money at once.[2]

The bespectacled Zakoji found the Kalispels floundering, their weekly planning meetings in Andrews' home poorly attended, random sessions where agency men and the Jesuit priest, Father Dominic Doyle, often out-talked the men and women of the tribe, debating conflicting schemes for economic development, each convinced that he knew what would be best for the Kalispels. Zakoji took Chairman Andrews aside to suggest minutes, an agenda, and rules of order to focus the deliberations, and drew an organizational diagram to sort committee tasks. By June 1963 the tribe had formed four committees representing their priorities for spending: one for youth development, another for a community building, a third for the family plan and housing, and a fourth for industrial development. But the committees were dominated by lean, sharp-featured Father Doyle, named to three, and agency men, William Bailey or John Weber, on the youth, housing, and industrial committees, and, Zakoji noted, "it was understood that Mr. Ensor, as Superintendent, would be involved in all committees."[3]

The industrial development committee listed only three possibilities—Manresa Cave as a tourist attraction, that cattle business, and a sawmill—demonstrating not so much a lack of imagination as the paucity of economic opportunity in Pend Oreille County. Without market surveys, nobody could think of a business from which inexperienced Kalispel managers might profit in remote Usk. Many offered suggestions: a retired economic analyst, Frederick C. Billings, urged the tribe to go into arts and crafts, not "in the typical tourist, dime-store sense . . . but rather quality artists and craftsmen," but few Kalispels practiced crafts. Moreover, the market might be inundated with Indian artifacts, for a federal agency, the Area Redevelopment Administration, had sponsored a development study for the Colvilles, the Spokanes negotiated with consultants to forecast the recreational prospects for their reservation, and a number of tribes fashioned 10-year economic plans at the request of the Secretary of the Interior.[4]

The committee's "sawmill" stemmed from preliminary talks with the Hedlund Lumber Company which proposed a chip-and-saw plant to make rough lumber and pulp chips. "Such an industry on the reservation would be a godsend to . . . the Kalispel tribe," asserted Ray Pierre, who succeeded Andrews as chairman, "and give their employable members a source of employment they have been lacking for years." But the Hedlund mill, projected to employ 75, depended on raising $730,000, more than half of it from the Economic Development Administration and $182,500 from the tribe, secured by a first mortgage. A second possibility: If the tribe would lend him $100,000, an Usk man, Stanton M. Culp, would reopen a bankrupt mill on Kalispel ground on the west side of the river as a remanufacturing plant employing Kalispels. Both prospects faded with the denial of Hedlund's application for federal assistance and Culp's sub-letting the mill to Georgia-Pacific.[5]

And that cattle business went a-glimmering with a negative report by the North Idaho agency land operations officer, Enos A. Anderson, late in 1963. In truth, Anderson simply pointed out the obvious: that a cattle herd would be "marginal," that $150,000 would need to be invested for irrigation and fertilizer, and that even so financed, herding would be seasonal and employ only two men fulltime. He concluded that "the odds appear to be against the success of a Tribal beef cattle enterprise." Four years later, however, some Kalispels who were still not convinced raised the cattle possibility again, only to receive a longer report from Ray P. Petterborg, soil conservationist at Lapwai, with the same result: "The area is marginal cattle producing area" and "good management is extremely important," implying that the Kalispels might not be up to managing the business. Asked to re-study cattle prospects, the agricultural scientists at Washington State University declined on the ground that the Anderson and Petterborg reports seemed conclusive.[6]

Early in the planning sessions, dissent surfaced among Kalispels. Some simply stayed away from meetings. Father Doyle clashed with bureau men; he recommended building a new church but the tribe refused; he seemed to doubt the Kalispels' ability to manage their judgment money, favoring a private trust that would distribute earnings from the principal equally among members of the tribe; and he warned that Indians would over-build under the housing plan. Clarence Campbell, whom Doyle customarily visited on Sundays, disagreed with the priest but could not bring himself to say so; Mary Campbell backed Doyle. Discords, jealousies, and grudges surfaced during the planning; they have not disappeared. In the long run, family loyalties and coalitions of large families prevail. At their meeting on February 19, 1964, for which Superintendent Ensor had prepared a new roster of eligible voters, corrected by Louis Andrews, a majority of the Kalispels voted to accept the plan developed by their committees.[7]

The plan called for giving at least $7,000 to each family, and more depending on family size, to build, buy, or remodel a home on or off the reservation—the "family plan;" $75,000 for a community hall; $10,000 to rehabilitate the church, and $1,000 for the cemetery; $1,000 toward a sanitary system that would be funded primarily by the Public Health Service; $250,000 for industrial development; $100,000 for the purchase of land; $260,000 for youth programs, including scholarships; and $761,000 to be invested with the proceeds to be used for tribal operating expenses. The plan represented the wishes of those Kalispels willing to take part in the planning—the work had fallen on no more than a dozen—and, if industrial development seemed vague and uncertain, it nevertheless expressed the tribe's determination to find some kind of business to support it. None of the money, in the majority's opinion, should be managed by a private trust.[8]

Sent to Washington, D.C., through channels, with assurances by attorney Dellwo and Superintendent Ensor that it truly represented the tribe's wishes, the plan came before the Senate Sub-Committee on Indian Affairs, chaired by Frank Church, Idaho, which was considering a bill to release Kalispel judgment funds. No Kalispels appeared before the committee because, Dellwo explained, "The Tribe had been assured that the Kalispel Bill was completely uncontroversial and would slide through in good fashion," but it did not, as senators bluntly signalled again their intention that Kalispel monies should go into a private trust and the tribe be terminated. The Kalispels also petitioned for two payments of $250 for each member from interest on their money, but "until the Kalispel bill passes they can't get a penny . . . either interest or principal." Senator Jackson lent Dellwo a transcript, and from it, two months after the hearing, the tribe learned that they were still among the guinea pigs for a senatorial experiment in termination and private trusts.[9]

"We had a meeting last Saturday and I saw two Indian mothers weep because it appeared that their hopes and dreams for getting the housing, education and per capita portion of the program this year was going aglimmering," Dellwo wrote Henry Jackson. He went on:

Here is a tribe that has had nothing. . . . Finally, after years of waiting it received its judgment fund. It set about planning for its use. It went to Congress with a complete program to show its good faith. It presented a bill that is identical to the Kootenai bill in Idaho, the Coeur d'Alene bill and others that have passed without incident. Suddenly it is faced with what appears to be an ultimatum from the Chairman of the Sub-Committee on Indian Affairs that this tribe can't get a dime of its judgment monies until it agrees to some plan of termination. You can imagine the shock and disappointment.[10]

Joe Garry tried to help; he wrote Jackson and Church: "I personally am vitally interested in the welfare of the Kalispels because some members of my family belong to it and I was myself an enrolled Kalispel until some years ago when I transferred to the Coeur d'Alene tribe." He attached a resolution of the Coeur d'Alenes stating that "a national or regional precedent may be set by the handling of the Kalispel bill" and urging its passage.[11]

Although he advocated termination of tribes, Jackson began to see the damaging effect termination might have on the Kalispels.

He softened. On the last day of July, the Senate published a report on the Kalispel bill directing the Bureau of Indian Affairs to look into the feasibility of a private trust for Kalispel funds and to draft legislation that would revoke the tribe's corporate charter and terminate them. On the next day, August 1, 1964, Chairman Jackson intervened to wrest the Kalispel bill from committee and push it to a vote. It passed. The threat of termination hung over the Kalispels ominously, like an approaching storm cloud, but now they might spend portions of the judgment money with approval of the bureau and the Senate committee.[12]

If planning polarized the Kalispels and roused sleeping quarrels, it also gave the tribe's leaders an exercise in management. The tribal officers and business committee, lacking office, file case, or typewriter, meeting in private homes, were learning to cope with the Indian bureau and grasping the political posturing that white men took for granted. As Zakoji observed in one of his frequent memos to Lapwai, "The Kalispels are beginning to contemplate their problems." He overheard three Indians agreeing that "it was hard to think about the problems of our community . . . because we've been living with them for such a long time."[13]

With divisions among the tribe, 11 families refused to take part in the proposed housing program but, on the other hand, the prospect of new dwellings drew a majority of the Kalispels closer. Almost from the moment they heard of their claim award, some had been sketching plans for new houses. A survey by the housing committee showed that 26 families proposed to build on the reservation, 19 to build or buy off it, and 27 to cooperate in a "mutual self-help program" to help each other build. A few Kalispels did not answer the committee's questionnaire, and the tribe did not know where to reach 18.[14]

With passage of the Kalispel bill releasing funds, lobbying began in the new session of Congress for approval of the tribe's plan. Dellwo took a delegation of Kalispels to Washington to talk with congressmen and appear before the Senate committee; he would say, "I have never seen a better presentation by the Indians themselves, made by the members themselves from material they had gathered and prepared. This is a new twist, because even in more advanced tribes they tend to rely on the tribal attorneys and sometimes the local Bureau personnel." Louis Andrews asserted that the 150 surviving members of the Kalispel tribe "live in abject poverty," and that the tribe would use a large part of its funds for housing. John Nomee, chairman of a tribal committee on health education, said a county nurse called theirs "a reservation of shacks with outside toilets and no running water."[15]

The committee had received a letter from the Pend Oreille County health officer and sanitarian describing Kalispel housing as "deplorable—beyond description. Some homes have only an outside wall, many roofs leak, foundations are rotten, wind and cold come through the floors. . . . There is overcrowding . . . with, in many cases, as many as eight (8) people in three (3) rooms." Of 19 houses for 154 Indians, eight had running water and 11 hauled theirs from an open stream. All houses "have outside privies which do not have fly or rodent control." Thirty Kalispels showed evidence of tuberculosis in x-rays.[16]

At one juncture in the delegation's meeting with the senators, after Ray Pierre criticized bureau services to the Kalispels, Senator Jackson asked Pierre if he didn't agree personally that the tribe would be better off with its funds in a private trust, perhaps the

The Kalispel Indian village where many Kalispels remained until new homes were built for them with judgment-fund monies in 1966. (Hazel Hunter album, Kalispel tribal collection)

Old National Bank of Spokane. In his quiet way, Pierre reflected and then replied firmly, "No, sir. That would be the first step to termination."[17]

The senators did not change their minds about trusts or termination, however, and the Kalispels found themselves unwilling targets in a confrontation between the committee and the Bureau of Indian Affairs over the future administration of Indian tribes. For any release of judgment funds, bureau support of the tribe seemed essential but while the Senate deliberated, a snag appeared: Father Doyle caught the ear of a newspaper reporter, Rowland Bond, whose articles in the *Spokane Daily Chronicle* oozed with the priest's scorn for the bureau. In one, Doyle, who as a boy rode with his father to deliver brick for Kalispel chimneys, was quoted as saying that all the bureau had done for the Kalispels since 1933 was install a few screen doors and once spray a pond to kill mosquitoes. Another quoted the Jesuit: "I don't believe the Kalispel people should be forced to subscribe to a plan that permits the Bureau of Indian Affairs to continue as guardian and banker." Meant well, intended to enlist citizen sympathy for the tribe, the stories also quoted Clarence Campbell: "We are worse off than any tribe in the area, completely isolated from the North Idaho Agency at Lapwai." If Ensor, sensing a personal attack, or other bureau employees thought the tribe had planted these items, the bureau might turn against the Kalispels at a critical point in their campaign for approval of the tribal plan. Dellwo hurried, by letters and telephone calls, to "de-fuse" the newspaper articles.[18]

Early in the 89th Congress, bills were offered for termination of the Quinaults and Colvilles of Washington. Indians of the northwest cried in protest, brandishing the chilling example of the Klamaths, terminated in 1959 when nearly two thousand received $44,000 each, sold their land, and squandered their awards. Although some managed prudently, destitute Klamaths soon swelled welfare rolls; dispossessed, without land, refuge, or prospects. (A smaller group of 473 Klamaths rejected termination to organize as a nonprofit trusteeship under Oregon law and keep some lands and cattle.) Even strong advocacy of Indian economic development by the current Commissioner of Indian Affairs, Philleo Nash, did not soothe northwest Indians; neither did Nash placate members of the senate interior committee who held strong individual opinions about Indians, were impatient with the bureau, and pressed toward termination.[19]

At Senator Jackson's insistence, however, the Senate committee unanimously resolved on August 25 to approve parts of the Kalispel plan and send it to Nash for action, stipulating that the bureau continue social and welfare services to the tribe. The resolution allowed distribution of approximately $1,232,000 for the family plan and housing, a community center, church rehabilitation, cemetery renovation, and waste disposal system; it did not release $1,371,800 for industrial development, land purchases, a youth program, or tribal operating expenses but again recommended that these funds go into a private trust, not managed by the Bureau of Indian Affairs.[20]

The committee's terms worried other Indians who feared that similar strings would be tied to new judgment awards. And indeed that was the intent, as Jackson told Dellwo: "We have an understanding to the effect that the same directive will be included in other legislation now before us. . . . In other words, this action is not pointed at the Kalispels only, but to several other groups around the country." At its September convention, the Affiliated Tribes of Northwest Indians—of which Joe Garry was first vice-president and the Kalispel, Louis Andrews, second vice-president—condemned "the practice of the United States Congress to attach . . . conditions to tribes' use and programming of judgment funds," citing the Kalispels.[21]

The Kalispels bowed to the Senate terms reluctantly, but gave in for fear that their houses might be put off even longer by "the determination of the Senate Committee to dictate to the Indian Bureau and the Tribe, what use should be made of the judgment funds." Dellwo urged Jackson, in conversation, to allow at least the $100,000 for land acquisition but Jackson repeated that the money must be handled by a private trust, and when Dellwo talked with the Commissioner of Indian Affairs, he found that the bureau would not go ahead with any of the plan "unless the Tribe expressed an unconditional acceptance of the changes . . . required by the Senate Committee." Faced with the Senate's stiff-necked insistence and the commissioner's meek deference, the Kalispels voted, 11 to one by a show of hands, for "a reluctant approval . . . given only to prevent a further delay in the Family Plan," as their resolution read. They wanted to start building houses "tomorrow, if possible."[22]

Twenty-eight families had drawn house plans by April 1965 when the tribe contracted with the Public Health Service for construction of domestic water and waste disposal systems, agreeing that the service would show Indians the best sites for new homes on their allotments, and the Kalispel owners would excavate and fill pipe trenches, install plumbing and septic tanks, and clean up after the work.[23]

With "family plan" funds released, Kalispels both on and off the reservation prepared to build or buy new homes. The business committee rejected pre-cut dwellings to contract with Joe Miller, a Spokane builder, for frame "expandable homes" ranging in size from 702 to 1,040 square feet and in cost from $9,000 to $12,000, not mansions, but houses comparable to so-called project housing in northwest cities. As building costs ran higher than expected, the

Under provisions of the "family plan" for use of judgment funds, many Kalispels built modern homes on and off the reservation. Most of the homes, like this one beside LeClerc road, are in forest settings or overlook the Pend Oreille.

The Kalispel tribal community center, on the site of the old Kalispel schoolhouse, was built with judgment funds. Important tribal meetings, youth activities, and similar functions convene here.

Kalispel business committee proposed $1,500 more for each family, but the bureau balked, offering its own resolution limiting an additional $1,500 to families buying less expensive houses. John Weber of the Lapwai agency told a tribal meeting that the bureau's resolution was the only one likely to be approved but nevertheless the Kalispels, tired of bullying from Senate and bureau, nearly turned him down, voting narrowly 15 to 13 for the bureau's resolution. Miller erected 38 houses on the reservation during the summer of 1966 and those Kalispels who still inhabited the old Indian village, the cluster of shacks and tipis that had sheltered them for a century, at last moved out.[24]

The next year, a Spokane contractor, N. H. "Dutch" Locher, built a new Kalispel community building, a one-story concrete block with kitchen and meeting rooms, for $79,555, on the site of the old schoolhouse which was burned. Some Kalispels cried as flames swept the familiar old structure. For the community hall, the Kalispels received a Housing and Urban Development grant of $44,624. Although $12,609 in judgment funds was spent for cost overruns, the building was not finished inside—door trim, mopboard, and interior paint omitted.[25]

The Kalispels now had houses for the 93 members of the tribe who lived on the reservation but had no jobs, and little prospect of any. Their income consisted of periodic pittances from interest on their judgment funds, requiring the tribe to send begging applications for "per capita payments" through channels—fiscal bandaids. Nine Kalispels drew state welfare assistance as aged, disabled, or dependent. Nine earned $1.75 an hour during 1967 as trainees in a tribal Community Action Program, largely lectures by agency personnel and a field exercise—construction of toilets for visitors at the Manresa Cave and the tribal swimming beach on the river, a task for which the agency requested "a working blueprint . . . not very detailed, and relatively easy to read." Three Kalispel men labored six months a year as fire suppression aides to the Forest Service.[26]

The bureau, meanwhile, looked on the reservation as farm land, characterizing its "highest and best use" as "leasing for grazing purposes, and for small scale logging activity, with the possibility of limited recreational development." Progress toward even such narrow uses seemed unlikely with judgment funds frozen by congressional mandate and a tribal leadership that, while improving, in the opinion of the bureau "suffers from lack of experience, formal training, and some lack of confidence on the part of individual tribal members . . . attributable in part to the limited number of adults available to run for, and be elected to, offices in tribal government."[27]

Lobbying continued, of course, for approval of other elements of the tribal program, sometimes shaking loose money such as the $447,280 to establish a trust fund (part of the family plan) for the education of 88 Kalispel children, placed in the National Bank of Washington branch at Newport, but the tribe needed a dramatic incident, a springboard to vault over the concerns of Congress, and discovered it in mid-1960 when Francis SiJohn proposed to sell Kalispel allotment 83 to a non-Indian, William Tombari, a Spokane real estate dealer. Although SiJohn's sale was not a key tract, it would whittle away scarce Indian land. Then, too, a good price might induce other Kalispels to sell, and the tribe's leaders could visualize their land base slipping away piecemeal. Dellwo urged Si-

John to give the tribe a chance to meet the highest bid, while the tribal business committee rushed through a resolution for a land-purchase program, "not yet fully formulated," that would enable the Kalispels to buy the SiJohn and any other allotments offered for sale.[28]

Moving fast on business decisions was difficult, however, because tribal meetings often failed to muster a quorum. Dellwo helped the Kalispels frame a new constitution that lifted earlier bars to tribal land purchases and placed the power to act on business matters in a new five-person business committee. Almost its first action was a resolve to buy the allotments leased to Culp on the west side of the river, regarding these as most vulnerable to purchase offers.[29]

Nothing since winning their claims case galvanized the Kalispels like the threat of losing their land base. The small business committee, made up of experienced individuals rotating positions among themselves, now held power to act and could move relatively fast.

For religious services, the Catholic Kalispels use a stone altar with flat rocks as pews in Manresa grotto. The tribe's economic development plan regards the cave as a tourist attraction.

Foremost among its members were such men and women as Stanley Bluff, Louis Andrews, Steve Pierre, Glen Nenema, Alice Ignace, Francis Cullooyah, Susan Finley, and a handful of others. Within a year the business committee adopted a Land Purchase and Consolidation Program, modelled on the Coeur d'Alenes' program, calling for the Kalispel tribe to acquire key allotments: the 160 acres west of the river, 80 acres surrounding Manresa Cave, lake lagoons as tourist attractions, another 300 acres as powwow grounds, and perhaps shoreline for marina development. Part of the program envisioned buying back land that once belonged to Indians but had been lost by encroachment of government or settlers, and another part, the purchase of allotments split among heirs which could be consolidated into tracts large enough for farming, industry, or housing development.[30]

The SiJohn allotment, however, sold to Tombari, heightening the urgency for land acquisition due to "increased pressure by Indian owners for sale of lands." The Portland area office approved and sent the plan to the Secretary of the Interior who also approved and sent it to the Senate recommending that Indian tribes with approved land-management programs should have preference in any sale of trust lands. Two months later the commissioner telegraphed the area office that the Kalispel purchase of lands with judgment funds had been authorized, subject to the usual oversight by the bureau and to annual federal appropriations for acquisition of lands in Washington state.[31]

With an initial $100,000 for the land program, the business committee's first purchases were allotments 31 and 33, next door to the church, from Joe Garry. In five years, the Kalispels acquired 34 allotments for approximately $156,000—an additional $50,000 was voted in December 1971—before running short of funds. The tribe thus took title to about 1,260 acres, roughly one-fourth of the reservation, land that might otherwise have melted away to non-Indian buyers. A good many Kalispels who sold to the tribe asked for monthly payments on their land, intending to live on the money. In a flurry of buying and trading, the tribe had protected its pivotal ground, including the acreage west of the river on which the Culp lease was cancelled in March 1971.[32]

The land program impelled the Kalispels to continue planning, for the Portland area director warned, at its outset, that "the success of the program . . . must be measured by the return which the tribal investment produces in terms of social and economic benefits for the whole tribal community." He required the business committee, in purchases of land, to defend the "economic soundness . . . to withstand every challenge and allegation of imprudence;" in other words, to buy only land for which it could foresee a use that would benefit the tribe. [33]

For a time, the business committee thought about reclaiming the LeClerc road through the reservation, badly in need of repairs, and the county engineer snorted that the Indians could have the road anytime they could maintain it. In the end, the county kept the road and improved it, but refused to impose residential speed limits through the reservation, explaining that the LeClerc was "the most heavily traveled county road in Pend Oreille." Meanwhile, the tribe rejected a proposal by the Pend Oreille County Historical Society to restore the old Jesuit mission; the Kalispels believed that might "lead to an influx of unwanted people on the reservation" that would "detract from its peace and calm." [34]

In the fall of 1967 the *Newport Miner* editorially demanded that the Kalispels open their reservation to county law enforcement officers, charging that "over 18 percent of the total crimes committed in this county are committed by Indians who constitute less than 1 percent of the total population," adding that Indians would not work and that although the tribe had been given $3,000,000, many families were on welfare. Two editorials elicited a reader's response: "When will the citizens of the county change their attitude that an Indian is born drunk and lazy? When will the Indian be given a fair opportunity on the job market?" The newspaper also provoked meetings among county and tribal attorneys and the State Board Against Discrimination—but no changes in practices or attitudes. The Kalispels had contracted with the Cusick police chief and a Newport judge for reservation law enforcement for more than a decade, and continued to do so until 1980 when a tribal law and order code provided for a tribal court; it was amended to allow the tribal judge to be elected from adult citizens of the county, and under it, the bureau, which regarded the reservation as "not a high crime area," stationed a police officer on the reservation for two years until the Kalispels trained their own. [35]

As the business committee justified each land purchase, a skeleton economic plan took shape: a ceremonial park for traditional Indian contests and Indian product shows to attract tourists; allotments consolidated into units large enough for grazing; smaller tracts as leased housing, and Manresa Cave, long regarded as a potential tourist and historical site.

In order to realize the best income from their judgment funds, the Kalispels, as parties to a broad lawsuit, sued the government to require investment of their monies at prevailing rates rather than simply dumping them in the federal Treasury at 4 percent. The attorney general settled with the Kalispels for $114,127 in unrealized interest after a court held that the government had a fiduciary duty to enhance tribal trust funds by prudent investments. [36]

Then a Cusick businessman, Ray H. Wilson, hoping the tribe could provide money, approached the Kalispels for a loan of $20,000 for his box company, operated from a shed near his home. With a loan from a friend, Wilson started the Aluminum Box Manufacturing Company in 1966 to make back-pack tool cases for carpenters working on Boundary Dam; he believed his unique boxes would sell throughout the country, and designed another case for campers, but he needed money for advertising, a dealer network, and cash flow. The Kalispels granted the loan, with concurrence of the bureau, for here, at last, seemed industrial opportunity. With prospects of industry, the tribe also obtained special legislation giving it authority to lease, buy, sell, or mortgage land. [37]

When Wilson—seeming always on the verge of success—needed more money, the Kalispel business council lent it, taking shares in the box company as security. The firm expanded to three locations, added gun and camera cases to its product line, and advertised, using the Kalispel name, in trade, outdoor, and camera magazines; it still did not profit, and the Kalispels lent more money for working capital, for raw materials, and even to meet Wilson's payroll taxes, taking more shares for each loan. During 1973 and 1974, the Kalispels continued to advance funds to keep the box company going until, by October 1974, the tribe had made Wilson nine loans totaling $294,689 and held 60 percent of the stock. Now apprehensive, censured by many members of the tribe for pouring their money down a rat hole, the Kalispel business committee refused Wilson more funds until the box firm could be evaluated and a financial and marketing program outlined by professional consultants. [38]

As their relationship changed—the Kalispels from lenders to majority stockholders and Wilson from part owner to hired manager—the Kalispels applied for a $300,000 grant from the Washington State Economic Assistance Authority to consolidate operations of the box company in a new structure on 20 acres of the tribe's property west of the river. This had been recommended by a consultant. Hearings on the application were frustrating—documents misplaced, changes in the authority's board, and long discussions about products appropriate for manufacture by an Indian tribe. Stan Bluff, baffled by the delays, once exploded: "We can make aluminum Indian arrows!" Silence around the table. No comment. Then, the discussion went on. There was some serious talk of making an aluminum canoe, with the traditional Kalispel sturgeon nose, but costs proved too high. At last the authority offered a grant of $200,000 and a loan of $100,064, one of its largest.

Then the state treasurer, Robert S. O'Brien, heeding the attorney general, refused to issue a warrant for the money on the

Kalispel Metal Products, the tribe's fabricating business near Cusick, manufactures steel and aluminum components to close tolerances. The structures beside the building are among 68 dock sections for Lake Chelan, Washington.

ground that aiding a private business was not the public purpose specified by law for spending state funds. To force release of the grant and loan, the members of the Economic Assistance Authority and the tribe sued O'Brien, and the state supreme court ruled in mid-1974 that "the reduction of unemployment and alleviation of economic distress for the Kalispel Indian Community is a proper public purpose." The Kalispels dedicated their new 20,000-square-foot plant a year later.[39]

In the meantime, a Spokane consultant, Livingston Management, completed a study of the box company that called for aggressive new management and tight production, marketing, and fiscal controls. Livingston found the firm loosely run, its distributors angered by slow deliveries and erratic sales practices, and the Kalispel business committee, untrained in financial reporting, allowing the factory to drift. In short, there seemed a demand for boxes but the company undermined its chances for profit by inept management. By the end of December 1974, the company had lost $302,566 since it started and owed the Kalispel tribe $312,667. The Kalispels' "investment has entirely disappeared," the consultant said, and the Kalispels had lost heart. As the company's problems grew more complex, the discouraged business committee paid it less attention.[40]

The consultant thought that, as a government-favored minority enterprise with products of fine quality, the company could be highly profitable—"the corporation has the capacity to become a multi-million dollar volume operation," in the consultant's phrase—but recommended discontinuing low-selling items including the original carpenter's and camper's boxes. The Kalispel plant had won Small Business Administration contracts for hospital carts, a low-demand product that disrupted the manufacture of its best sellers, gun and camera cases. To rescue their investment, the consultant warned, the Kalispels would have to devise clear policies, hire expert managers, oversee the company closely, and be prepared to lend it more money.

One purpose of the box company, of course, was to train and employ young Kalispels. Some of the training was offered under the supervision of Spokane Community College, and in this respect the firm succeeded, although not all employees were Indians.

Kalispel Metal Products employs both Indians and non-Indians, among the latter skilled metal workers who leave jobs in large cities for the rural lifestyle of Cusick. The company trains Kalispels for manufacturing and office employment.

With reorganization, the factory, renamed Kalispel Metal Products, expanded its line from gun and camera cases to specialized fabrication of components for suppliers of the Department of Defense and the manufacture of marine structures, largely floating steel docks, for industrial customers, the Corps of Engineers, and the National Park Service. And if Kalispel Metal Products did not make the tribe rich, it was a boon to Cusick, generating jobs and money—the biggest business in town, its fiscal condition the topic of common gossip in bars and restaurants up and down the river.

Convinced that only another change in management would save the struggling company, the Bureau of Indian Affairs recruited Robert E. Knouff, flotation systems manager for United McGill of Columbus, Ohio, designer of some marine structures the Kalispel plant made. Knouff knew the Cusick firm because he visited several times a year for his Ohio employers. The Kalispel business committee agreed to hire Knouff, who took over on March 1, 1982. The bureau, in addition, arranged a 30-year direct federal loan and subsidized bank credit to Kalispel Metal Products for operations and new capital. Knouff hired skilled technicians who preferred the woodsy lifestyle of rural Cusick and the close personal climate of a small company. In his first year, Kalispel Metal Products broke even financially with three basic lines: aluminum gun cases, steel marine structures, and general metal fabrication to close tolerances.[41]

For a decade, Metal Products had eclipsed other parts of the Kalispel's plan for turning their land and judgment funds into businesses for the future. The business committee, by its dogged buttressing of the factory, widened dissent within the tribe. A number of Kalispels refused to take part in tribal meetings and, as a result,

Begun as a box-making company, Kalispel Metal Products continues to produce special-purpose aluminum boxes for campers, truckers, photographers, and others. The products are advertised and distributed nationally.

the business committee strengthened its role, reluctantly perhaps, for it bore the tribe's burdens. As the Kalispels continued long-range planning, they concluded that their land base, the reservation, was too small, particularly for tourism.

The planners kept a wary eye on Congress, for the threat of termination still hung over northwest tribes, although the bureau now leaned toward a conciliatory policy of Indian self-determination. President Kennedy's Commissioner of Indian Affairs, Robert L. Bennett, and his successor, Louis R. Bruce, advocated changing the bureau from an agency that managed Indians to one that served them, a reversal baffling to many longtime employees in the field, who were unaccustomed to listening to Indians. Attorney Dellwo, visiting Washington, had strolled with Senator Jackson into the Senate's confirmation hearing for Bennett to listen as Jackson, Church, and Clinton Anderson of New Mexico, with "loaded questions" (Dellwo's phrase), squeezed Bennett to promise faster progress toward termination. Bennett sidestepped and shortly after, adroitly shifted the onus for termination from the bureau to Congress, declaring that whenever a tribe reached a social, economic, and political level like that of a surrounding white population, he would notify Congress in order that Congress might decide if the tribe should be terminated. Under Bennett's regime, termination talk softened. Although the commissioner, at Jackson's request, would draft a bill to terminate the Kalispels, he did so with evident reluctance, telling Jackson that the bureau was "unable to make any commitment with respect to it," and urging that the Kalispels be allowed to vote on termination. The tribe protested that they would not consent to termination and that the renewed "threat of termination . . . brought development and planning on the Kalispel Reservation to a standstill."[42]

But planning did not stop and termination did not occur. Although the Kalispels, at one time, seemed on the verge of knuckling under to the obdurate senators, when Forrest Gerard, a noted Blackfoot, succeeded James Gamble on Jackson's staff, Jackson himself turned face. He no longer offered his annual bill to terminate the Colvilles; he backed reinstatement for the terminated Menominees; and he stilled his demands that the Kalispels be terminated when they received the balance of their judgment funds. Gamble, with Clinton Anderson, had been a prime instigator of the Senate committee's termination and trust-fund policy; he drafted bills to pattern Colville termination on the Klamath—bills which a majority of the Colvilles first favored and then rejected, taking a stand against termination under the leadership of Lucy Covington. Jackson's about-face was not lost on his colleagues. Senator Edward M. Kennedy remarked, "The Interior Committee, which during the termination period of the fifties had been the source of dislocation of the native American and weakening of his tribal institutions, has under the distinguished leadership of the Senator from Washington become a forceful spokesman for the interests of the Indian community." The Kalispel judgment funds finally slipped through Congress with the Indian Judgment Funds Distribution Act, which radically changed the way Congress reviewed awards. Much of the money released was invested in certificates of deposit, and unexpended family-plan funds went into a minors' trust with the Spokane National Bank to be paid out to young Kalispels in instalments at age 18 or in full at 21.[43]

While senators were shifting position, a wave of Indian militancy swept across the nation, ephemeral alliances coalescing around the American Indian Movement, which picketed and stormed bureau offices in Washington and other cities, including Portland. The movement attracted mainly urban Indians. As rural people, the Kalispels, Colvilles, Coeur d'Alenes, and Spokanes firmly denounced AIM through Alex Sherwood, Joe Garry, and Covington, saying it gave all Indians a black eye. After the invasion of the bureau's building in Washington, the government scattered bureau offices through the cavernous Department of the Interior, making it even more cumbersome to deal with.

Funded by the bureau, which contracted for economic studies of many reservations, still another consultant prowled the Kalispel reservation. Pacific Consultants of Everett, assessing the tribe's economy, termed the metals company "a very viable business" and recommended that the Kalispels consider, in addition, a cattle feedlot, a shopping center, and an "integrated recreational complex" centered on Manresa Cave.[44]

These recommendations paralleled an economic plan being devised for all Pend Oreille County. In an era of economic plans, launched by the Economic Development Administration, the residents of depressed areas tried to think of ways to create businesses for themselves. In a three-county consortium, the Trico Economic Development District, the populace of Pend Oreille concluded that outdoor recreation and tourism offered their best prospects. Since the depression of the thirties, local farmers had been moving away from grains and vegetables and toward beef and dairy cattle. In 1964, for example, 51.5 percent of farm sales had been beef cattle, and 18 percent, dairy products. Consequently, the cattle business might expand a little, and the county's hardworking people (said the plan) might work in specialized manufacturing if it could be lured to northeastern Washington, but forest and mining industries seemed to have peaked. All timber went out of the county for processing and only one lumber mill now employed more than 20 men.[45]

From their self-examination, the people of Pend Oreille County concluded that "the recreational potential . . . is very great," and talked of restoring the old Idaho & Washington Northern railroad, a heritage village to show pioneer living, cleaning and stocking the river for fishing, the Kalispels' old mission, recreational lodges set beside forested lakes, their caves, skiing, and seasonal and annual celebrations, all designed to bring tourists into the county. Thus the county's plan—tourism, cattle, specialized industries, and events—sounded much like the Kalispels'.

Both plans reflected the limited choices available to remote rural districts. But the consultants' report more or less summed up the inclination of the Kalispel business committee: the metals factory with perhaps other industrial plants on their west-side site, animal herding to use pasture land, and outdoor recreation to lure tourists. As a member of the committee, Steve Pierre promoted a pork-producing plant, guessing its annual operating costs at $603,000, but an informal study showed little hope for success and, as another of the committee remarked, "One sick hog—and your business is gone." On the other hand, a buffalo herd could reach a specialized market and symbolize the Kalispels' past; shaggy bison would be a fitting backdrop for traditional Indian games and crafts at the tribe's ceremonial grounds.[46]

The Kalispels' buffalo roundup usually occurs late in the fall. Although the animals are in fenced pastures, they are unpredictable and can be dangerous, especially in stampedes. (Photo: Jimi Lott, Spokesman-Review/Spokane Chronicle*)*

Learning from the bureau that the Theodore Roosevelt National Memorial Park north of Medora, North Dakota, would dispose of buffalo surplus in its herd, the business committee quickly spoke for the animals without waiting for community approval, and sent Davis Bluff with a truck to pick them up. He returned with 12 head, five bulls and seven cows. The park service eventually turned over 16 more cows and four bulls to the Kalispels who pastured them between the community hall and the river, near the ceremonial grounds, a picturesque reminder of times when Kalispel hunters rode to the plains. As the herd grew to 75, the tribe hired a herd manager—one of several hired employees, including planner and accountant—and in 1983 slaughtered a few animals for a first public sale of meat and trophies. Each year a few have been butchered to distribute meat among members of the tribe.[47]

The committee also asked its attorney, Dellwo, to clarify its legal rights to water and river frontage, both important in the development plan for irrigated pasture and tourist attractions. By tribal resolution the Kalispels invited the bureau to inventory tribal water resources, and formally appropriated all ground and surface waters of the reservation for the tribe. Three years later, Dellwo was still trying to induce the bureau to survey the resources, pointing out that backwater from Box Canyon Dam created a permanent "river lake" with recreational value, bordering the reservation, and the Kalispels needed to know more about it to develop a marina and beaches. In the meantime, the attorney had successfully challenged a proposal for a flood-control zone by the State Department of Ecology which would have allowed flooding of the Kalispels' industrial site on the west bank and as much as two-thirds of the reservation.[48]

In their efforts to plan, the Kalispels felt the distance between them and the North Idaho agency was too great. Lapwai was more responsive under Ensor's successor, Thomas St. Clair, but 185 miles and a state border created barriers to cooperation. Not long after the bureau opened a Spokane agency in 1970, the Kalispels petitioned to be transferred to it, encouraged by the Spokanes. St. Clair opposed the switch but the bureau, taking its opportunity to attach the Kalispels to an agency in Washington state, approved the transfer in 1974. A few years later, in a further gesture of friendship, the Spokane tribe granted full fishing and hunting rights on their reservation to Kalispels—but civilized protocol intruded: Kalispels were asked to carry their identification cards.[49]

The Kalispels and the federal government, as joint plaintiffs, filed suit against the Pend Oreille County Public Utility District, alleging that water backed behind Box Canyon Dam illegally raised the river level six to ten feet, flooding pasture and eroding riverbank. Near the end of August 1983, a federal district court ruled in favor of the Kalispels, opening the way to further suits to recover damages and negotiate a water level. In a separate case, the tribe sued to quiet its title to the riverbed. The courts declined to dismiss the suit and ordered it to trial, producing an historic decision that the State of Washington had not received clear title to the Pend Oreille riverbed when it became a state.[50]

By the late seventies, the Kalispels seemed well on their way to putting their corporate house in order, but their land base remained a compelling issue, as it had been since 1895 when the tribe accepted 40-acre individual tracts rather than abandon their homeland. Any sound plan for developing outdoor recreation demanded more land—the space, forests, and waterways to lure sportsmen and vacationers. In 1977 and again in 1978, tribal resolutions stated the Kalispels' "intent to persue [sic] . . . a more adequate land base," as Francis Cullooyah advised the agency. The Kalispels uncharacteristically called a press conference at which Sonny Tuttle, assigned by the bureau as natural resources director for the tribe, revealed that the Kalispels, with the advice of consultants, had fixed on a so-called Brown's Lake corridor—8,321 acres, 83 percent Forest Service and 17 percent state land, extending from the

Young Kalispel men on the Pend Oreille River, 1917, in a birch-bark canoe with traditional sturgeon nose. Note the beaded vest on the seated man. The Kalispels were the southernmost tribe to utilize bark canoes. (Frank Palmer photo, Eastern Washington State Historical Society)

The tribal office building, constructed with donated materials and Kalispel labor, stands beside the restored Our Lady of Sorrows Church. The white structure, center, is part of playground equipment. Behind it—dots in a field—is the buffalo herd.

upper half of the reservation northeasterly into the hilly country of Browns and Half Moon lakes and the creeks and forests around them. Browns had long been popular for fly fishing. When they heard that the Kalispels wanted back some of their old land, Portland bureau officers thought it "a somewhat unique project." [51]

With their proposal to reverse the territorial shrinkage that had pinched them progressively for 125 years, the Kalispels had come full circle—from unwilling participants in councils that would take away their land and curb their wanderings to spirited competitors in the paper chase for federal and foundation grants. One of their largest grants for the ceremonial grounds, $100,000, came from a Wisconsin foundation.

Designating itself an economic development committee, the business committee conducted yet another study, as their resolution said, to produce "a comprehensive plan . . . for planning and future development" and "to have and maintain a Tribal Overall Economic Development Plan to qualify for various government programs and assistance."

Issued late in 1983 as a spiral-bound, 130-page photocopy book with a red-lettered cover that depicts Kalispels fishing from a sturgeon-nosed canoe, the study is the tribe's basic business guide. A companion study of recreation prospects was conducted by the Thoreson-Peterson Planning Group, a Spokane economic consulting firm.[52]

The "OED," as everyone in the tribal office calls the development study, envisions linking Browns Lake to the reservation by horseback-riding trails and suggests many uses for the corridor: campgrounds, fishing and hunting, hiking, cross-country skiing, snowmobile trails, boat and canoe rentals, and youth camp. Perhaps the tribe will stock the forest with elk for limited hunting. User fees and rentals will return the tribe enough money to maintain the recreation area and realize a small profit, the study predicts. The tribe, obviously, must acquire the land or receive federal use permits for it.

The Kalispel business committee meets in the tribal office building. From left to right: tribal counsel Robert D. Dellwo (back to camera); Darlene Auld, secretary; Glen Nenema, chairman; Francis Cullooyah, and Edo Pierre. One member, Stanley Bluff, was absent from this 1984 meeting.

The plan, of course, incorporates the other Kalispel endeavors: the metal products company; ceremonial grounds and buffalo herd; a tribal store to sell tax-free liquors, Indian craft work, and buffalo meat and products; the Manresa historical site; a mobile-home park overlooking the Pend Oreille; pasture leasing; and the improvement or replacement of reservation homes. (Three houses were rebuilt and 16 repaired during 1981 and 1982 with Housing and Urban Development funds. The Kalispels charge that the original construction was shoddy—walls have cracked and the plumbing leaks.) All of these plans require political acumen and money. Washington State argues that tribal stores should be licensed and buy their liquor supplies from the state (an earlier tribal trading post opened in 1979 survived only two years), and consultants point out that realizing their plan will cost the Kalispels millions and depend on promotion and competent management.[53]

The Kalispels' economic environment may improve dramatically, and that of Pend Oreille County, with construction of the Ponderay Newsprint Company, a $210 million newsprint mill proposed by a consortium of newspaper publishers. The mill, near Usk, is supposed to double the tax base of the county and employ 140 persons; it will displace the Kalispel metals factory as the biggest employer in the area.

The new mill notwithstanding, the land is fundamental to the future of the Kalispels, who clung to the last shred of ancient homeland as white settlement and government fiat tore the rest from them. And there remain problems that are not economic. A generation now emerging, for example, favors keeping the "blood quantum," a specified amount of Kalispel blood for tribal membership, but knows this will slowly reduce the size of the tribe and perhaps, in time, extinguish it. The Kalispels will continue to hold onto their land, for earth is the foundation of their heritage, the record of what they have been; it sings with voices of the present, as Kalispels gather each January at Hi Nick's house to dance again the ancient Blue Jay ritual, and it echoes with voices from their past.

Notes

The following abbreviations are used in the notes:

BIA   Bureau of Indian Affairs
CIA   Commissioner of Indian Affairs
CR   H. M. Chittenden and A. T. Richardson, *Life, Letters and Travels of . . . De Smet,* 4 volumes.
Dellwo   Files of Dellwo, Rudolf & Schroeder
FRC   Federal Records Center, Seattle
HBC   Hudson's Bay Company
NA   National Archives and Records Service, Washington, D.C.
OPA   Oregon Province Archives, Society of Jesus, Gonzaga University
RCIA   *Report of the Commissioner of Indian Affairs* with year
Wilkinson Files from Wilkinson, Cragun & Barker relating to Kalispel claims case, etc., turned over to Dellwo, Rudolf & Schroeder
WSU   Washington State University

Other abbreviations are standard for legal citations, congressional documents, names of federal agencies, and land descriptions.

Parentheses do double duty; some parenthetical words identify passages in the text to which a cited source refers, and some indicate the location of sources.

When a location is not cited, the source remains with the office indicated in the note or text, is in Kalispel tribal files, or is so generally available that no specific location is necessary.

Chapter 1. White Man's Religion; White Man's Vengeance

1. C. M. Drury, *Nine Years with the Spokane Indians,* 76, 114.

2. J. Joset, "Origin of St. Ignatius," MS (OPA).

3. A number of writers have described Indian appeals for Jesuit missionaries, e. g., R. I. Burns, *Jesuits and the Indian Wars of the Northwest,* pp. 44–48; J. Fahey, *Flathead Indians,* pp. 64–88; and G. J. Garraghan, *Jesuits of the Middle United States,* 2:246–47, 288–89.

4. CR 2:472, 460. There is a question about the identity of tribes camped on the Clark Fork. De Smet called their chiefs Chalax and Hoytelpo, one of whom, Chalax, was a noted Pend Oreille shaman.

5. For names of additional Jesuit missionaries, see W. P. Schoenberg, *Paths to the Northwest,* pp. 17–52; Fahey, *Flathead Indians,* pp. 80–81. According to Drury, *Nine Years,* 190, 301, Eells and Walker regarded the Kalispel mission as closing the field to them and evidently stopped going to Pend Oreille River bay after 1843.

6. A. Hoecken, St. Ignatius mission baptismal summary (OPA); CR 2:456–57, 468; Schoenberg, *Paths,* p. 36; W. L. Davis, *History of St. Ignatius Mission,* pp. 10–11; Joset, "Origin of St. Ignatius" (OPA).

7. G. Suckley in *Reports of Explorations and Surveys,* 12:296; Drury, *Nine Years,* p. 77.

8. Joset, "Origin of St. Ignatius Mission" (OPA), and "Loyola" (OPA); Suckley, p. 297.

9. CR 2:478; Schoenberg, *Paths,* p. 37; P. J. De Smet, *Oregon Missions,* pp. 94, 105.

10. Suckley, p. 297; Drury, *Elkanah and Mary Walker, Pioneers among the Spokanes,* pp. 130–31, describes the ash as about six inches deep.

11. Joset, "Origin of St. Ignatius Mission" (OPA); Fahey, *Flathead Indians,* pp. 83–84.

12. Drury, *Nine Years,* pp. 317, 322; a Kalispel tribal resolution, May 8, 1975, eliminates Indian-custom marriage which had been accepted.

13. Joset, "Origin of St. Ignatius Mission" (OPA); Hoecken to De Smet, quoted in CR 4:1229; De Smet, *Western Missions and Missionaries,* pp. 296–303.

14. Suckley, p. 296 (game).

15. Fahey, *Flathead Indians,* p. 87 (quotation).

16. Joset, "Origin of St. Ignatius Mission" (OPA); Davis, *St. Ignatius,* pp. 19–20; CR 4:1232–33; Schoenberg, *Paths,* p. 59. Alexander, a Pend Oreille chief, chose the site, according to Hoecken's letterbook 1855–56 (OPA).

17. Burns, *Jesuits and Wars,* p. 50; Stevens to CIA, Dec. 6, 1853 (NA); K. D. Richards, *Isaac I. Stevens,* p. 147; A. H. Smith, *Archaeological Survey . . . 1957,* p. 53 (bones).

18. *Reports of Explorations and Surveys* 1:149, 151 (on p. 151 Stevens calls Kalispels "Pend Oreilles of the Lower Lake);" Stevens to CIA, Dec. 29, 1853 (NA); C. M. Gates, ed., *Messages of the Governors of the Territory of Washington*, p. 4.

19. Joset, "Origin of St. Ignatius Mission" (OPA).

20. For a description of Stevens, see Richards, *Isaac I. Stevens*, pp. xi, 18.

21. Menetrey to Stevens, Sept. 25, 1855 (NA).

22. Stevens to Bolin, Aug. 20, 1855 (NA), and letter of instructions, Stevens to Crosbie, Aug. 28, 1855 (NA). Stevens, who spelled the agent's name "Bolon," designated Bolin special agent, assigning him the tribes between the Cascades and the Bitterroots. See Stevens to Bolin, Mar. 23, 1854 (NA).

23. N. W. Durham, *History of the City of Spokane and Spokane Country* 1:274; G. W. Fuller, *History of the Pacific Northwest*, pp. 304–05; Stevens to CIA, Aug. 30, 1855 (NA).

24. Stevens to Lansdale, Oct. 26, 1855 (NA).

25. Lansdale to Stevens, Nov. 7, 1855 (NA).

26. The draft treaty and council minutes were transmitted with a letter, Stevens to CIA, Sept. 2, 1856 (NA).

27. *Ibid.* As translated by Revais, Victor referred to lands north and south of the Pend Oreille. I have inserted east and west to conform to the river's change in course from westward to northward.

28. Burns, *Jesuits and Wars*, p. 145, gives Lansdale's informal understanding; Stevens to CIA, Sept. 2, 1856 (NA).

29. Yantis to Supt. J. W. Nesmith, May 17, 1857 (NA); Steptoe to Gen. N. S. Clarke, Oct. 19, 1857 (NA). Hoecken left the missions in 1861 due to poor health.

30. C. H. Rumrill, major, 1st Washington Territory Infantry Volunteers, to Supt. C. H. Hale, June 30, 1854, in *RCIA 1854*, p. 75.

31. The Steptoe expedition has been discussed by many writers, e.g., Burns, *Jesuits and Wars*, pp. 199–220; Burns, "Pere Joset's Account of the Indian War of 1858," *Pacific Northwest Quarterly*, 38 (1947), pp. 285–307; and R. Ruby and J. Brown, *Spokane Indians*, pp. 105–13. See *Report of the Secretary of War 1858–59*, pp. 59–82. Questions about Steptoe's motive and actions continue to puzzle historians. Ruby and Brown, *Spokane Indians*, pp. 109–10, quote Steptoe as complaining that conflict no longer excites him. Richards, *Stevens*, p. 431 *n* 33, cites a letter in which Steptoe describes himself as brooding and sick with a malady later diagnosed as a brain tumor.

32. J. Teit, *Salishan Tribes*, p. 371.

33. Teit, *Salishan Tribes*, p. 369 (40 Kalispels); Joset's untitled account of 1858 war (OPA). See Burns, "Pere Joset's Account."

34. A. G. Brackett, *History of U.S. Cavalry,* p. 182, quoted in Burns, *Jesuits and Wars,* p. 230.
35. C. W. Frush, "A trip from The Dalles to Fort Owen," *Contributions to the Historical Society of Montana,* 2 (1896), pp. 340–41.
36. Teit, *Salishan Tribes,* p. 37.
37. Teit, *Salishan Tribes,* p. 37 (Spotted Coyote), p. 371; L. Kip, *Army Life on the Pacific,* p. 64.
38. Burns, *Jesuits and Wars,* p. 297, says that Wright "had lost the war," and in pages 298–319 describes the Jesuits' role in bringing about peace. On page 299, Burns disputes the usual version that the slaughter of horses forced an Indian capitulation; he says the herd belonged to the Palouse, Tilcoax, and that its destruction probably did little more than wipe out Tilcoax's wealth and improve the market for horses during the next few months. Wright to Joset, Sept. 10, 1858 (OPA).
39. Wright's report of the Spokane council appears in Senate Executive Doc. 1, 35th Congress, 1st sess. (1858, serial 975), pp. 399, 407–08. In article 5 of Wright's agreement, the army renounces vengeance. Wright's superiors criticized him for agreeing to these terms.
40. CR 3:967–70.
41. CR 2:766–67; 4:1574–75; Burns, *Jesuits and Wars,* 343–46; Fahey, *Flathead Indians,* p. 109.

Chapter 2. Kalispel Country

1. Morris Swadesh, "Salish Phonologic Geography," *Language,* 28:237, puts the Spokanes, the Pend Oreilles including the Kalispels, and Flatheads in one language group. About 1823 a Hudson's Bay Company trader reported the spread of Salish, HBC 208/e/1. G. Mengarini, "Memoirs" (OPA), speaks of conversing from the United States to the Willamette in Salish. V. F. Ray, *Sanpoil and Nespelem,* p. 10, classifies interior Salish by dialect. J. Giorda, J. Bandini, and G. Mengarini, *Dictionary* (1877–79). According to his deposition, p. 37, June 18, 1951 in Indian Claims Commission Docket 94, A. H. Smith could not determine when the Kalispels first occupied the Pend Oreille valley.
2. F. W. Hodge, *Handbook of American Indians,* part 1, pp. 51–52, 646; Lucy Peuse also told this story of mistaking a camas field for a lake; J. Teit, *Salishan Tribes,* pp. 296, 298; R. G. Thwaites, ed., *Original Journals of the Lewis and Clark Expedition,* 4:119; J. Joset, "Foundation of St. Ignatius Mission among the Kalispels," MS (OPA). Many Kalispels say they never heard these names.
3. Teit, *Salishan Tribes,* pp. 252, 358, identifies Kettle Falls as the trade center, but D. H. Chance, "Influences of the Hudson's Bay Company," p. 23, could not find evidence in documents of trading there, al-

though much gambling went on. D. Thompson, *Narrative,* Glover ed., p. 336, calls Kettle Falls "a general rendezvous for News, Trade, and settling disputes;" G. Ayars, et al., "Cultural Resource Survey of the Kalispel Trail," 1: 24, 39, 58–59, reported no artifacts found on the old trail; F. Libra, "Hudson's Bay-Kalispel Trail," *Big Smoke 1978,* pp. 11–24; V. F. Ray, in testimony, p. 190, Indian Claims Commission Docket 94, is careful to explain that the terms Upper and Lower Pend Oreille "do not necessarily imply a cultural relationship."

4. Teit, *Salishan Tribes,* pp. 349–50; Joset's letter to an unnamed Jesuit, June 24, 1883 (OPA); E. S. Curtis, *North American Indian,* 7: 71–72.

5. J. Fahey, *Flathead Indians,* pp. 66–67 (Iroquois); Teit, *Salishan Tribes,* pp. 349–50.

6. See D. Collier, et al., *Archaeology of the Upper Columbia Region,* pp. 110–14; *Newport Miner,* Oct. 13, 1927; Curtis, *North American Indian,* 7: 71–72, is virtually alone in saying that a small bone spike or dentalium shell in the nasal septum was in vogue until about 1845.

7. A. H. Smith, petitioner's exhibit 65, Indian Claims Commission Docket 94. His pagination relates to sections of a manuscript from which he extracted information; it is uninformative and therefore not used in this or subsequent citations. Smith spent more time among the Kalispels than any other investigator, the summers of 1936, 1937, and 1938, with later brief visits; Ray spent a week or two in the mid-thirties; Leslie Spier, a day or two; and Stuart Chalfant, a few weeks in 1952. Teit seems to have relied on Michel Revais, a Flathead with Kalispel relatives, for much of his data and quotes Revais from time to time.

8. Smith, ex. 65, *passim;* in his testimony before the commission, pp. 95–96, Smith estimates 800 Kalispels lived in a winter village between 1850–60 "on the present reservation;" Teit, *Salishan Tribes,* pp. 345–46 (caribou).

9. V. F. Ray, "Native Villages and Groupings of the Columbia Basin," *Pacific Northwest Quarterly,* 27 (1936), pp. 128–29, lists 14 Kalispel villages, more or less permanent; Smith, ex. 65, provides a gazeteer which, in general, confirms Ray's list. Specific sites, although in the same general areas, moved for dry wood and other supplies.

10. Smith, ex. 65, *passim;* Joset, "Ethnology of the Rocky Mountain Indians," MS (OPA).

11. Unless otherwise noted, descriptions of Kalispel digging, hunting, and fishing generally follow Smith, ex. 65. The Kalispel tale is from the recollections of Lucy and Antoine Peuse, 1970. Alston V. Thoms, principal investigator for Washington State University's Calispell Valley Archaeological Project, in a personal communication to the author, observes that thousands of earth ovens—"more than anyone dreamed"—were built on both sides of the river through the millennia. Almost every place where four natural resources come together, camas oven sites can be found be-

tween Newport and Jared. The resources are: sandy sediments that provide easy digging and a dry work place; adjacent forest for firewood; rocky slopes below high terraces that provide rocks; and nearby wet meadows that produce camas. The valley apparently contains thousands of ovens and hundreds of thousands of fire-cracked rocks used in their construction. Project workers excavated portions of a 100-acre tract where a paper mill may be built, finding ovens dating from 4,150 years ago to recent times. On the basis of tools unearthed in the project area, however, only initial processing appears to have taken place at oven sites. Except for cooking relatively small quantities of meat, there is little artifact evidence that other activities occurred at those sites. Once cooked in the ovens, the roots may have been dried before being carried to villages where they were ground or pounded into cakes. This secondary processing of camas, as well as the manufacture and maintenance of stone tools, and other domestic activities, apparently took place at residential sites. At short-term residential sites on both sides of the river, archaeological searchers also found evidence of what may be the floors of prehistoric mat lodges.

12. Thoms, personal communication; Thompson, *Narrative*, Glover ed., p. 298.

13. The practice of breaking off branches is described in F. B. Schmid's recollections, *Colville Examiner*, Feb. 12, 1927.

14. Kingfisher tale, Antoine Peuse, Aug. 17, 1980.

15. C. M. Drury, *Nine Years*, pp. 113–14 (quotation).

16. Curtis, *North American Indian*, 7:88 (dance).

17. *Ibid.*, 7:88.

18. Ray, "Cultural Distributions: Plateau," Univ. of Calif. *Anthropological Records*, 8:2, 228.

19. Curtis, *North American Indian*, 7:75.

20. *Ibid.*, 7:89 (Skaip).

21. Smith deposition, pp. 47–48, Indian Claims Commission Docket 94.

22. Teit, *Salishan Tribes*, p. 351, quoting Revais on acquisition of the horse. See Francis Haines, "Northward Spread of Horses among the Plains Indians," *American Anthropologist*, 40 (1938):429–37.

23. Ray, *Sanpoil and Nespelem*.

24. Teit, *Salishan Tribes*, pp. 312–13, describes the separate groups; De Smet, CR 3:995, mentions the divisions, calling them Upper and Lower Kalispels; Suckley, on the basis of Hoecken's information, also notes two bands, *Reports of Exploration*, 1:291–301; Smith, Indian Claims Commission Docket 94, deposition, p. 89, indicates that Kalispel participation in buffalo hunts were limited to a few families each year responding to a Flathead invitation; Antoine Peuse, Aug. 17, 1970 (Coyote).

25. Lucy and Antoine Peuse, July 21, 1970; Ray, "Cultural Distribution," p. 229 (women in assemblies).

26. "Ethnology of Rocky Mountain Indians," MS (OPA); Antoine Peuse, n.d. (boy).

27. W. P. Winans to Supt. S. Ross, Aug. 1, 1870 (Winans papers, WSU).

28. Ray, *Cultural Relations in the Plateau of Northwestern America,* p. 149, names the Colvilles and others "as the most representative of older levels and the fundamental aspects of Plateau cultures"; F. W. Hodge, *Handbook of American Indians,* 1 : 51–52 (scalping); Teit, *Salishan Tribes,* p. 360 (wars).

29. Thompson, *Narrative,* Glover ed., p. 331 (white earth); Antoine Peuse, Aug. 17, 1970 (smoking).

30. Teit, *Salishan Tribes,* p. 315; Ray, *Sanpoil and Nespelem,* p. 21, says the 1782–83 epidemic killed from one-third to one-half the Indians of the area.

31. Biographical information on Thompson, *Narrative,* Glover ed., pp. xiv–lxvii. Scholars who traced his path include T. C. Elliott, "David Thompson's Journeys in the Pend Oreille Country," *Washington Historical Quarterly,* 23 (1932), pp. 18–24, 88–93, 173–76, and Allan H. Smith, "David Thompson in the Pend Oreille River Valley, 1809," *Record, 1961,* pp. 8–15. The text follows Smith.

32. Thompson's journal appears in several edited editions. The text relies on those edited by J. B. Tyrell, 1916, and Richard Glover, 1962. Both editors used T. C. Elliott's accounts. The occurrences in the text appear in Thompson, *Narrative,* Glover ed., pp. 295–96.

33. J. Hector in *Palliser Papers,* pp. 467–68.

34. Thompson, *Narrative,* Glover ed., pp. 297–98.

35. *Ibid.,* pp. 298–99. Elliott says Thompson went only as far as Cusick but Smith argues that he reached the vicinity of Tiger, 26½ miles below Cusick. Second trip, Glover ed., pp. 307–09.

36. Joset, "Foundation of St. Ignatius Mission among the Kalispels," MS (OPA).

37. George Simpson to Governor and Committee, HBC, Nov. 25, 1841, speaks of "exhaustion" of the Colville district, HBC D.4/59/49–56, quoted by D. H. Chance, *Influences,* p. 53. In table 15, Chance shows the purchases of Indian products, including leather lodges, leather shirts, leggings, gum, roots, and berries, bark, horses, etc., and Indian products exported, table 12. On p. 65, Chance lists the Pend Oreilles among the traders of horse accoutrements at Colville, 1827–28, by which he appears to mean Kalispels. (See his terms, p. 10.) Thompson, *Narrative,* Glover ed., p. 304 (woolens).

38. Antoine Peuse (Sandpoint); Chance, *Influences,* 42 (repairs); Alexander Ross report, Mar. 10, 1825, HBC B.69/e/1 (Saleesh); C. T. Heron journal, HBC B.45 / a / 1 (council); Thompson, *Narrative,* Glover ed.,

p. 303 (canoes), p. 331 (couriers), p. 332 (near Spokane House); Francis Heron to John McLoughlin, Jan. 15, 1830, quoted by Chance, p. 105 (horses).

39. Joset, "Foundations of St. Ignatius;" Chance, *Influences*, table 1, p. 19, shows Pend Oreilles [Kalispels] trading each month between April and October, 1830, and table 8, p. 56, lists furs received from tribes in 1830; on p. 99, he quotes Duncan Finlayson's journal, 1834, on Kutenai incursions; Winans census, June 1870 (horses) (Winans papers, WSU).

40. Thompson, *Narrative*, Glover ed., pp. 332–34; Spokane district journal, HBC, 1822–23, quoted by Chance, *Influences*, p. 88; Joset, "Origin of St. Ignatius Mission," MS (OPA), and "A Quarter of a Century among the Savages," MS (OPA).

Chapter 3. Promises

1. Supt. J. W. Nesmith to CIA, Nov. 19, 1858 (NA).
2. Yantis to Nesmith, July 20 and Dec. 7, 1857 (NA).
3. Lugenbeel to Supt. E. R. Geary, July 18, 1859 (NA). Four companies of the 9th Infantry opened the post on June 21, 1859.
4. Yantis to Nesmith, Dec. 7, 1857 (NA).
5. H. Bancroft, *Works*, 31: 231–32, 251; D. H. Meinig, *Great Columbia Plain*, p. 214 (trails); W. J. Trimble, *Mining Advance*, pp. 25–26.
6. J. Fahey, *Flathead Indians*, pp. 107, 109; G. W. Fuller, *History of the Pacific Northwest*, pp. 304–05, summarizes interior gold rushes 1855–64.
7. Yantis to Nesmith, May 17, 1857 (NA).
8. R. M. Kvasnicka and H. J. Viola, *Commissioners of Indian Affairs*, p. 83 (Greenwood), p. 90–91 (Dole). In testimony before the Indian Claims Commission, docket 81 (Coeur d'Alenes v. U.S.) Nancy O. Lurie, a noted anthropologist, calls "the location of various agencies and various districts . . . extremely confused" between 1855 and 1873. See transcript, pp. 19–20.
9. Charles Hutchins, Flathead agent, to Supt. Hale, June 30, 1863 (NA); R. I. Burns, *Jesuits and the Indian Wars of the Northwest*, p. 115.
10. N. W. Durham, *History of the City of Spokane and Spokane Country*, 1: 276; the California volunteers were replaced in 1862 by Washington Territory volunteers and they, by Oregon volunteers in 1865. Six months later, a company of the 14th Infantry, regulars, returned. Regulars would garrison Colville until it was closed in 1882.
11. Kvasnicka and Viola, *Commissioners*, p. 91; the end of treaty-making was written into the appropriations act of March 3, 1871, 16 *Stat.* 514.
12. J. Teit, *Salishan Tribes*, pp. 310–11, says Chewelahs are Ka-

lispels who moved into the Colville valley, which modern Chewelahs confirm. Marie Grant, interviewed Nov. 22, 1983, says that her great-great-grandfather was among the Kalispels who settled halfway between the Colvilles and Kalispels after marrying Colville women. J. Joset, "Colville Mission," MS (OPA), speculates that the Chewelahs were Kalispels who moved, after the closure of St. Ignatius in 1854, to be nearer to the Colville mission. The Chewelahs, consequently, appear to be Kalispels living in the Chewelah area. In her memoirs, Alice Abrahamson, a Chewelah, in the *Inland Register,* Feb. 29, 1984, says Nez Perces, Colvilles, and some Canadian Indians joined the Chewelah band. On Moses: W. N. Bischoff deposition, p. 159, Ind. Cl. Com. Docket 94; *RCIA 1874,* p. 82 (renegades).

13. Durham, *History of Spokane,* 1:291 (memorial), 1:267, 269 (Pinkney City); W. P. Winans to Terr. Supt., July 31, 1871 (Winans papers, WSU).

14. Special Commissioner J. P. C. Shanks in *RCIA 1873,* p. 163 (Winans); Joset to an unnamed Jesuit, June 24, 1883 (OPA); W. P. Schoenberg, *Gonzaga University,* p. 48 *n 7,* says that in 1877 one Jesuit out of 43 worked exclusively among whites; by 1893, 27 of 142 served among whites and 51 in Indian missions.

15. Winans, *RCIA 1870,* p. 464; Winans' annual report to CIA, Sept. 1, 1871 (Winans papers, WSU). Winans was well acquainted with whites and Indians of the area; he lived 13 years in the Colville valley, held various county offices, and served in the 1871 territorial legislature.

16. Winans, abstract of articles issued to Indians for the quarter ended Sept. 30, 1870 (Winans papers, WSU); *RCIA 1870,* p. 486; Schoenberg, *Gonzaga,* pp. 19, 22 (Tosi); Winans to Terr. Supt., 1870 report (Winans papers, WSU).

17. C. J. Kappler, *Indian Affairs: Laws and Treaties,* 1:915; *RCIA 1873,* pp. 294–95.

18. Winans to Supt. T. I. McKenny, May 27, 1872 (Winans papers, WSU).

19. Winans to McKenny, June 30, 1872 (Winans papers, WSU).

20. Terr. Supt. R. H. Milroy in *RCIA 1873,* p. 294; E. H. Ludington, inspector general, to CIA, Aug. 11, 1872 (NA); Winans to Terr. Supt., Feb. 5, 1871 (war) (NA); John Egan, Capt., 33rd Inf., to CIA, Dec. 24, 1870 (60 soldiers) (NA).

21. Exec. Order, July 2, 1872; *RCIA 1873,* pp. 295–96 (quotations).

22. Shanks in *RCIA 1873,* p. 163; Winans to Garfielde, July 15, 1872 (Winans papers, WSU).

23. R. Ruby and J. Brown, *Spokane Indians,* p. 157 *n 45;* Bancroft, *Works,* 31:280 *n 33* ("winds"); note, n.d., no signature, attached to Winans' copy of Ex. Doc. 102, 43rd Cong., first sess., "Proposed Indian Reservations in Idaho and Washington Territories," (Winans papers, WSU); Shanks, "Report on Indian Frauds," p. 457 (Simms).

24. S. T. Sherwood, agency farmer, to Winans, July 31, 1872 (quotations) (Winans papers, WSU); Simms in *RCIA 1874,* pp. 328–29.

25. Fahey, *Flathead Indians,* p. 169 (buffalo). Winans, in letters to the terr. supt., Jan. 31 and March —, 1871, reported the Spokanes, Okanogans, and Calispels coming for medicines and blankets (Winans papers, WSU).

26. The commission's report, *RCIA 1873,* pp. 157–62, dated Nov. 17, 1873. Shanks and the other commissioners conferred with Indians as scattered as Wyoming and California. Shanks, "Frauds," pp. 16–17 (power to hold).

27. Shanks commission report, *op. cit.* The parentheses are Shanks'.

28. Shanks found religious competition especially troublesome on the Nez Perce reservation, and the quotation refers to this, but also mentions religious rivalry in the Colville area.

29. Simms in *RCIA 1874,* p. 328.

30. Shanks, *RCIA 1873,* pp. 163–64; *RCIA 1874,* pp. 14–15.

31. See Sen. Misc. Doc. 32, 43rd Cong., first sess., Jan. 20, 1874, a letter from the Secretary of the Interior to the Chairman, Committee on Indian Affairs, asking a reservation for Indians of the Colville agency, naming the Kalispels among prospective residents; report of a civil and military commission to the Nez Perces, *Report of Secretary of Interior 1877,* p. 611.

32. Joset, "Colville mission," MS (OPA) (dreamer); see also report of civil and military commission to the Nez Perces, *op. cit.,* pp. 607–13, esp. 608–09.

33. *RCIA 1874,* p. 82; Fuller, *History of Pacific Northwest,* pp. 273–74 (Smohalla).

34. Burns, *Jesuits and Wars,* p. 407 (Cataldo); Joset to Simms, July 4, 1877 (OPA); Gazzoli to Blanchet, Aug. 30, 1877 (undated clipping from *Oregonian,* (OPA). See House Ex. Doc. 1, part 2, "War of 1877," vol. 1, 45th Cong., second sess. (serial 1794).

35. W. J. Pollock, Indian inspector, to Secretary of Interior, Nov. 30, 1880, stamped "received" Oct. 14, 1915 (NA); Durham, *History of Spokane,* 1: 325–27, describes settlement.

36. Burns, *Jesuits and Wars,* pp. 416–18; *Report of Secretary of War 1877,* p. 647 (serial 1794); P. Ronan, Flathead agent, to CIA, Jan. 2, 1878 (corrals) (NA).

37. *Report of Secretary of War 1877,* p. 581; Victor's letter, written by Simms, enclosed with Simms to CIA, Oct. 27, 1877 (NA).

38. A. Diomedi, "Indian Missions," *Woodstock Letters,* 8 (1879), p. 32–41.

39. *Ibid.*

40. Ronan to CIA, Dec. 10, 1877 (NA).

41. Ronan to CIA, Jan. 2, 1878 (NA).

42. Cain to Howard, Dec. 12, 1877, in *Report of Secretary of War 1877,* pp. 639–41.

43. Interstate Commerce Commission Valuation Docket 959 (1929): *Northern Pacific Railway et al., passim;* p. 603 sketches a brief railroad history. See also *United States v. Northern Pacific Ry. et al.,* Equity E 4389, Eastern Washington district court (1939) (FRC).

44. Joset to unnamed Jesuit, June 24, 1883 (OPA). Joset does not name the chief.

45. S. Waters to CIA, June 26, 1884 (NA).

46. *Ibid.*

47. Waters' obituary, *Spokesman-Review,* Dec. 24, 1902; Waters to CIA, Dec. 26, 1884, referring to a similar letter, Nov. 29, 1884 (NA).

48. *RCIA 1885,* 183; *RCIA 1887,* 449.

49. Waters to CIA, July 23, 1886 (NA). Fort Coeur d'Alene was established on Lake Coeur d'Alene in 1878 and later renamed Fort Sherman.

50. F. P. Prucha, *Indian Policy in the U.S.,* pp. 27–29; *Report of the Indian Rights Association 1884,* p. 5.

51. Kvasnicka and Viola, *Commissioners,* pp. 158–59 (Hayt), pp. 186–87 (J. D. C. Atkins, CIA 1885–88); Prucha, *Indian Policy,* pp. 27–28 (quotation).

52. Northwest Commission to CIA, Apr. 3, 1887 (NA); Van Gorp is characterized by Schoenberg, *Gonzaga,* p. 149. For the work of the commission, see House Ex. Doc. 63, 30th Cong., first session (1888), serial 2557. The commission also thought Sandpoint a cheaper place to hold a council because they would not have housing on the Pend Oreille River (pp. 40–43). *Spokane Falls Morning Review,* Feb. 25, 1887 (quotation).

53. House Ex. Doc. 63, 30th Cong., first session, pp. 40–46.

54. *Ibid.*

55. Lee's letter to the Northwest Commission, June 17, 1887, appears with its printed report, *op. cit.*

56. For example, W. Smead, Flathead agent, to CIA, Sept. 23, 1902 (NA), calling the unratified "treaty" the "cause of much complaints from these Indians." See House Ex. Doc. 63 (1888), p. 12, terms; report of meeting, pp. 40–46; printed contract, pp. 56–58.

Chapter 4. **Settlement Along the Pend Oreille**

1. Lloyd Crown in *Big Smoke 1975,* p. 35.

2. "Kalispel Land Acquisitions," Indian Claims Commission Docket 94 (acres); R. L. Dingee, *Historical Sketches of Pend Oreille County,* pp. 27–29; *RCIA 1889,* p. 283; L. Hudson et al., *Cultural Resource Overview,* 2: 345; C. R. Barker in *Spokesman-Review,* March 29, 1953.

3. L. J. Jared in *Big Smoke 1979,* p. 32; commanding general, Depart-

ment of the Columbia, telegram to Adjutant General of the Army, Aug. 7, 1889 (haystacks) (NA); CIA to C. S. Vorhees, April 28, 1888 (NA); CIA to Secretary of Interior, July 27, 1889 (NA).

4. *RCIA 1890*, p. 218.

5. [Demersville, Montana] *Inter-lake,* March 28, 1890, quoted in C. B. Haskell, "On Reconnaisance for the Great Northern;" Fahey, *Flathead Indians,* p. 258 (towns); *Oregonian,* Jan. 1, 1892 and June 18, 1893 (Great Northern).

6. "Kalispel Land Acquisitions," *op. cit.;* Bureau of Land Management master title plats: the areas nearest the river, T 33 and 34N, R44EWM, and T 31, 32, 33, and 34N, R43EWM, were surveyed in 1891 and 1892; *Spokesman-Review,* Sept. 3, 1893 (*Dora*).

7. *RCIA 1891*, p. 443; *Spokane Chronicle,* Nov. 14, 1892, quoting Peter Ronan (Kutenais).

8. BLM master title plats.

9. Northern Pacific grants, Stevens County deed books, C, p. 79 (1894) and pp. 168, 208, 222, and 269 (1895).

10. J. W. Bubb to CIA, Nov. 30, 1894 (NA).

11. Mullan and McCammon to CIA, Dec. 11, 1894 (NA); CIA to Secretary of Interior, March 13, 1896 (counsel for tribe) (NA).

12. The land contested is lots 1, 6, and 12, Sec. 30, T 34N, R44EWM, for which LeClerc applied May 28, 1894; first asst. secretary, Dept. of Interior, to CIA, Oct. 20, 1909 (NA); deposition of John Brown, settler, to C. Hunt, Sept. 25, 1909; deposition of N. LeClerc, Oct. 1, 1909; Masseslow deposition, Sept. 23, 1909 (NA).

13. Bubb to CIA, Nov. 3, 1893 (NA) and April 19, 1894 (NA); Bubb pension file 1187057 (NA); records of inspection, No. 9026: Colville, Dec. 16, 1895, reports alleged kickbacks, etc. (NA).

14. Bubb to CIA, Nov. 30, 1894 (NA).

15. M. C. Howe, *Historical Sketches of Pend Oreille County,* pp. 11, 15–16; CIA to Wilson, n.d. (NA).

16. Bubb to CIA, Aug. 29, 1895 (NA). The claims are in T 33 and 34N, R44EWM, three on the west side of the river near modern Cusick. Bubb found no white claims for these three. The list of Indian claims also is in General Land Office file 1895/98978 (NA).

17. Bubb to CIA, Aug. 29, 1895 (NA).

18. Special Agent Clair Hunt to CIA, May 24, 1909, mentions the Kalispels' use of land (NA); forest reserve, 29 *Stat.* 903; Senate Doc. 105, 55th Cong., first sess., (1897); the Priest River reserve was closed in 1908 and sections transferred to the Kaniksu and Pend Oreille forests.

19. Department of Interior, *Annual Report 1905,* p. 72 ("moral right"); GLO to Britton & Gray, Northern Pacific attorneys, July 21, 1896; Northern Pacific to CIA, March 3, 1899; Willis Van Devanter, asst. atty. gen., to Secretary of Interior, Feb. 26, 1899 (all NA). Dept. of Interior, *Annual*

Report 1906, pp. 167–68, says the Northern Pacific gave the U.S. a quit claim deed to 2,711.86 acres of Kalispel land. The railroad relinquished its claim under an act of July 1, 1898 (30 *Stat.* 620), revising the terms for land exchange.

20. *Spokesman–Review,* Sept. 3, 1893.

21. Pend Oreille County deeds, book A, pp. 66, 117, 451–52; BLM cadastral survey plats; *Spokesman-Review,* Sept. 3, 1893 (house and meadow); *Spokesman-Review* magazine, May 8, 1949 (*Volunteer*); Howe, *Historical Sketches*, p. 43 (*Metaline*); *Newport Miner,* July 20, 1911 (home). There were four LeClerc brothers—Napoleon, Felix, Arsen, and Joe—but Joe's name does not appear on deeds. Apparently only Felix married.

22. *Newport Miner,* June 25, 1908, dates major floods of the settlement period in 1887, 1894, 1903, and 1908.

23. *Spokesman-Review,* Feb. 22, 1896, reports a bill for river improvement; A. E. Davidson to Rep. S. C. Hyde, quoted in *Spokesman-Review,* Feb. 28, 1896.

24. Bradley bought in T 32, 33, and 34N, R43EWM; T 32, 33, 34, and 35N, R44EWM; T 31 and 32N, R45EWM, T 31 and 32N, R46EWM, according to the *Newport Miner,* June 20, 1912.

25. Coeur d'Alene & Spokane Ry., Kootenai County, Idaho, articles of incorporation No. 89, Oct. 21, 1902; Blackwell was among the incorporators of the Spokane & Inland Empire in 1904, *Poor's Manual of Railroads 1909,* p. 1300; *Spokane Daily Chronicle,* June 14, 1905 (merger by stock increase).

26. U.S. Forest Survey Release No. 2: *Forest Statistics: Pend Oreille County, Washington,* estimates that Pend Oreille County was 95 percent timbered with 525,000 acres of merchantable timber, an estimated nine billion board feet. Not all species were salable, at the time, and 31.4 percent of the county's land was held in forest reserves.

27. Panhandle Lumber Co., articles of incorporation, Kootenai County No. 611, March 20, 1906; Idaho & Washington Northern, Kootenai No. 372, March 25, 1907. Of 9,402 shares issued in the railroad, 7,700 (82 percent) were held by Illinois and Pennsylvania stockholders.

28. The map appears in *Railway Age Gazette,* 49:21 (Nov. 18, 1910), p. 962; B. A. Sharp, Coeur d'Alene supt., to CIA, Dec. 17, 1927 (NA) (compensation). Three Kalispel claimants, Amos Nick, Isabel Abrahamson, and Mary Andrews selected allotments formerly occupied by Tse-Tse-ah (or CCA) after the railroad filed right-of-way maps, approved by GLO April 4, 1910; report of special meeting, directors of the I&WN, March 20, 1909 (Secretary of State, Washington state, No. 3665).

29. According to the *Newport Miner,* Dec. 15, 1938, "30 Years Ago," Panhandle bought Usk for $22,500 and the Stecker site for Ione for $10,400.

30. *Newport Miner,* Sept. 7, 1911; according to Howe, *Historical*

Sketches, 23, F. G. Jordan produced cement there in 1901 but soon gave up.
    31. *RCIA 1897*, p. 168; CIA to B. F. Barge, chairman of the commission, March 14, 1897 (NA).
    32. J. M. Webster, Colville agent, to CIA, July 18, 1905 (NA) and April 3, 1909 (NA) summarizing a series of letters on the Kalispel situation; *Annual Report 1931*, Association of Graduates, West Point, June 10, 1931, pp. 115–16, contains Webster's obituary with a brief review of his career. Webster gave a "notice" to Masseslow, dated June 15, 1907, that the chief could show, declaring the Indians' right to their land.
    33. C. F. Hauke, 2d asst. commissioner, to Webster, n.d. [Sept. 1911] (NA); Prucha, *Indian Policy*, pp. 39–40, quotes the *Report of the Indian Rights Association 1886*, p. 9 (Dawes); Webster to CIA, April 3, 1909 (NA).
    34. CIA to Webster, Oct. 28, 1908 (NA); Webster to CIA, April 3, 1909 (NA); *Newport Miner*, Jan. 14, 1909 (LeClerc) and Jan. 21, 1909 (jail).
    35. CIA to Webster, Feb. 2, 1909 (Jones); Webster to CIA, April 1 (smallpox) and April 3, 1909 (well off) (all NA).
    36. Webster to CIA, May 5, 1910 and Feb. 26, 1912 (NA); *Spokesman-Review*, Sept. 30 and Oct. 9, 1911 (Fair).
    37. Webster to CIA, May 5, Oct. 1, and Dec. 20, 1910 (NA); Supervisor Oscar H. Lipps to CIA, Aug. 19, 1911 (Cusick) (NA). Miles, at Fort Spokane, had been turned over to the Department of the Interior Aug. 28, 1899, for an Indian school after the army closed it, and was used temporarily as an agency and sanitarium.
    38. CIA to Hunt, April 22, 1909; Hunt to CIA, Nov. 8 and 9, 1909, with depositions of Brown, LeClerc, and Masseslow (all NA); Poindexter offered a bill in Congress (HR 32516, Feb. 4, 1911) for LeClerc's relief, which did not pass. Hunt, incidentally, would become Stevens county engineer and state surveyor general, 1920–24.
    39. Hunt to CIA, Nov. 9, 1909 (NA). The acreage is authorized by amendment, Feb. 28, 1891, to the Dawes act.
    40. Hunt to CIA, Nov. 9, 1909; Webster to CIA, Jan. 20, 1912, reviews Hunt's and Hill's work (NA).
    41. Powersite withdrawal No. 72, July 2, 1906; revoked, according to the *Newport Miner*, Dec. 21, 1911, which lists the land affected; May 16, 1912, water right; CIA to Poindexter, July 19, 1912, on legislation necessary to allot withdrawn areas (NA).
    42. GLO to CIA, May 13, 1909, denying permission on the ground that the law "did not permit the cutting of timber"; *Spokesman-Review*, July 2, 1911 (visit). In a brief autobiography written in 1958, Taelman says he was the only Salish-speaking priest then at Gonzaga; he misstates the date of Masseslow's appeal as 1910 (OPA).
    43. *Spokesman-Review*, April 1, 1912 ("pitiful"); *Newport Miner*, Feb. 8, 1912; McChesney, supt. of Spokane Indian school, to CIA, April 15, 1912 (NA).

44. *Newport Miner,* Feb. 1, 1912; Taelman autobiography (OPA).
45. W. P. Schoenberg, *Paths to the Northwest,* p. 282 (Gonzaga); *Spokesman-Review,* Sept. 23, 1912 (music) and Jan. 1, 1913 (church).
46. Taelman in *Spokesman-Review,* Jan. 1, 1913.
47. Taelman MS, n. d. (OPA).
48. Schoenberg, *Paths,* p. 299.
49. Webster to CIA, Feb. 26, 1912, commenting on the recommendation of Supervisor Fred L. Baker, stated in Baker to Webster, Feb. 13, 1912 (FRC). Baker drafted proposed legislation for a Kalispel school. *Newport Miner,* Feb. 1 and March 21, 1912.
50. *Newport Miner,* July 20 and Aug. 3, 1911. Merryweather sold subsequently to Lee Wood, Spokane (*Miner,* Dec. 2, 1937).
51. Memo, Lane to President, March 21, 1914 (NA); Ex. Order No. 1904, March 23, 1914; J. Cole, register, to Commissioner, GLO, April 7, 1914 (NA).

Chapter 5. **Learning Through Neglect**

1. Griva diary, box 2, Griva papers (OPA); typescript autobiography, pp. 45, 82–83, 84 (OPA).
2. Griva autobiography, pp. 106, 118; diary, March 19 and 20, 1914; Chancellor, Diocese of Seattle, to Griva, Feb. 12, 1914 (OPA). Eastern Washington would fall under the Spokane diocese established a month later, on March 18, 1914.
3. Griva autobiography, p. 107 (OPA).
4. *Ibid.,* pp. 120–21; *Spokesman-Review,* March 26, 1915, estimated the cost of the church at $2,000.
5. CIA to Colgrove, Oct. 22, 1912; Report on Coeur d'Alene agency 1914, n.d. (received in the Indian office June 29, 1915); Colgrove to CIA, Jan. 30, 1914, reports four bids for construction of the Kalispel and Kutenai schools, the lowest by D. W. Parks at $3,650 plus $60 for wells and $45 for outhouses (all NA).
6. J. M. Johnson, Colville superintendent, to CIA, Sept. 2, 1915, estimating that 23 percent of the Colville children are in public schools (FRC); Indian office circular 1014 (tuition).
7. Colgrove to CIA, April 25, 1915 and Oct. 30, 1916 ("intention") (FRC).
8. Otis B. Goodell, supervisor, to CIA, Sept. 30, 1916 ("careless"); William E. Humphries, supervisor, to CIA, Dec. 13, 1916 (English) (NA).
9. Humphries' report, Dec. 9, 1919; Colgrove to CIA, Oct. 30, 1916 (godsend) and April 29, 1918 (jobs); Inman, incidentally, was attempting to resign to transfer to clerical work (NA).
10. Resolution, Pend Oreille County commissioners, Aug. 8, 1939, for

replacing bridge; J. C. Stegner, county engineer, to supervisor, Kaniksu National Forest, March 28, 1939, gives history of bridge at Usk (Pend Oreille County engineer's files); *Newport Miner,* May 18 and Nov. 16, 1911 (I&WN service); D. T. Mason, *Timber Ownership and Lumber Production in the Inland Empire,* p. 13 (profits); *Poor's Manual of Railroads 1916,* p. 510 (I&WN); Blackwell borrowed heavily from Panhandle trying to forestall foreclosure; Blackwell Lumber Co., certificate of amendment to articles of incorporation, Kootenai County No. 61, June 19, 1916. Blackwell died in 1922.

11. U.S. Forest Service, *Forest Statistics: Pend Oreille County* (1937), pp. 2–4.

12. *Newport Miner,* Jan. 25, 1912 (taxes), June 24 and July 1, 1920 (quotations).

13. Alice Ignace testimony, Indian Claims Commission Docket 94 (influenza); Goodall to CIA, Sept. 30, 1916 (NA).

14. Colgrove to CIA, April 28, 1915 (NA).

15. Colgrove, 1915 Coeur d'Alene agency report (NA).

16. Supervisor F. A. Baker to CIA, Dec. 27, 1911 ("demoralizing"); *Spokesman-Review,* Sept. 30 and Oct. 11, 1911 and Sept. 9, 1917. In 1911 the *Spokesman-Review* counted 21 tribes numbering 696 Indians at the Fair: Oct. 9, 1911. The state attorney general ruled in 1913 that Indians must have fishing licenses, according to the *Spokesman-Review,* Oct. 25, 1913.

17. Coeur d'Alene superintendent, annual report, June 30, 1928 (FRC); letter, unsigned, received at the Coeur d'Alene agency July 30, 1935 (FRC).

18. See R. M. Kvasnicka and H. J. Viola, *Commissioners of Indian Affairs,* pp. 226, 234–35.

19. Humphries to CIA, Dec. 19, 1919 (Inman); Coeur d'Alene superintendent Lawshe annual report 1920; Lawshe to CIA, Nov. 10, 1920; Humphries report 1920 (NA). Under Knox, 15 or 16 attended.

20. Prucha, *Indian Policy,* p. 42; Indian Office circular 771, Sept. 18, 1913 and circular 857, April 5, 1914; Kvasnicka and Viola, *Commissioners,* pp. 246–47; Colgrove to CIA, Feb. 18, 1914 (NA).

21. CIA to Otto Gut, Colbert, Wash., Oct. 19, 1916 (NA).

22. Colgrove to CIA, Feb. 9, 1916, gives history of the island, including a deposition by Paul Masseslow, Feb. 5, 1916; Lawshe to CIA, Aug. 15, 1923 (relinquishment); Indian Office internal memo, Aug. 24, 1923, drops reservation of Indian island (NA).

23. Panhandle Lumber Co. to Secretary of Interior, Sept. 15, 1913; CIA to Panhandle, Nov. 3, 1913 (NA); Lawshe to CIA, Jan. 20, 1925 (Dalkena); T. White, forester, to Lawshe, 1920 timber report (NA); E. E. Hupp, county agent, to CIA, July 26, 1924 and reply, Aug. 13, 1924, on T. N. Parks' application (NA); CIA to Lawshe, Nov. 8, 1921 (Diamond)

(NA); general timber sale regulations, April 10, 1920; C. M. Knight to CIA, Dec. 8, 1919, reports lumber companies paying $4 to $4.35 per thousand for Coeur d'Alene reservation timber (NA).

24. Lawshe to CIA, Jan. 20, 1925 (NA).

25. *Spokesman-Review*, Nov. 20, 1911, named attorney Harve Phipps; Feb. 28, 1915 (guardian); Sept. 21, 1905 (ITA); Jan. 4, 1912 (Toppenish); April 18, 1916 (lobby).

26. Opinions of the Washington state attorney general 1935–36, p. 127.

27. Act of March 3, 1863, 12 *Stat.* 765; quotation from the noted Indian counselor, Ernest L. Wilkinson, "Highly Speculative Nature of Indian Tribal Suits," a paper quoted by Nancy O. Lurie, "Indian Claims Commission Act," *Annals of the American Academy of Political and Social Science*, 311: 57. Lewis description based on report of physical exam for Washington National Guard, Feb. 11, 1908 (Washington state archives), a letter from Spokane attorney Philip S. Brooke, Sr., to me, Nov. 21, 1983, and a story and photo in *Spokane Woman*, Sept. 23, 1926.

28. PL 68-235; see House Report 566, 68th Cong., first sess. (1923); Lewis to Jones, Jan. 8, 1925 (Jones papers, University of Washington); HR 9160, 68th Cong., first sess.

29. *Congressional Record*, 66, part 4, pp. 3908–09 (stipulations); HR 9270 and S. 3185, 69th Cong., first sess.; Jones's bill, S. 3185; *Congressional Record*, 67, part 8, p. 8625, quoting Rep. Louis C. Cramton of Michigan.

30. 29 Supreme Court Reports 463 (1929); House Doc. 493, 70th Cong., 2d sess. (1928), is the attorney general's review of the pocket veto process.

31. *Spokesman-Review*, Oct. 30–Nov. 5, 1925.

32. *Spokesman-Review*, July 17–28, 1926; Lewis quotation, July 17, 1926; resolutions, July 25, 1926.

33. Garry's work based on interviews with Alice Ignace O'Connor and Celina Garry Goolsby; *Newport Miner*, March 29, 1928; Hill's HR 5574 was combined with Jones's S. 1480, 70th Cong., first sess., which passed. See *Congressional Record*, 69, part 1, pps. 475, 5778, 8044, 9064–65. Unlike the Kalispels, the Spokanes had ceded land by treaty in 1887.

34. *Congressional Record*, 69, part 1, p. 5778 (Hill's remarks), pp. 9064–65 (veto).

35. *Colville Examiner*, Sept. 8, 1928. According to the *Examiner*, Feb. 6, 1926, John Bigsmoke died at age 57 after serving 15 years as chief.

36. Lewis left Spokane in 1931 and died in Los Angeles on March 18, 1941; undated clipping in Lewis papers, Eastern Washington State Historical Society, gives the figure of $10,000; CIA to Wesley Jones, Sept. 27, 1929 (Jones papers, University of Washington).

37. Annual report, Coeur d'Alene agency, June 30, 1928 (NA), esti-

mates an aggregate income of $5,825 of which $4,000 was wages; Antoine Peuse recollections (Sandpoint); *Newport Miner,* Sept. 14, 1911 (game laws), Aug. 9, 1928 ($50 fine).

38. *Newport Miner,* Aug. 9, 1928 (jurisdiction), Aug. 19, 1926 (G. McMath letter and tribes attending), Aug. 18, 1927 (Indian police, Saluskin, stick games).

39. Annual report, Coeur d'Alene agency, June 30, 1928 (NA).

40. *Ibid.*

41. CIA to Lawshe, Nov. 6, 1920, directs him to proceed with allotment; Annual report, Coeur d'Alene agency, 1928; Nels O. Nicholson, forester, report for 1922; Lawshe to CIA, Jan. 20, 1925 (all NA).

42. The patent dates are from the Bureau of Land Management master title plat files; the Andrews and Bigsmoke allotments are Nos. 7 and 14, lots 1, 6, 7, and 12, Sec. 30, T 34N, R44EWM.

43. Lee Muck, forest evaluation engineer, to CIA, May 27, 1927 (Dalkena); Coeur d'Alene annual report, 1928 (clamoring); Lawshe to CIA, March 4, 1926 (Ignace); T. C. White, ranger, to CIA, June 9, 1926 (Coeur d'Alene); B. A. Sharp to CIA, July 16, 1927 (Kaniksu fire compact) (all NA).

44. George M. Nyce, senior forest ranger, and Muck to CIA, Nov. 7, 1927 ("not opportune"); CIA to Sharp, Feb. 17, 1928, authorizes the sale; contract approved, July 7, 1928; CIA to Thomas C. Carter, forest assistant, Spokane, Dec. 12, 1928 (camps) (all NA). The prices were in line with stumpage rates at the time. Technically, Panhandle had individual contracts with each allottee.

45. Coeur d'Alene agency report 1930; Coeur d'Alene superintendent A. G. Wilson to CIA, Jan. 4, 1938, recapitulates Panhandle contract; Wilson to CIA, Nov. 17, 1938; certificates of completion, 1928–1938, by allotments (all NA); *Newport Miner,* March 21, 1929 (homes).

46. Wilson to CIA, Nov. 17, 1938 (NA), enclosing a summary by James W. Overton, forest ranger; annual forestry and grazing report, North Idaho agency, 1939 (FRC).

47. Records of the Pend Oreille County engineer; C. P. Mathes, North Idaho realty officer, to Louis Andrews, Oct. 9, 1970, with attachments, details road agreements of July 7, 1911, June 1, 1928, and June 24, 1930, and other information.

48. *Newport Miner,* Aug. 18, 1927. Although Ignace Garry was prominent among the Kalispels and Coeur d'Alenes, his son, Joe Garry, lists him as a Spokane on his application to Haskell Institute (FRC).

49. *Colville Examiner,* Sept. 8, 1928 (colorful); *Spokesman-Review,* Sept. 12, 1932 (Many Wigwams).

50. *Spokesman-Review,* Oct. 25, 1965, Garry obituary; interview with Celina Garry Goolsby.

51. *Spokesman-Review,* July 23, 1926 (Burke) and Sept. 12, 1932, picturing Garry in costume at the dedication of Garry Park, Spokane; July 24, 1926 (monument).
52. Indian office circular 2551, Feb. 15, 1929; *Newport Miner,* March 30, 1939, "10 Years Ago." No copy of the Kalispel report has been located. The Indian office was particularly upset by an article by Vera Connolly, "Cry of a Broken People," in *Good Housekeeping,* Feb. 1929.
53. Prucha, *Indian Policy,* pp. 32–34; *RCIA 1933,* pp. 108–09.
54. 48 *Stat.* 984, signed June 18, 1934; Kvasnicka and Viola, *Commissioners,* p. 278; Indian office circular 3001, June 22, 1934 ("powers") and circular 3015, Aug. 16, 1934 ("splendid cooperation").

Chapter 6. Organizing

1. Pend Oreille County commissioners' journal, book 2, p. 624 (Nov. 25, 1933) and book 3, p. 17 (Oct. 6, 1934). The purpose of the IRA is clarified, in part, in Bryan L. Stevens v. Commissioner of Internal Revenue, 452 Fed.2 741 (1971), as rebuilding a land base into economic units, partly through land acquisition.
2. Coeur d'Alene agency report, 1928, June 30, 1929; Indian office circular 3015, Aug. 16, 1934 (NA).
3. E. M. Johnston, land field agent, to J. M. Stewart, director of lands, Office of Indian Affairs, April 1, 1937 (FRC).
4. Secy. Ickes to Controller General, Oct. 12, 1934 (NA); Indian office circular 3033, Oct. 22, 1934, designating Washington Emergency Relief Administration (WERA) as agency to distribute cattle; penciled note attached to 1937 extension worker's report (FRC); Alice Ignace O'Connor ("hay"); Stan Bluff ("on their feet"); annual report of North Idaho agency extension workers, Jan. 3, 1939 (FRC); Wilson to CIA, June 2, 1941 (FRC). A search of WERA files yielded no information on Kalispel cattle. Under the program, an Indian paid for cattle by returning a calf for each adult animal received, and the government then transferred title for the ID cattle to the Indian. See Indian office circulars 3096, Aug. 15, 1935, and 3112, Nov. 8, 1935.
5. Extension report, Jan. 3, 1936; extension report for 1937 indicates the association has disbanded (FRC).
6. Wilson to CIA, Nov. 23, 1934 (NA). The team visited the Coeur d'Alene and Nez Perce reservations twice, the Kalispel once, on Nov. 12. The Coeur d'Alenes voted 76–73 against, and the Nez Perces 249–211 against reorganizing under IRA. In a report titled, "North Idaho Withdrawal program: Kalispel Reservation," 1952, p. 27, the superintendent

says: "The resident leaders and spokesmen . . . are Flathead and Spokane Indians." (FRC).

7. Collier to Indians of the Kalispel Reservation, Jan. 22, 1935 (Coeur d'Alene files, NA).

8. See Cohen, "Indian Self Government," in A. Josephy, *Red Power,* pp. 29–41; R. D. Dellwo interview on the process of charter writing; Indian office circular 3134, Mar. 7, 1936, establishes three classes of Indians.

9. George P. LaVatta, field agent, to E. M. Johnston, land field agent, April 6, 1937 (FRC).

10. The constitution was approved by the Secretary of Interior March 24, 1938, and the corporate charter, May 28, 1938; CIA to Secretary of Interior, Dec. 10, 1937 (FRC).

11. Alice Ignace O'Connor (Bigsmoke).

12. R. M. Kvasnicka and H. J. Viola, *Commissioners of Indian Affairs,* pp. 278–79 (charters and funding); Indian office circular 3001, June 22, 1934, explains that the act passed on almost the last day and that tribal referendums would be held within a year.

13. Application to Haskell, June 19, 1930 (FRC); *Spokane Daily Chronicle,* April 5, 1941, Dec. 17, 1953, and Dec. 14, 1956; *Spokesman-Review,* Nov. 16, 1940 (quotation); interview with Celina Garry Goolsby, Joe's sister.

14. North Idaho agency, 1936 report of extension work (FRC); Business Committee of the Lower Kalispel Indians to CIA, June 17, 1929; instructions, CIA to superintendent, June 25, 1929 (NA).

15. Coeur d'Alene agency annual reports, 1931–35 (FRC). Although the income figures are estimates, usually recopied from one report to the next, they may be taken as indicative. CIA to Wilson, Nov. 5, 1931, indicates that agency funds have been diverted for relief of needy Indians and cautions against buying clothing because the department hopes to obtain war surplus clothing; Wilson to CIA, Dec. 18, 1931 ($51) (NA).

16. Pend Oreille County commissioners' journal, book 2, 434, Oct. 9, 1929, stating road priorities to comply with chapter 88, session laws of 1929; Bigsmoke to CIA, n.d., received April 30, 1934 ($386); Wilson to CIA, May 10, 1934 (CWA); CIA to Sen. Burton Wheeler, Jan. 19, 1934 (wages) (NA).

17. Bigsmoke to CIA, received April 30, 1934; Wilson to CIA, May 10, 1934; CIA to Bigsmoke, May 17, 1934 (NA).

18. Annual reports of extension workers for Kalispel reservation, 1936 and 1939 (FRC).

19. See E. E. Hupp, "Land Purchase and Forest Renewal," *Big Smoke 1980,* pp. 12–18; H. D. McCullough, credit agent, to E. M. Johnston, land field agent, May 1, 1937, with copies to other offices (FRC).

32. *Emergency Conference of the National Congress of American Indians,* Washington, Feb. 25–28, 1954, mimeographed; Kalispel minutes, July 22, 1954. The Kalispel resolution naming Garry was doubtless drafted by Garry and Dellwo who, at the time, drafted all Kalispel resolutions and public statements.

33. W. E. Washburn, *Red Man's Land,* pp. 90–91; Kvasnicka and Viola, *Commissioners,* pp. 302–05; *New York Times,* Aug. 15 (Oregon) and Sept. 25, 1956 (Garry quotation). See C. F. Wilkinson and E. R. Biggs, "Evolution of the Termination Policy," 5 *American Indian Law Review* 139 (1977).

34. Interviews with Alice Ignace O'Connor, R. D. Dellwo, and Helen L. Peterson ("unfriendly").

35. Kalispel school census, 1940 (FRC); Department of the Interior, "Indian School Population," June 30, 1941, table V; Fourth Annual Report, 1938–39, Washington superintendent of public instruction to CIA, Sept. 9, 1939; Phinney to CIA, June 18, 1948 (FRC). The federal government paid for public schooling through Indian Education Funds awarded to the state and apportioned among districts having Indian pupils.

36. Based on review of sparse tribal minutes and interviews with Dellwo and O'Connor.

37. Tribal minutes and resolution, Sept. 15, 1954; Dellwo on PUD.

38. BIA, *Indian Reservations of the Northwest,* Oct. 1960, pp. 83–85.

39. *New York Times,* Nov. 4, 1950 ($14 billion), Jan. 4, 1956 (70%), and May 28, 1956 (LaFarge); transcript of hearing, Jan. 21, 1952 (Wilkinson); Washburn, *Red Man's Land,* pp. 104–05, describes the commission's quarters and attitude; Arthur V. Watkins, who became a commissioner in 1959, in House Report 1854, 89th Congress, 2d sess., 11.

40. Smith deposition, June 18, 1951, in Indian Claims Commission Docket 94; transcript of hearing, pp. 66–170; Petitioner's Exhibits 63 (map) and 64 (overlay). When the Wilkinson firm represented the Flatheads in their claims case, Smith and Ray signed affidavits dated July 2, 1957, which in effect reduced the territory claimed for the Kalispels in Montana because it conflicted with Salish claims in Docket 61.

41. Findings of Fact, Indian Claims Commission Docket 94, June 8, 1958; interlocutory order, June 9, 1958, to proceed to an agreement on land values; contracts Sept. 29, 1961 and Sept. 20, 1962 with appraisers (Wilkinson); valuation report by Saunderson. Hobbs used BLM tract records for his sampling and, by weighting, arrived at 1907 as "the average date of taking for this entire area," a procedure used in earlier claims cases. His maps are Petitioner's Exhibits 50 and 51. The Kalispels were not consulted on the date.

42. Wilkinson office memo, n.d. (Wilkinson). There had been considerable discussion also between the BIA and Wilkinson firm over the

20. Douglas Clark, asst. land field agent, to J. M. Stewa lands, Indian office, Sept. 3, 1941 (FRC); resolution, April 1! The area had been logged by Diamond Match and traded t forest for stumpage.

21. This and following paragraphs are based on: annual tension workers, North Idaho, 1944, 1947, and 1948 (FRC); agency report, "Administration of relief for the welfare of I 11, 1941, outlining policies and reporting expenditures 19 Wilson report on social security assistance to Indians, Ma Pearl Wright, Pend Orielle County welfare department, to agency, Jan. 3, 1945, enclosing a list of Indian recipients, 1946; Archie Phinney, North Idaho supt., to Wright, June FRC).

22. Taelman to Very Rev. Father Asst., Oct. 28, 1940 (O

23. *Newport Miner*, June 29 and July 6, 1944; *Inland Regi* diocesan newspaper, July 14, 1944.

24. See Kvasnicka and Viola, *Commissioners*, pp. 279, 28

25. *Ibid.*, p. 285; 60 *Stat.* 1049.

26. *Spokesman-Review*, Nov. 16, 1940; March 18, 1950; A *Spokane Daily Chronicle*, Dec. 17, 1953; Dec. 4, 1956; De typescript biography; interviews with Celina Goolsby, R. D. Helen Peterson.

27. Simmons' contract, BIA No. I-1-ind 42429, amended Sept. 11, 1950 (Wilkinson); Wilkinson association, Nov. 16 19 BIA); R. D. Dellwo interview; *New York Times*, July 14, 1950 Simmons contract did not carry an expiration date.

28. The Gonzaga contract, although Father Bischoff's serv in 1950, was not signed until 1963 (Wilkinson); Kvasnicka and *missioners*, p. 294.

29. Kvasnicka and Viola, *Commissioners*, p. 295; PL 83-2 757, approved Aug. 15, 1953, lifted the long-standing prohib sale of liquor to Indians. Sen. W. G. Magnuson of Washington of three bills to allow liquor sales, but all were defeated, and sneaked the authority into HR 1055, 83rd Cong., first sess., federal discrimination against Arizona Indians.

30. "Summary data pertinent to the preparedness of Indian to dispense with services. . .," BIA, June 30, 1952 (FRC); N "Withdrawal program—Kalispels" (FRC).

31. See F. P. Prucha, *Indian Policy in the United States*, Kvasnicka and Viola, *Commissioners*, pp. 296–97; PL 83-2 George Abbott, counsel for the House Committee on Interior a Affairs, to an emergency conference of the National Congress of Indians, Feb. 25, 1954 ("general framework").

Gonzaga contract which the BIA held up for 31 months on the ground that the Kalispels had "never acted intelligently" to approve it, according to a draft letter, Glen A. Wilkinson to Secretary of Interior, n. d. (Wilkinson). Memo, David Bonga to Dellwo, May 10, 1983, says the stipulation to compromise and settle does not say the Kalispel title has been extinguished but merely approves compensation for 2,373,000 acres.

43. Wilkinson draft to Secretary of Interior, n. d. (Wilkinson); testimony of Louis Andrews and Alice Ignace before the Indian Claims Commission, Docket 94. Dellwo attended at Sherwood's invitation and the account is based partly on his recollection.

44. PL 88-25, May 17, 1963, a supplemental appropriation bill which includes Kalispel funds; Hobbs to Andrews, June 20, 1963 (Wilkinson).

Chapter 7. **The Plan**

1. Charles Hobbs to Louis Andrews, June 20, 1963 (Wilkinson); memo of tribal meeting June 5, 1963, at which bureau men discounted the need for an attorney; conversation with Stan Bluff, Glen Nenema, and Andrews, May 6, 1983 ("neglect"); contract Oct. 12, 1963, with Dellwo, Rudolf & Grant, approved by BIA March 20, 1964; Zakoji memo July 17, 1963 (FRC).

2. Conversation with John Weddel, Portland area BIA, May 10, 1983; Dellwo to John Webber [*sic*], Lapwai, Oct. 18, 1963; Dellwo to Sen. Jackson, July 27, 1964 and response, Aug. 3, 1964; Dellwo to J. H. Gamble, Senate staff, Aug. 16, 1965: interview with Dellwo. The Coeur d'Alenes had not had a formal family plan; Kalispels apparently were the first to formalize the concept in a written plan. Colvilles used 80 percent of their judgment monies for per capita distribution.

3. Zakoji memo, July 17, 1963 (FRC). Bailey was a BIA community planner, and Weber, assistant Lapwai superintendent.

4. *Ibid.* Economic studies for various tribes are filed in the National Archives.

5. Hedlund application to EDA, June 2, 1966 (Dellwo); Culp to North Idaho agency, Oct. 11, 1963 (FRC). Culp in 1966 assumed the leases of the bankrupt McDonald Lumber Co. on allotments west of the river (FRC).

6. Anderson to W. Ensor, Dec. 4, 1963; Petterborg to T. St. Clair, Oct. 23, 1967 (BIA Portland); conversation with E. E. Eggleston, range management officer, Portland BIA, May 10, 1983; conversation with Bluff, Nenema, and Andrews, May 6, 1983.

7. Dellwo to J. J. Weber, April 14, 1965; Zakoji memo, April 6, 1965 (Doyle); "Brief Report on the Housing Program," housing committee of

Kalispels, July 7, 1964; Ensor to R. D. Holly, area director, March 10, 1964 (all FRC).

8. Copies of the plan are in the Dellwo offices, Portland BIA, and Senate Interior and Insular Affairs Committee files. Members of families could "pool" their entitlements under the family plan. For example, by pooling, a family of two parents and five children might receive $30,000 for housing.

9. S. 2608 and HR 10973, and Senate Report 1287, Kalispel judgment bills, 88th Congress, 2d sess.; Dellwo to Jackson, July 21, 1964 (Dellwo).

10. Dellwo to Jackson, July 21, 1964 (Dellwo).

11. Garry to Church and Jackson, July 24, 1964, with Coeur d'Alene resolution 15 (65) (FRC).

12. Senate Report 1287, 88th Cong., 2d sess.; PL 88–412 (1964); "Statement of Kalispel tribe, Re: HR 10973 and S. 2608," n.d. (Dellwo). HR 10973, a bill by Rep. Walt Horan, allows the use of judgment funds for any purpose determined by the tribal council and approved by the Secretary of the Interior, but defers implementing the use until the BIA determines the feasibility of a private trust.

13. Zakoji to Weber, Aug. 11, 1965 (FRC).

14. "Brief report on the housing program," *op. cit.; Spokane Daily Chronicle,* Oct. 17, 1966 (11 families).

15. *Spokane Daily Chronicle,* April 22, 1965; Dellwo to Gamble, April 28, 1965 (Dellwo).

16. Dr. R. W. Winston and R. T. Olson to Committee on Indian Affairs, Dec. 4, 1964 (Pend Oreille County); *Spokane Daily Chronicle,* April 22, 1965 (tuberculosis).

17. Conversation with Dellwo, Jan. 5, 1984.

18. *Spokane Daily Chronicle,* Aug. 13, 16, and 17, 1965; conversation with Nenema and Larry Goodrow, Kalispel tribal planner, June 14, 1983 ("de-fuse").

19. HR 788 (Quinaults) and HR 5925 (Colvilles), 89th Congress, first sess.; R. H. Kvasnicka and H. J. Viola, *Commissioners of Indian Affairs,* pp. 306, 314–15; S. 1442, by Jackson and Magnuson, 88th Cong., 2d sess., called for one-step termination of the Colvilles on the Klamath model.

20. Jackson to Dellwo, Aug. 31, 1965; CIA to Portland BIA, Sept. 28, 1965 (Portland BIA). Of family plan funds, a substantial amount that belonged to minors was placed in a minor's trust account in the Spokane National Bank.

21. Jackson to Dellwo, Aug. 3, 1964; resolution Sept. 25, 1965 (Dellwo).

22. Kalispel tribal resolution Oct. 2, 1965; Dellwo to Gamble, Aug. 16, 1965.

23. Contract with PHS, Aug. 27, 1965, and report of the tribal planning committee, same date (FRC).

24. Miller, then at 8705 N. Weipert St., estimated the costs at $11.50 to $13.50 a square foot which, at the time, would be low for urban housing. Fred N. Wessels, construction superintendent, to North Idaho agency, April 21 and May 11, 1966 (FRC); *Spokane Daily Chronicle*, Oct. 17, 1966.

25. Contract and construction data in Lapwai files (FRC).

26. "Socio-Economic Report for the Kalispel Band," Jan. 1968, 5 (FRC); W. Bailey to L. Staley, North Idaho agency, Sept. 6, 1967 (toilets and CAP training) (FRC). Seven Kalispels had received vocational training since 1952 through the state, but in 1968 none was employed in a field he had trained for.

27. "Socio-Economic Report," 1968.

28. Dellwo to SiJohn, June 1, 1966 (Dellwo); tribal resolutions June 8, 1966; *Spokane Daily Chronicle*, Feb. 18, 1968 (educational trust).

29. Revised constitution and by-laws, approved by the Secretary of Interior July 27, 1967, allow the tribe to reconsider and modify any action of the business committee within 35 days.

30. Kalispel resolution 68-2, Aug. 1, 1967.

31. *Ibid.* (quotation); Portland BIA to Kalispel business council, Nov. 8, 1967; Secretary of Interior to chairman, Senate Committee on Interior and Insular Affairs, April 22, 1968 (NA); telegram, CIA to Portland BIA, June 21, 1968.

32. Garry sales at $3,200 and $3,400, July 10, 1968, and deeds, Aug. 12, 1968; Culp cancellation, March 3, 1971, a friendly transaction; Kalispel resolution 72-14, Dec. 15, 1971, adds $50,000; C. P. Mathes, Lapwai realty officer, report of Kalispel land-acquisition program, March 6, 1972.

33. A. W. Galbraith, acting Portland director, to Kalispel business council, Nov. 8, 1967 (FRC).

34. Dellwo to Superintendent, Lapwai, Aug. 19, 1968 (mission); S. Bluff to County Engineer E. L. Barcklay, Jan. 25, 1972, and H. A. Pease, county engineer, to Kalispel tribe, Aug. 24, 1976 (Pend Oreille County engineer's files).

35. *Newport Miner*, Oct. 5, 12, and 19, 1967; Dellwo to Prosecuting Attorney, Pend Oreille County, Oct. 25, 1967, and to editor, *Miner*, Oct. 24, 1967; *Law and Order Code of the Kalispel Indian Community*, 1980; tribal resolution, July —, 1980; interview with Gerald F. Rodgers, Portland BIA, May 10, 1983. See Allan Baris, "Washington's Public Law 280 Jurisdiction on Indian Reservations," 53 *Washington Law Review* 701 (1978). In brief, the state assumed jurisdiction over reservation lands only on petition of a tribe.

36. See Cheyenne-Arapahoe, et al., v. U.S., 206 Court of Claims 340 (1975). Interest on Indian funds had been set by 45 *Stat.* 1164 (1929) which put the rate at 4 percent when no other rate was specified by law or

treaty. For this suit, the Kalispels again turned to Wilkinson, Cragun & Barker. Patricia L. Brown, WC&B, to Kalispel Indian Community, Oct. 16, 1980, reports the settlement, which the Kalispels proposed spending for tribal government operations, according to the Kalispel resolution of May 6, 1981.

37. *Spokesman-Review,* Dec. 2, 1973; case study, 1976, by Eastern Washington University business class, of which a typescript is in the Dellwo files; Report to Kalispel tribe, Oct. 1, 1975, by Livingston Management, Spokane; PL 92-182 and House Reports 92-542 and 92-640, 92d Congress, first sess., on bills conferring statutory authority for land acquisition which adopt Dellwo's language in "Statement of Kalispel Indian Community Re: Kalispel Land Consolidation Bill," n.d.

38. Untitled report on Aluminum Box Mfg. Co., July 9, 1975, listing dates, purposes, and amounts of nine loans.

39. Pacific Consultants, Everett, feasibility study for economic development, 1972; BIA Portland to Dellwo, Aug. 10, 1972, enclosing summary report; Robert Anderson, et al., v. O'Brien, 524 Pac.2 390 (1974); amicus curie brief by Dellwo, Rudolf & Schroeder, Wash. supreme court No. 42818; court decision, en banc, July 11, 1974; *Spokesman-Review,* July 17, 1975 (dedication). The parking-lot paving and access road relied on a $25,000 grant from the Farmers Home Administration.

40. Livingston Management, "Report to the Kalispel Tribe of Indians: Aluminum Box Manufacturing Co. Feasibility Study," Oct. 1, 1975.

41. Conversations with Portland BIA personnel May 10, 1983; Knouff interview, Nov. 22, 1983; conversation with tribal executive council, May 6, 1983; quarterly financial reports, KMP.

42. Kvasnicka and Viola, *Commissioners,* p. 327; Dellwo to R. Pierre, April 11, 1966; Bennett to Jackson, enclosing draft bill, Nov. 11, 1968 (Dellwo); Kalispel resolution, Feb. 28, 1968, passed 5–0.

43. *Congressional Record,* 120, part 45, 5924, in a memo on S. 1017, 93rd Cong., 2d sess. (Kennedy); Indian Judgment Fund Distribution Act, PL 93-134, Oct. 19, 1973, 87 *Stat.* 466, requires the Secretary of Interior to prepare a distribution plan, freeing the Senate committee from judgment legislation; Wilkinson, Cragun & Barker, notice to clients, May 24, 1973; conversation with R. Dellwo. Gerard would become Assistant Secretary of Interior—Indian Affairs.

44. Pacific Consultants, "Report Summary of Economic Development Feasibility on the Kalispel Reservation, Cusick, Wash.—August 1972." Many such studies for Indian tribes were financed under the Indian Reservation Development Act of 1967.

45. *Overall Economic Development Plan for the Trico Economic Development District,* 1970, *passim;* Pend Oreille County Rural Development Committee, *Report,* 1969. Trico includes Stevens, Ferry, and Pend Oreille counties.

46. The business committee asked the Portland BIA for a feasibility study of hogs in 1968 but an informal review proved discouraging; Alice Ignace O'Connor (quotation).

47. O. J. Cotes, ed., *Kalispels,* p. 33; *Spokesman-Review,* Nov. 14, 1983; conversation with Nenema, Bluff, and Andrews, May 6, 1983.

48. Tribal resolution, Oct. 14, 1970; memo by Dellwo, March 19, 1973; Dellwo to Department of Ecology, April 8, 1971; Asst. Atty. Gen. Wick Dufford to Dellwo, April 30, 1971, saying the department "makes no contention of jurisdiction over Kalispel lands."

49. Kalispel resolution 73-23, Jan. 10, 1973; conversation with David Bonga and R. Dellwo, June 30, 1983. No doubt the Kalispels also resented Ensor's attempts to undermine Joe Garry by supporting Coeur d'Alene dissidents in framing a new tribal constitution which failed to pass. Spokane chairman to Kalispel chairman, n. d. 1980.

50. U.S. and Kalispel tribe v. Pend Oreille County PUD No. 1, U.S. District Court, Eastern Washington, No. C-80-116; *Spokane Daily Chronicle,* July 12 and Aug. 29, 1983. Box Canyon, completed in 1955, evidently did not produce the headwater anticipated, because in June 1961 the PUD amended its license to allow two feet rather than one foot backwater at Albeni Falls. There was some caving of shoreline at this time. The government's motion to dismiss the United States as involuntary plaintiff in the riverbed suit was denied May 25, 1984, and the case ordered to trial.

51. Cullooyah to G. Campbell, Spokane agency, Nov. 10, 1980; Kalispel resolutions 1977-56 and 1978-10; memo, M. P. Wheeler and F. G. Malroy, BIA, to planning support group, May 16, 1978 ("unique"); *Spokane Daily Chronicle,* Feb. 10, 1977; consultants were Thoreson-Peterson Planning Group, Spokane; "Briefing Paper on the Kalispel Land Acquisition Project," prepared for the press conference. The land is in T 33 and 34 N, R44 EWM.

52. *Tribal Overall Economic Development Plan,* June 1982; BIA contract No. POOC 1420 7080, PL 93-638. Although it carries a 1982 date, the plan was not issued until October 1983. Kalispel resolution 1982–84, Oct. 29, 1982. Apparently there is little precious metal in the area sought, according to "Preliminary Mineral Inventory of the Kalispel Reservation and Proposed Annexation Lands," April 1982, by the Council of Energy Resource Tribes, Englewood, Colorado.

53. In an attempt to enforce its regulations, the State of Washington seized $21,000 worth of liquor enroute to the Kalispel store in January 1984; *Spokane Chronicle,* Jan. 4, 1984; HUD contracts 1981 and 1982, including carryover (BIA Portland).

Bibliography

Like many histories of American Indian peoples, this study of the Kalispels stands at its base on such documents as field reports, annual reports, correspondence, and inspectors' reports of the federal Indian service preserved in the National Archives or one of its regional depositories—in this case, the Federal Records Center at Seattle. Modern Kalispels recall little of their past and the elders who once might have offered oral continuity died a generation or two ago.

In addition to government archives, this history relies on the archives of the Oregon Province of the Society of Jesus at Gonzaga University and on the files of attorneys who represented the tribe.

The Oregon Province holdings consist of approximately nine hundred archival boxes of mission records and the papers of individual Jesuits who served in Washington, Oregon, Idaho, Montana, and Alaska. The collection also includes manuscripts, photographs, newspaper clippings, about five thousand volumes on Indian subjects, and selected documents on microfilm from European and Canadian archives.

The attorneys' files are those of the Wilkinson firm of Washington, D.C., and Dellwo, Rudolf and Schroeder of Spokane. The Wilkinson files relating to the Kalispels' suit before the Indian Claims Commission, four large cardboard boxes, have been turned over to the Dellwo firm. For the Kalispels' claim, and for other suits, the two firms copied hundreds of documents from public and private archives and from published sources relating to the Kalispel people. In addition, Dellwo has counseled the Kalispels since the tribe's incorporation under the Indian Reorganization Act and, therefore, holds the most complete record of the tribe's business in recent times.

Tracing the Kalispels' history since 1855 is complicated by the fact that the tribe never had its own agent but was attached to that of another. At times nobody knew who was in charge of the Kalispels. Consequently, documents relating to the Kalispels, by that name or others, are scattered among the records of the Coeur d'Alene (now, North Idaho), Colville, Spokane, and Flathead agencies.

The papers of Senator Wesley B. Jones of Washington at the University of Washington, and those of the erstwhile Indian Agent, William Park Winans, at Washington State University, don't disclose much concern for the Kalispels but the Winans papers do supplement agency and Indian Office reports for the period of Winans' employment in the Indian service. The papers of the Spokane attorney and historian, William S. Lewis, held by the Eastern Washington State Historical Society, contain little reference to Lewis's legal work; they are mostly letters and drafts for his historical studies.

I interviewed a number of persons for aspects of the Kalispel story and searched Indian service and county files for context. They are cited in the notes where the information can be credited to the source, but I acknowledge with appreciation the assistance of Robert D. Dellwo, tribal counsel, and Alice Ignace O'Connor, longtime tribal secretary and unofficial tribal historian, who supplied details I could not find elsewhere. Hudson's Bay Company documents, excerpted from materials gathered for my earlier study of the Flatheads, are quoted with permission of the governor and council of the company. Legal files, congressional documents, reports of government agencies, and similar sources are cited fully in the notes and, consequently, not repeated in this bibliography, except for a few that have achieved a separate standing, such as the report of Isaac Stevens' explorations for a northern railroad route.

The following list of sources shows manuscripts, books, articles, and periodicals consulted in preparation of this book. Abbreviations of location are the same as those in the notes.

Unpublished

"Calispell Valley Archaeological Project," Washington Archaeological Research Center no. 45-PO-139, Washington State University, Pullman, Washington, 1985.

Chalfant, Stuart A. "Aboriginal Territory of the Kalispel Indians," typescript, Indian Claims Commission Docket 94, n.d. Under examination, Chalfant explained that this study was based on others' fieldwork.

Daugherty, Richard D. "Archaeological Research in the Boundary Dam Area," typescript, Pullman, Wash.: Washington Archaeological Research Center, 1962 (?).

Delisio, Mario P. "Final Report: Archaeological Survey of the U.S. Corps of Army Engineers: Land on Lake Pend Oreille and the Pend Oreille River," typescript, Boise, July 31, 1974.

"Emergency Conference of American Indians on Legislation," mimeographed summary of meetings Feb. 25–28, 1954, of the National Congress of American Indians in Washington, D.C. Provided by Helen L. Peterson, former NCAI secretary.

Griva, Rev. Edward M., S.J., "History of 50 Years of My Missionary Life among the Indians and Whites from July 1894 till the end of September 1944," typescript, n.d. (OPA).

Indian Claims Commission Docket 94, "Testimony and Exhibits: Lower Pend Oreille or Kalispel Tribe v. the United States," microfilm (NA, RG 279).

Joset, Rev. Joseph, S.J., ["Narrative of the 1858 Indian War"], untitled manuscript (OPA). See R. I. Burns' edited version in the *Pacific Northwest Quarterly,* listed among articles.

———, "Ethnology of the Rocky Mountain Indians," manuscript (OPA).

———, "Foundation of the St. Ignatius Mission among the Kalispels," manuscript (OPA).

———, "Loyola, an Indian chief," manuscript (OPA).

———, "Origin of St. Ignatius Mission," manuscript (OPA). In the Kalispels' claim case, Indian Claims Commission Docket 94, this is petitioner's exhibit 16, labeled from the California Province, but Oregon documents once filed in the California Province have been transferred to the Oregon archives at Gonzaga.

———, "Quarter of a Century among the Savages," manuscript (OPA).

———, "Short Chronology of the Beginnings of Catholic Missions in the Rocky Mountains," manuscript, circa 1880 (OPA).

"Land Purchase and Consolidation Program of the Kalispel Indian Community," Usk, Wash.: Kalispel Tribal Council, Aug. 1, 1967.

"Lower Pend Oreille or Kalispel Tribe v. United States," Indian Claims Commission Docket 94, 6 *Ind. Cl. Com.* 353, 369 (1958).

Livingston Management, "Report to the Kalispel Tribe," Spokane: Livingston Management, Oct. 1, 1975.

Mengarini, Rev. Gregory, S.J., "The Rocky Mountains: Memoirs of Father Gregory Mengarini," n.d. (OPA). Originally in Italian, the memoirs have been translated by Gloria Ricci Lothrop for a dissertation and book.

"Overall Economic Development Program for the Trico Economic Development District," typescript, Colville, Wash.: Trico Economic Development District, May 31, 1970, with occasional updating. Trico consists of Stevens, Ferry, and Pend Oreille counties.

Pacific Consultants, "Report Summary of Economic Development Feasibility on the Kalispel Reservation, Cusick, Wash.—August 1972," Everett, Wash.: Pacific Consultants, Aug. 1972.

Pend Oreille County Rural Development Committee, "Report," duplicated by the committee, 1969.

"Reservation Goals 1964–75: Kalispel Indian Reservation," Lapwai, Idaho: North Idaho Agency, 1964.

Smith, Allan H., "Gazetteer of the Kalispel Country: Field Notes, 1936–39," typescript, n.d., for the Kalispels' claim case (Wilkinson).

"Socio-Economic Report for the Kalispel Band of Indians of the Kalispel Reservation, Wash.," Lapwai, Idaho: North Idaho Agency, Jan. 1968 (FRC).

"Statement of the Kalispel Tribe, Re: H.R. 10973 and S. 2608," typescript, n.d. (Dellwo).

Thoreson-Peterson Planning Group, "Briefing Paper on the Kalispel Land Acquisition Project," Spokane: Thoreson-Peterson, 1977.

"United States and Kalispel Indian Tribe v. Pend Oreille County Public Utility District 1," No. C-80-116 in U.S. District Court for Eastern Washington.

Books and Pamphlets

Ayers, Gary, et al. *Cultural Resource Survey of the Kalispel Trail.* Sandpoint, Idaho: Cultural Resource Consultants, Inc., 1979. Produced under contract with the Colville National Forest, USDA.

Bancroft, Hubert H. *History of Washington, Idaho, and Montana, 1845–1889.* (Vol. 31 of *Works*). San Francisco: The History Co., 1890.

Burns, Rev. Robert Ignatius, S.J. *The Jesuits and the Indian Wars of the Northwest.* New Haven: Yale University Press, 1966.

Carriker, Robert C. *The Kalispel People*. Phoenix: Indian Tribal Series, 1973.

Chance, David H. *Influences of the Hudson's Bay Company on the Native Cultures of the Colvile* [sic] *District*. Moscow, Idaho: Northwest Anthropological Research Notes, 7, No. 1, Part 2, 1973.

Chittenden, Hiram Martin, and Alfred Talbot Richardson. *Life, Letters and Travels of Father Pierre-Jean De Smet, S.J., 1801–1873*. 4 vols. New York: Francis P. Harper, 1905.

Collier, Donald, Alfred E. Hudson, and Arlo Ford. *Archaeology of the Upper Columbia Region*. Seattle: University of Washington Press, 1942. University of Washington Publications in Anthropology, 9, No. 1, pp. 1–178.

Cotes, O. J., ed. *The Kalispels: People of the Pend Oreille*. Usk, Wash.: Kalispel Tribe, 1980, with a grant from the Washington Commission on the Humanities. Printed at Brigham City, Utah, by the Office of Technical Assistance and Training.

Coues, Elliott, ed. *New Light on the Early History of the Great Northwest: Manuscript Journals of Alexander Henry and David Thompson*. 3 vols. New York: F. P. Harper, 1897.

Curtis, Edward S. *The North American Indian*. 20 vols. Edited by Frederick Webb Hodge. Seattle: Curtis, 1907–30.

Davis, Rev. William L., S.J. *A History of St. Ignatius Mission*. Spokane: C. W. Hill Printing Co., 1954.

De Smet, Rev. Peter John, S.J. *New Indian Sketches*. New York: D. & J. Sadlier & Co., 1863.

———. *Oregon Missions and Travels over the Rocky Mountains*. New York: E. Dunigan, 1847.

———. *Western Missions and Missionaries: A Series of Letters*. New York: P. J. Kenedy, 1859.

———. See Chittenden and Richardson.

Dingee, Ruby Lusher. *Historical Sketches of Pend Oreille County, Washington*. Newport, Wash.: *Newport Miner*, 1930.

Drury, Clifford M. *Elkanah and Mary Walker, Pioneers among the Spokanes*. Caldwell, Idaho: Caxton Printers, Ltd., 1940.

———. *Nine Years with the Spokane Indians: The Diary, 1838–1848, of Elkanah Walker*. Glendale: Arthur H. Clark Co., 1976.

Durham, Nelson W. *A History of Spokane and Spokane Country, Washington, from Earliest Times to the Present*. 3 vols. Spokane, Chicago and Philadelphia: S. J. Clarke Publishing Co., 1912.

Fahey, John. *The Flathead Indians*. Norman: University of Oklahoma Press, 1974.

Fay, Keith L. *Developing Indian Employment Opportunities.* Washington: Bureau of Indian Affairs, 1972.

Garraghan, Rev. Gilbert Joseph, S.J. *Jesuits of the Middle United States.* 3 vols. New York: America Press, 1938.

Indian Reservations of the Northwest. Portland: Bureau of Indian Affairs, Oct. 1960.

Josephy, Alvin M., Jr. *Red Power.* New York: American Heritage Press, 1971.

Kappler, Charles J., comp. *Indian Affairs: Laws and Treaties.* 4 vols. Washington: Government Printing Office, 1905–29.

Kip, Lt. Lawrence. *Army Life on the Pacific: A Journal of the Expeditions against the Northern Indians, the Tribes of the Coeur d'Alenes, Spokans, and Pelouzes, in the Summer of 1858.* New York: Redfield, 1859.

Kvasnicka, Robert M., and Herman J. Viola, eds. *The Commissioners of Indian Affairs, 1824–1977.* Lincoln: University of Nebraska Press, 1979.

Law and Order Code of the Kalispel Indian Community. Spokane: Kalispel Tribal Council, 1980.

Mason, David Townsend. *Timber Ownership and Lumber Production in the Inland Empire.* Portland: Western Pine Manufacturers Association, 1920.

Meinig, Donald W. *The Great Columbia Plain: A Historical Geography, 1805–1910.* Seattle: University of Washington Press, 1968.

Meriam, Lewis, and Associates. *Problems of Indian Administration.* Baltimore: Johns Hopkins Press, 1928.

Palliser, John. *Papers of the Palliser Expedition, 1857–60.* Edited by Irene M. Spry. Toronto: The Champlain Society, 1968.

Preliminary Mineral Inventory of the Kalispel Reservation and Proposed Annexation Lands. Englewood, Colo.: Council of Energy Resource Tribes, April 1982.

Price, Monroe E. *Law and the American Indian: Readings, Notes and Cases.* New York: Bobbs-Merrill Co., Inc., 1973.

Prucha, Rev. Francis P., S.J. *Indian Policy in the United States: Historical Essays.* Lincoln: University of Nebraska Press, 1981.

Ray, Verne F. *Cultural Distributions: Plateau.* University of California Anthropological Records 8:2. Berkeley: University of California Press, 1942.

———. *Cultural Relations in the Plateau of Northwestern America.* Los Angeles: Southwest Museum, 1939.

————. *Sanpoil and Nespelem*. Seattle: University of Washington Press, 1933. University of Washington Publications in Anthropology, vol. 5.

Reports of Explorations and Surveys to Ascertain the Most Practicable and Economical Route for a Railroad from the Mississippi River to the Pacific Ocean . . . 1853–4. 12 volumes in 13. Washington: Government Printing Office, 1855–60. Senate Executive Document 46, 33rd Congress, 1st session (serial 992) and House Executive Document 91, 33rd Congress, 2d session (serial 791).

Richards, Kent D. *Isaac I. Stevens: Young Man in a Hurry*. Provo, Utah: Brigham Young University Press, 1979.

Ruby, Robert H., and John A. Brown. *The Spokane Indians: Children of the Sun*. Norman: University of Oklahoma Press, 1970.

Schoenberg, Rev. Wilfred P., S.J. *Gonzaga University: Seventy-Five Years, 1887–1962*. Spokane: Gonzaga University, 1963.

————. *Paths to the Northwest: A Jesuit History of the Oregon Province*. Chicago: Loyola University Press, 1982.

Sewell, James A., and Associates. *Pend Oreille County, Washington: A Comprehensive Water and Sewer Plan*. Newport, Wash.: Sewell, April 1971.

Smith, Allan H. *Archaeological Survey of the Pend Oreille River Valley from Newport to Jared, Washington, August, 1957*. Olympia: Washington State Department of Conservation, February 1958.

Teit, James A. *Salishan Tribes of the Western Plateaus*. Edited by Franz Boas. *Forty-fifth Annual Report, Bureau of American Ethnology, 1927–28*. House Doc. 380, 70th Congress, 2d session (1930).

Thompson, David. *David Thompson's Narrative, 1784–1812*. Edited by Richard Glover. Toronto: The Champlain Society, 1962.

————. *Narrative of Explorations in Western America, 1784–1812*. Edited by J. B. Tyrell. Toronto: The Champlain Society, 1916.

Thwaites, Reuben Gold, ed. *Original Journals of the Lewis and Clark Expedition, 1804–1806*. 8 vols. New York: Dodd, 1904–05.

Tribal Overall Economic Development Plan. Usk, Wash.: Kalispel Tribe of Indians, June 1982.

Trimble, William J. *The Mining Advance into the Inland Empire*. Madison: University of Wisconsin *Bulletin 638*, 1914. Reprinted with an introduction by Rodman W. Paul, New York: Johnson Reprint Corporation, 1972.

United States Forest Service. *Forest Statistics: Pend Oreille County, Washington*. Missoula, Mont.: Northern Rocky Mountain Forest and

Range Experiment Station, Forest Survey Release No. 2, March 1937.

Walker, Deward E., Jr. *Indians of Idaho.* Moscow, Idaho: University Press of Idaho, 1978.

———. *Myths of Idaho Indians.* Moscow, Idaho: University Press of Idaho, 1980.

Washburn, Wilcomb E. *Red Man's Land/White Man's Law.* New York: Charles Scribner's Sons, 1971.

Articles

Barker, Charles I. "Early Explorers Awed by Albeni Falls Scenery," *Spokesman-Review,* March 29, 1953.

Burns, Rev. Robert Ignatius, S.J. "Pere Joset's Account of the Indian War of 1858," *Pacific Northwest Quarterly,* 38, No. 4 (October 1947): 285–314.

Chalfant, Stuart A. "Ethnological Field Investigation and Analysis of Historical Material relative to the Coeur d'Alene Indian Aboriginal Distribution," in *Interior Salish and Eastern Washington Indians, I,* New York: Garland Publishing Co., 1974, pp. 37–155.

Clark, Donald H. "Pinckney City and Fort Colville," *Spokesman-Review* magazine, May 3, 1953, p. 3.

Collier, John. "Indians Come Alive," *Atlantic,* 170, No. 2 (Sept. 1942), : 75–81.

Connolly, Vera L. "Cry of a Broken People," *Good Housekeeping,* 88, No. 2 (Feb. 1929): 30–31, 226, 228, 229–37.

Crown, Lloyd. "Cattle Raising in Pend Oreille County," *Big Smoke 1975,* pp. 35–38.

Davis, Rev. William L., S.J. "Peter John DeSmet: The Journey of 1840," *Pacific Northwest Quarterly,* 35 (1944): 29–34, 121–42.

de Rouge, Etienne, S.J. "L'Indien du Nord-Quest," *Etude* (France), 49 (1890): 400–500.

Diomedi, Rev. Alexander, S.J. "Indian Missions," *Woodstock Letters,* 8 (1879): 32–41.

Elliott, Thomas C. "David Thompson's Journeys in the Pend Oreille Country," *Washington Historical Quarterly,* 23 (1932): 18–24, 88–93, 173–76.

Frush, Charles W. "A Trip from The Dalles to Fort Owen," *Contributions to the Historical Society of Montana,* 2 (1896): 337–42.

Haeberlin, H. K., James A. Teit, and Helen H. Roberts, directed by Franz Boas. "Coiled Basketry in British Columbia and the Surrounding Region," *Forty-first Annual Report, Bureau of American Ethnology,* 1919–24, pp. 133–484.

Haines, Francis. "Northward Spread of Horses among the Plains Indians," *American Anthropologist,* n. s., 40 (1938): 429–37.

Haskell, C. F. B. "On Reconnaissance for the Great Northern," *Spokesman-Review* magazine, Jan. 2, 9, 16 and 23, 1949. Letters by Haskell, edited by his son, Daniel C. Haskell, published by the New York Public Library, 1948.

"Hot News from Pinckney City: A Murder and a Hanging," *Spokesman-Review* magazine, March 30, 1958, p. 19.

Hunt, Clair. "War Dance of the Spokanes." *Wide World Magazine* (London), Sept. 1912: 436–43.

Hupp, Erle E. "Land Purchase and Forest Renewal," *Big Smoke 1980,* pp. 12–18.

Kingston, Ceylon S. "Mary Moody, First Steamboat on Lake Pend Oreille," *Spokesman-Review* magazine, July 6, 1952, p. 2.

Lurie, Nancy O. "Indian Claims Commission Act," *Annals,* American Academy of Political and Social Science, 311 (May 1957): 56–70.

Laut, Agnes C. "Red Men of the Northwest," *Review of Reviews,* 77, No. 2 (Feb. 1928): 183–94.

Libra, Flossie. "Hudson's Bay-Kalispel Trail," *Big Smoke 1978,* pp. 11–24.

Mooney, James. "Ghost Dance Religion and the Sioux Outbreak of 1890," *Fourteenth Annual Report, Bureau of American Ethnology,* 1892–93, part 2, pp. 641–1104.

Peterson, Helen L. "American Indian Political Participation," *Annals,* American Society of Political and Social Science, 311 (May 1957): 116–26.

Ray, Verne F. "Kolaskin Cult: A Prophet Movement of 1870 in Northeastern Washington," *American Anthropologist,* n. s., 38, No. 1 (Jan. –March 1936): 67–75.

———. "Native Villages and Groupings of the Columbia Basin," *Pacific Northwest Quarterly,* 27 (1936): 99–152.

Rousch, J. F. "Legislative Reapportionment in Washington State," *Pacific Northwest Quarterly,* 23, No. 3 (July 1937): 263–300.

Smith, Allan H. "David Thompson in the Pend Oreille River Valley, 1809," *The Record 1961* (Washington State University), pp. 8–15.

Swadesh, Morris. "Salish Phonologic Geography," *Language,* 28 (1952): 232–48.

Wilkinson, Charles F., and Eric R. Biggs. "Evolution of the Termination Policy," *American Indian Law Review,* 5, No. 1 (1977): 139–84.

Newspapers, Periodicals, and Directories

American Indian Law Review
Big Smoke, annual publication of the Pend Oreille County Historical
     Society
Colville Examiner
Inland Register, weekly newspaper of the Spokane Catholic Diocese
Inter-lake, once published weekly at Demersville, Montana
Newport Miner
New York Times
Oregonian (Portland, Oregon)
Pacific Northwest Quarterly, journal of the Washington Historical
     Society
Poor's Manual of Railroads, annual
Railway Age Gazette
The Record, annual publication of Washington State University Library
     and Friends of the Library
Spokane Chronicle, formerly *Spokane Daily Chronicle*
Spokane Woman, once a monthly publication of Spokane federated
     women's clubs
Spokesman-Review (Spokane, Wash.)
Washington Law Review
Woodstock Letters, annual publication of the Society of Jesus

Index

Abrahamson, Isabel: 86
Abrahamson, John: 136
Affiliated Tribes of the Northwest: 151, 170
Agricultural Adjustment Administration, U.S.: 146
Alexander (Pend Oreille chief): 25, 192n. 16
Allotment: *see* General Allotment Act
Ambrose (Kalispel subchief): 38
Anderson, Sen. Clinton: 182–83
Andrews, Bazil: 125
Andrews, Joseph: 136
Andrews, Louis: 151, 162, 164, 165, 168, 170, 175
Andrews, Mary: 86, 114
Antoine (Colville Indian): 57
Archaeological finds: 29, 195n. 11
Army, U.S.: 12, 14, 19, 48, 50, 60–62, 74; service by Kalispels, 146; *see also* Steptoe, Col. Edward; Wright, Col. George

Bigsmoke, Baptiste (Kalispel chief): 120, 123, 136, 144
Bigsmoke, John (Kalispel chief): 100, 109, 120, 125, 207n. 35
Bischoff, Rev. William N.: 151–52
Blackfeet Indians: 4, 7, 10, 15, 38, 39
Blackwell, Fred A.: 84–86, 103
Blanchet, Rev. Francis N.: 4, 6
Blue Jay ritual: 190
Bluff, Davis: 185
Bluff, Solomon: 136
Bluff, Stanley: 175
Bolin, A. J.: 16
Bond, Rowland: 169

Brotherhood of North American Indians: 116
Brown, John: 79, 91
Brown's lake: 187–88
Bubb, Capt. John W.: 77–80, 91
Buffalo: 38, 39, 55–56, 196n. 24; Kalispel herd, 184–86, 190
Burke, Charles H.: 131
Burke Act of 1906: 109
Byrne, Rev. Cornelius E.: 151

Calispell Lake: 27, 30, 32
Camas: *see* foods
Campbell, Clarence: 136, 142, 156, 163, 165, 169
Canoe, Kalispel: 28
Cataldo, Rev. Joseph: 60, 61
Cattle program: 135–36, 209n. 4; business, 135, 139–40, 144–45, 163–65
Cayuse Indians: 11, 15
Chalfant, Stuart A.: 158
Charter, Kalispel: 140, 210n. 12; *see also* Indian Reorganization Act
Chewelah Indians: 26, 51, 68, 198n. 12
Chicago, Milwaukee, & St. Paul Railroad: 103
Chiefs, unnamed: 19, 29, 43–44, 63, 104
Claim suits: *see* Indian Claims Commission; judgement funds; land
Clark Fork river: 28, 34
Clothing: 31, 35, 44, 68, 104
Citizenship: 116
Coeur d'Alene Indians: 6, 7, 15, 20, 22, 23, 27, 32, 50, 53, 56, 60, 61, 70, 100, 115, 126, 129, 136, 151, 161, 166, 183, 209n. 6
Cohen, Felix S.: 139